940.548641

AUTHOR .....JOHNSON, S.....

TITLE ..AGENTS....EXTRAORDINARY

		20. 07.
	17. 09.	16. 07. 79
	78. 74. 77	12. 09. 79
		04. 09.
07. 04. 74	30. 10. 74	
	03. 11. 76	04.
27. 07.	12. 12. 78	15. 02.

D1612848

100 070 456 3D

Agents Extraordinary

ALSO BY STOWERS JOHNSON

Branches Green and Branches Black
London Saga
The Mundane Tree
Mountains and No Mules
Sonnets, They Say
Before and After Puck
When Fountains Fall
Gay Bulgaria
Yugoslav Summer
Turkish Panorama
Collector's Luck
The Two Faces of Russia

Agents
Extraordinary

STOWERS JOHNSON

Illustrated with photographs and a map

WANDSWORTH PUBLIC LIBRARIES ★

ROBERT HALE · LONDON

© Stowers Johnson 1975
First published in Great Britain 1975

ISBN 0 7091 5162 4

Robert Hale & Company
Clerkenwell House
Clerkenwell Green
London EC1R 0HT

940.548 642 JOHN

100070456

M64694

Printed in Great Britain by
Clarke, Doble & Brendon Ltd
Plymouth

Contents

	Acknowledgments	8
	Note on Orthography	10
1	Balkan Background	11
2	Retrospective Biography I The Making of an Agent: Major Mostyn Davies	13
3	Retrospective Biography II (i) Dragon School to Winchester: Frank Thompson, shades of T. E. Lawrence (ii) New College, Oxford (iii) Undergraduates at War	16
4	Parachutist for 'Special Duties'	29
5	With the Partisans in Macedonia	32
6	Tserna Trava: Topography of Resistance	40
7	The British Mission Arrives: the Mountain Victory	48
8	Enemy Reprisals	55
9	The Augmented Mission of 'Mulligatawny'	62
10	Spring Offensive	69
11	Defence in Balkan Style	73
12	Extrication	83
13	At Tempo's Headquarters: Partisan Warfare, Ambushes and Reprisals	88
14	Retrospective Biography III Sergeant of Signals: Kenneth Scott	95
15	Out of the Soup into 'Claridges'	98
16	On the Run across Encirclement	102
17	A Parallel Mission: Kenneth Syers	112
18	Thompson's Private Army: the Long March Begins	121
19	The Anti-Communist Policeman: a Tangle of Agents	126
20	On the Bulgarian Mountains	131
21	Ambush at Batulia	140

22   The Trap   147
23   'Prisoners of War'   155
24   The Faked Trial: Agent Murders Agent   162
25   Working 'Under Gestapo Orders'   168
26   Liberation Day   177
27   Retribution   184
28   Left-wing Double Agent against Right-wing Double
     Agent: Kim Philby versus Geshev   187

Illustrations

facing page

1 Mostyn Davies at Herringswell   32
2 Kenneth Syers with the C.O. of his Yugoslav squadron   32
3 Frank Thompson   33
4 Kenneth Scott   33
5 Tempo parading the British Mission with Mostyn Davies, on the balcony at Kičevu, September 1943   48
6 Tserna Trava   49
7 Before the watermill, Tserna Trava   49
8 General Apostolski, Major Mostyn Davies, General Tempo (copy of a photograph found on Mostyn Davies at Dobro Polje)   64
9 Captain Stoyanov's headquarters, the school at Gorni Bogrov   64
10 The Bulgarian soldier deserters forming the Hristo Botev partisans   65
11 Tempo addressing his partisans in the snow, February 1944   80
12 The road to the frontier above Tserna Trava in summer   80
13 'The Long March': British soldiers marching with the the Second Sofia Brigade, May 1944   81
14 Jordanka with her hand grenades leading an attack to liberate a frontier village   112
15 The baker martyrs of Litakovo: Maria and Haiden Haidenov and their bakehouse with basket as put out for the partisans   113
16 Eleshina town hall   128
17 The Bulgarian frontier forests   128
18 Frank Thompson's grave above Litakovo   129
19 Thompson Railway Station, Bulgaria   129

PHOTO CREDITS

S. Sekretariat za Informacije, Beograd: 5, 11; Museum of the Revolutionary Movement in Bulgaria: 10, 13, 14.

Acknowledgments

The Author wishes to thank all who have so generously given their time and assistance in his quest for information, in particular the following:

For personal interviews: K. A. J. B. Scott Esq., D.C.M.; Kenneth Syers Esq.; Mme Vera Nacheva Ivanova (Sofia); Mrs T. Thompson (mother of Frank Thompson); Mrs Brenda Ross (formerly Mrs Mostyn Davies); Mrs I. Mays-Smith (sister of Mostyn Davies); Bickham Sweet-Escott Esq. (author of *Baker Street Irregular*); Mr P. Bozov (former cultural attaché, the Bulgarian Embassy, London); Robert Conquest, Esq.; Mm Dobrila Djukić (Savezni Sekretarijat za Informacije Beograd); Mr G. Djagarov (President, Bulgarian Society of Writers, Sofia); Mr Nicola Dontchev (Society of Bulgarian Writers, Sofia); Professor Michael R. D. Foot; Anthony Forster, Esq.; Duke Grandjean Esq. (former Treasurer Communist Party of Britain); James Klugman Esq.; Mr Pavel Konyarov (Society of Writers, Sofia); Mr Radomir Kostadninović (schoolmaster and author of *Tserna Trava and Tserna Travians*); Donald H. McLachlan Esq. (first editor of *The Sunday Telegraph*); Professor Jovan Marjanović (Beograd); Miss Iris Murdoch; L. Pliatzky Esq.; Mr B. Ristić (counsellor, Yugoslav Embassy, London); Professor Hugh Seton-Watson (School of Slavonic Studies, London; author of *The East European Revolution*); Mr I. Sobajeff (London); Mr T. Stojanov (former cultural attaché, the Bulgarian Embassy, London); Commander Edgar Young R.N. (retired).

For correspondence: General Mihailo Apostolski (Director Institut za Nacionalna Istorija, Skopje); Mrs M. Blaschko; Edward Blinmen Esq.; H. Branden Esq., Q.C., M.C.; General-potpukovnik Petar Brajović (Beograd); J. B. Brown Esq.; Noel Carrington Esq.; Potpukovnik Dane Cekov (Beograd); Mrs M. Coles; Miss Rose E. B. Coombs (librarian, Imperial War Museum, London); J. C. Dancy Esq.; H. G. Dixey Esq. (former headmaster, Dragon School, Oxford); Professor K. J. Dover (University of St Andrews); J. G. Griffith Esq. (Jesus College, Oxford); E. Hattersley-Smith Esq.; Lord James of Rusholme (vice-chancellor, University of York); Professor D. H. N. Johnson; Francis W. King Esq.; J. H. R. Lynam Esq.; John S. McNair Esq.; Mrs Margaret Matthews; R. B. Moberley Esq.; H. H. Monroe Esq., Q.C.; Slobodon Parunović (Amsterdam);

J. B Poynton Esq; A. Retey Esq.; Cyril E. Robinson Esq.; Miss
M. E. M. Ross; J. Shepard Esq. (former editor of *The Wyke-
hamist*); Mrs B. M. B. Stevenson; Mrs Ann Slughe; Professor E.
P. Thompson (brother of Frank Thompson); David Wolfers Esq.;
N. H. Wilkinson Esq.; Mr Zoran Vesić (Savenzni Sekretarijat za
Informacije, Beograd).

The author has also to thank the following newspapers for pub-
lishing his various letters and requests for information: *Birming-
ham Evening Mail, Birmingham Post, The Guardian, John o'
London, The Listener, Liverpool Echo, Liverpool Daily Post,
Manchester Evening News, The Morning Star, The New Statesman,
The Observer, The Scotsman, The Sun, The Sunday Times, The
Western Mail, The Yorkshire Post, The Times Literary Supple-
ment, T.V. Times, Literaturen Front* (Sofia).

Apart from the enormous amount of information to be found in
the publications of the national historical institutes in Beograd and
Skopje—in particular the vast collection of partisan diaries, records,
anecdotes and historical documents still being published at Beograd,
which has already amounted to run into its second hundred volumes
(*Zbornik Dokumenata i Podataka o Narodno-oslobodlačkom ratu
Jugoslovensjih Naroda*), and the records of the Institute of History
in the Museum of the Revolutionary Movement, Sofia—much of the
author's information has had to be obtained abroad in the field by
word of mouth. He therefore wishes to express his gratitude to all
the townsfolk of the Tserna Trava district, its doctor, schoolmaster
and tavern-keeper with all their friends for their good-humour and
patience; and across the Bulgarian frontier to the Society of Writers,
to the mayors and town councils of Botevgrad and Litakovo for their
hospitality; and to the townspeople of Eleshina and Gorni Bogrov,
all of whose memories were vivid and who had a great deal to tell.

Note on Orthography

For personal and place names on the Yugoslav side, where there is an alternative Romic to the Cyrillic alphabet, this has been retained except where it would confuse English readers, e.g. Nish instead of Niš or Tserna instead of Crna.

On the Bulgarian side, since there is no current alternative transliteration to Cyrillic, the traditional version has been followed. The following expressions need to be understood:

Cheta   Guerilla band or company, used by all armies in Yugoslavia whether of Tito or Mihailović.

Chetnik   Member of a *cheta*, but in World War II came to denote only members of the anti-Communist armies, chiefly followers of Mihailović.

Odred   Guerilla detachment.

Odbor   Committee.

mahala   Village district, hamlet.

planina   Downland type of Balkan mountain.

haidouk   Old-time legendary hero.

1: Balkan Background

The ancient medieval Bulgarian Empire once dominated the Balkans from Byzantium to the Adriatic. In 1878 Russian influence and the Treaty of San Stefano almost re-established this, but then the Western powers asserted themselves to reduce Bulgaria's territory, which her own misfortunes in the Balkan Wars and World War I continued to diminish, so that west and south of Sofia from the Aegean to Skopje, in the land called Macedonia, were peoples who spoke a language which could be understood all over Bulgaria, yet they were domiciled outside the Bulgarian boundaries, in Yugoslavia or in Greece. The Greeks had driven out their Macedonian-speaking population as far as possible. In Yugoslavia they were supposed to be Serbianised as a part of the Royal Yugoslav state, just as was attempted with the Albanian peoples north of Ohrid Lake.

When Hitler invaded Royal Yugoslavia in 1941, he gave the Albanian-speaking territories into the Italian jurisdiction of Mussolini's Albania, but all the Macedonian-speaking areas he bestowed to become a larger Bulgaria. Many were highly content with this re-establishment of Imperial Bulgaria. The Royal Bulgarian Army moved in and began to root out every trace of Serbianisation, even to surnames and the printed word. They burned and they 'Bulgarised', installing new Bulgarian mayors, lawmen and tax-gatherers. The old frontier had gone and a new Demarcation Line indicated the larger Bulgaria.

This new wartime territory was infested with pockets of Serbs, Mohammedans and Communists, all of whom became activated under the inspiring leadership of Tito's Montenegrin deputy, Svetosar Vukmanović, known by his party name of 'Tempo' and assisted by his Commander-in-Chief, General Mihajlo Apostolski. Everywhere they organised revolt against the Royal Bulgarian troops and the persecutions, forming guerrilla bands into companies and re-forming them into territorial 'brigades'.

The Royal Bulgarian Army was closely supervised by the Abwehr and the Gestapo. The Germans traditionally regarded the Bulgarians as 'demi-civilised' and, while keeping their own tight military discipline, tended to despise rather than check the brutalities by which such 'savages' complied with their commands. The Abwehr exerted maximum pressure on Royal Bulgarian authorities to preserve communications and safeguard installations and depots and they chose to ignore the primitive terrorism by which villages were destroyed at random. But though the Bulgarian staff and police might comply, the rank and file of that Bulgarian Army was shocked when ordered to 'Bulgarise' peasants who spoke their own language and who might indeed be distantly related to many of them. Hence the desertions which increased as the campaign went on.

To understand the complications of this muddled military and guerrilla scene it must be realised that an old Royal Yugoslav Army still existed in the area under the quisling Nedić, who also complied with Nazi demands. At the same time here and there villages gave allegiance to Mihailović, whose *chetnik* overlords—though professing allegiance to the exiled King of Yugoslavia and to the British—terrorised the districts, bandit fashion, with the temporary and quiescent approval of the Germans, of Nedić's Royal Yugoslav Army and also of the Royal Bulgarian Army.

When the British authorities gradually became puzzled about many such complexities over which hovered the legendary figure of Tito, Captain F. W. Deakin was sent out from H.Q. of S.O.E. at Cairo to explore the situation and make contact with the true partisans. Actually he was head of section, but, so important was this crucial fact-finding and so desperate the shortage of operational officers, that he himself had to be dropped into Yugoslavia on the night of 29th May 1943. Though wounded, he at once sent a stream of regular messages back to Cairo giving the first accurate details about Tito's partisans and his contacts with Tito in person. Churchill immediately grasped the significance of this and Fitzroy Maclean was sent out with the rank of brigadier general to take over British liaison duties and continue Captain Deakin's work. As the British emissary to Tito, his task was to balance those two hated Allied missions, the British and United States teams that were cultivating Mihailović and his *chetniks*.

When he arrived the situation had worsened and become incredibly difficult. The British and the United States were advertised as assisting Mihailović—who, instead of attacking the Germans, had chosen to lie low and make his own private war. Using the slogan "Death to Communism!" his *chetniks* made treacherous assaults against all partisans. In this way, with the approval of German and Royal Serb alike, they survived; indeed, some *chetnik* commanders lived openly at German and Italian headquarters as liaison officers.

Worst of all, Brigadier Maclean had to hear complaints against London's B.B.C., for the Royal Yugoslav Government was using British Radio to announce decorations of *chetnik* officers for fighting against Tito's partisans when, in the same bulletins, degradation notices were published to disgrace regular Yugoslav Army officers who under Tito were actively fighting the Germans![1]

To S.O.E. at Cairo the name of Tito's deputy, 'Tempo', who ruled in the southern section of Macedonia and Montenegro, was even more mysterious than that of his leader. His district from Skopje to Nish was the very hub of the Balkans, controlling road and rail communication to Bulgaria and Greece. The Germans insisted on its complete pacification by a regime which knew only brutality as the method of maintaining power. Tempo was operating in one of the most primitive and passionate, as well as isolated, sections of World War II.

Bickham Sweet-Escott had taken over the Balkan Desk at Cairo S.O.E. in the early spring of 1943, and he prepared a parallel mission to that of Maclean to make the link with Tempo so that, almost simultaneously with Maclean's famous mission, the British mission of Mostyn Davies was parachuted—a mission which came to be surrounded not with fame but with the administrative curtains of oblivion, which this book makes some attempt to draw back.

First it is interesting to look into the lives of the two liaison officers, nurtured as they were in their different spheres in that Engand between the wars and propelled into rather than trained for an unwanted war.

2: Retrospective Biography I
The Making of an Agent:
Major Mostyn Davies

Mostyn Llewellyn Davies was born on 26th June 1910. He went to Charterhouse School and on to Magdalen, Oxford, his father by then having become Squire of Herringswell in Suffolk. Mostyn took up Spanish at Magdalen and attended the courses of Saragossa University that were held at Jaca in the Pyrenees, as a result of which he was selected one of the team of Oxford and Cambridge delegates led by Philip Guedalla to visit South America as guests of Buenos Aires University.

After Oxford he had become a Member of Lincoln's Inn, and, like his father, had joined the Inns of Court Territorial Regiment. Possibly his low degree (*aegrotat*) at the university had brought him

[1] H. Seton Watson, *East European Revolution*, Methuen, 1950, page 129.

down to reality, for he took up accountancy as a career in earnest, passing all the qualifying examinations to become a fully-fledged accountant.

Very soon after qualifying Mostyn Davies had sought admission to the Civil Service and became a Deputy Accountant for Trinity House. This was no mere office post near Tower Hill, for it involved making trips out to lighthouses and lightships to inspect accounts on the spot. His zest and sense of humour must have brought a welcome relief to the men he visited.

In the stir that accompanied the rise of Hitler's Germany and around the time of Munich, various new Ministries were being formed for which the usual circulars had been sent to all Civil Service departments asking for volunteers. Mostyn Davies sent in his application. He had become restless at Trinity House. The routine irked him. He fretted at such stability which laid down a complete map of his promotion prospects for years to come. Accordingly, leaving Trinity House at the age of twenty-nine, he served in the Ministry of Information, the Ministry of Supply, in Lord Beaverbrook's Ministry of Aircraft Production and in the Ministry of Transport and Shipping. He had become Private Secretary to Lord Llewellyn, with whom he was taken to his various Ministries when transferred, an unusual tribute as the custom was to accept a new secretary at each new Ministry.

The nation was now at war, but Mostyn Davies found himself tied down in a reserved occupation. By nature daring and impetuous, he could not be contented with his circumstances. Friends and colleagues had gone nearer the fighting front and he wished to see action. Weekends hunting with Lord Burleigh or shooting at Herringswell only made him more restless. "Now is the time," he would say to his family, "and the only time, when a young man can achieve something by taking the risk."

Hitler invaded Norway, native land of Mostyn's mother, Clara Lina Andrea. Though he did not speak Norwegian, Mostyn immediately volunteered for special work there. Then came the Government's momentous appeal over the B.B.C. for maps, photographs and documents from pre-war holiday-makers. Mostyn took all his collection to the War Office with a renewed appeal to be of service.

During this period the organisation that came to be known as S.O.E. (Special Operations Executive) had been gathering. Presenting itself as the Statistical Research Department of the War Office and known to its members as Section D, it had been evolved after Munich "with the object of doing those things which assisted the execution of His Majesty's Government's policy but which His Majesty's Government preferred not to acknowledge as the action of its agents".[1] From the country house known as 'The Frythe', nor far from Hatfield in Herfordshire, it had moved into more anonymous premises at St Ermine Hotel in the West End of London, and, as No 64 Baker Street, was to be the hub of a miscellaneous activity about which even its own members knew little. One of the chief secret men in the secretariat was Gladwyn Jebb, a Magdalen man whose former tutor at Magdalen, Professor Namier, was also associated in the venture. Colin Gubbins, who had been involved raising the independent companies in Norway, had been posted to No 64 Baker Street as a brigadier.

It was then accepted that one of the easiest ways of getting into enemy-occupied France was by way of the Pyrenean frontier, and, as Mostyn Davies had special knowledge of this as well as of the Spanish language, there is no doubt his application attracted attention. It was never the policy of S.O.E. to allow anybody into enemy territory with immediate special knowledge that could be useful if extracted by enemy torture or drugs, so Mostyn Davies, with his experience in so many Ministries, was passed over for the action he desired. Instead, it was his knowledge of .Canada and his South American connections that sign-posted his selection, and Spain was not to be his goal.

On 7th December 1941 the Japanese attack on Pearl Harbor had brought the United States into the war with a jolt which revealed the deficiencies of their international intelligence system. From June 1941 Colonel William Donovan had been working as Co-ordinator of Information and he now began to create for the U.S.A. a similar organisation to the British S.O.E. He had toured the Balkans during the first years of the war and had been receiving in New York full co-operation from the English representative, Colonel William Stephenson. Stephenson was now sent an English mission to assist Donovan's organisation and work under his direction.

By this time Mostyn Davies had succeeded in becoming "attached to the War Office", to be despatched secretly as an important member of S.O.E. to West Africa. Lord Llewellyn had tried to persuade his young secretary to accompany him to the Board of Trade, but Mostyn, at last on the scent of a more difficult job than Civil Service routine, found the prospect of military action more alluring. He had been sent out nominally as a civilian working for the West African Governors' Conference Secretariat in Lagos. His chief here was Louis Franck, and it was not surprising that when Franck was recalled to London and briefed to take charge of the mission to join Colonel Stephenson in New York, he selected

[1] Bickham Sweet-Escott, *Baker Street Irregular*, Methuen, 1965.

Mostyn nominally as adviser on West African affairs but actually with a view to developing South American connections. The others in that mission were Bickham Sweet-Escott, adviser for Western Europe, Thomas Masterson for the Middle East and Balkans and John Keswick for western Asia.

After many characteristic ventures in the U.S.A., and also after his marriage, Mostyn Davies flew to Cairo S.O.E. to join Force 133. Here he renewed his acquaintance with his colleagues, Bickham Sweet-Escott and the others of the United States mission with Stephenson. He began to train for that action in the field which he so much desired, being designated as leader of the British mission to contact Bulgarian resistance in the central Balkans.

The period of training was short enough, understandably, for he had already been so long advising for the S.O.E. school in Canada and for the training of potential guerrillas for South America.

In September, 1943, he was dropped, now with the rank of major, into the very heart of the Balkans.

But the sequence of events of which this was the beginning was totally unlike what befell other missions, being not only extra-ordinary, but also a chapter which all the authorities concerned have chosen to keep tightly closed. The story to be unfolded in this present narrative, coming as it does chiefly from foreign sources, contains far more than is known to those archives.

3: Retrospective Biography II
(i) Dragon School to
Winchester: Frank Thompson,
Shades of T. E. Lawrence

Later to join Major Mostyn Davies was another Oxford man, Captain Frank Thompson, ten years younger and with the impetuous idealism which seizes the young in that first flush of wider read-ing which Oxford gives its freshmen. For he went up to Oxford in 1938 and, like so many of his contemporaries, volunteered at the outbreak of war after only one year at New College—snatched away, so to speak, in the first fluttering of the winds from Helicon. In complete contrast to Mostyn Davies, William Frank Thompson had been brought up to be a poet. His father, Edward Thompson, was then well known as poet and historian as well as a successful novelist. During World War I Edward Thompson had won the M.C. as a chaplain. His son Frank had been born at Darjeeling on 17th August 1920. The family came to Oxford and settled in the residential district of Boar's Hill. Here Edward Thompson established himself as a man of letters and sent his sons to the Dragon School, one of the most esteemed and famous of preparatory schools in Great Britain.

The home atmosphere of the Thompsons at Boar's Hill was bound to inspire great expectations for the young. Bridges, Masefield, Gilbert Murray, Sir Arthur Evans—all were to be met. Edward Thompson was also friendly with Henry Nevinson, Geoffrey Garratt and Lord Lothian. During Frank's boyhood Robert Graves, a close friend of Edward Thompson, was living at Islip and the family used to see a great deal of him. Graves's book *Revolt in the Desert*, about T. E. Lawrence, had been published in 1927, the same year as Edward Thompson's novel about Townshend's Desert Army. St John Philby was also well known there and his book on Arabia often came into discussions. There was a tolerant, international sympathy which radiated in the home and made friends from India specially welcome.

In September 1933 he began life at Winchester, with that feeling of excitement coupled with isolation which separates the young from their home life. Frank Thompson soon found his feet there, absorbed in the ways of that institution which he entered with the sturdy independence so characteristic of the Dragon School, energetic, untidy and uninhibited. It was as if the legends of T. E. Lawrence's eccentric mischief and fun of which he had heard so much had rubbed off upon himself. He knew most of the Oxford gossip about the Lawrence house at No 2 Polstead Road and the two young Arabs in costume who rode around with him on ladies' bicycles in the pre-war days, the bizarre carelessness of the hero's dress, the firing of blank cartridges from windows of Jesus College into the Turl. Such extravaganzas of Lawrence as that satirical hanging of the Croix de Guerre around the neck of the dog belonging to his patron Hogarth, the Magdalen don and Keeper of the Ashmolean, were part of the gossip at the Thompson house on Boar's Hill.

There is no doubt that as he moved up through the school Frank Thompson's zest for life drew him into wider channels than the linguistic paths of Classics. Following the tradition of his father, he began to declare himself for freedom, for the open-necked shirt and for what in the Thirties was known as the 'Open Society'.

Francis King was the first master who really influenced him. They shared an interest in the poetry of Cecil Day Lewis, who at that time, 1936, was a member of the Communist Party. The Fascist rebellion in Spain was uppermost in the minds of thinking people of those days, and his friends the Carritts grew restless with the news of Spanish atrocities and Hitler persecutions. The two older brothers went to Spain to fight Fascism and one, Antony, lost his life there. The younger Carritt brother, who had left the Dragon School having won their first scholarship to Bryanston, took up a vacancy that matured at Eton. Here this young Carritt was to shock all and sundry by joining the Young Communist League and collecting money at Eton to buy milk for Spanish children, also by raising funds to educate young German Jewish refugees.

Frank Thompson was not so active in the serener atmosphere at Winchester. Once in a small form debate at the Dragon School he had actually defended capitalism with some success, but now, caught up with the humour of contrast, he devoted his energies and enthusiasm to supporting the Communist Party in the Wykehamist Debating Society election, the object really being to tantalise and infuriate as many Old Boys as possible and provoke angry letters of protest from an aged Establishment.

The tragic death of T. E. Lawrence in May 1935 shocked the Thompson household as much as any in Oxford, where not a few had seen his intent, uniformed figure as he sped by motor-cycle to break his journey with a call on Dr Hogarth.

Despite his display of red, Frank found himself attending parades as a member of the Officers' Training Corps training for drill competition with bayonet drills and the usual two hours a week of spit and polish on uniform and equipment which he could only lament as "sheer drudgery". The usual field day came along, an operation prefaced by the hour's journey in a bus that shuddered at the latest popular songs, vociferous and unreasonably cheerful.

Such events are haphazard and chaotic, and Frank's first experience was no exception. The cadets 'debussed' and technically 'took up positions' in various gorse bushes where the time passed easily in munching chocolate and reading, until after a couple of hours all were informed that 'the enemy' were coming. At a prearranged signal the lads each let off a few blank cartridges and then charged forward, running 'at the double' for two uphill miles without stopping. Once at the summit, rifles down, flopping with exhaustion and reaching for sandwiches, the order came to 'take up a position'. Here again the detachment settled down to sandwiches and reading, when, interrupting the laziness of such stolen leisure, an umpire briskly arrived for 'inspection'. Sandwiches, books all vanished and the slating began. The 'position' was all wrong. A new and totally different 'position' was necessary, though there was no further uphill for it. Off everybody went until, after a few more blanks had been discharged somewhere, the bugle blew for cease-fire. There was a break for tea before 'embussing'. The popular songs on the return home lost their variety as the bawling of them grew more deafening and of course, because the expedition was so late back, the water had gone too cold for baths.

All his clique liked to be slightly outrageous in a mood which consisted of mildly supporting Communism. Frank Thompson, however, let everyone see how deeply he was stirred by the Spanish War in which his two friends, the elder Carritts, were involved. He gave news of them with bated breath. Sometimes the discussions would move to the subject of Lawrence's death and his role as Aircraftsman Shaw, and here Rex Campbell-Thompson assumed a conclusive knowledge, for Lawrence had worked for his father in the days of the Carchemist excavations.

Frank always joined the parties wearing a red tie, but his manner otherwise seemed nonchalant, perhaps a trifle ironical in conversations, shrugging off his refusal to be confirmed, to accept religion or loyalty to set political ideals, much as with declarations of laziness he rejected any overemphasis on athletic prowess. His friends, looking back on these traits, can recognise that he might have been consciously casting himself into the mould of Lawrence, were it not that Frank only exaggerated that satirical affectation of indolence so common to those pre-war years.

He left the Officers' Training Corps and joined the Scouts, find-them more interesting and relaxing. However much he might feign idleness and affect to shirk effort, that same year found him back in the O.T.C. furiously working for qualifications and looking forward to the O.T.C. camp, though, as he wrote to a friend: "If I can reach a certain standard of efficiency in blasting people up and reading military maps, I am awarded a Certificate A which gives me the inestimable pleasure of being an officer next time there's a war. That means that I shall have the comfortable certainty that I shall be killed in three weeks, whereas had I been a private I might have lasted three months."

He now began to potter with linguistics. He mentions, in spite of other pressures, attempts such as Hugo's *Italian in 3 Months*, Dante side by side with translation, German efforts, hopes to go to a work camp near Vienna, and so on.

For Frank Thompson the event which was to have the greatest significance to him was the visit of Sir Bernard Pares to make a prize presentation. That great pioneer of Russian studies in England; one-time Gentleman Usher of the first Russian Duma (Parliament); holder

of the Soldier's Cross and Medal of St George; Russian correspondent of the *Daily Telegraph*; an authority, lecturer and traveller both
in the Russia of the Czars and of the Soviets; who had seen Russia
in both war and revolution and who knew Siberia; held his audience
of Wykehamites spell-bound, despite their ignorance, even hostility,
to the great background of which he spoke. He was then Professor
of Russian at London University and Director of the School of
Slavonic Studies in days when events in Russia had reached the
doldrums of English interest.

"Everyone who could", he told the boys, "should learn Russian!"
He went on to detail the European situation where Russia was
winning respect through the cool diplomacy of Maisky on the Non-
intervention Committee, attempting to combine with England and
France to prevent Fascist interference in Spain and avert a European
war, although in this very Spain Stalin had to deal with the
Trotskyite following that were as deadly enemies to him as Franco
himself. Hitler's intrigues in Austria were transforming the murderers of Dolfuss into heroes. Pares was one of the few who really
knew what this meant and its effect on France by breaking down
her old *cordon sanitaire* against Bolshevism. And in his speech the
shadow of the coming European war darkened intensely, but only
momentarily, for he dangled before his audience the attractions of
encountering one of the greatest modern literatures, a glorious new
world of music, and the baffling Slavonic mind of the people. "Everyone who could", he challenged, "should learn Russian!"

There was no Russian class and no Russian teacher at Winchester,
but the challenge was taken up and Frank Thompson entered his
name for the class that was promised. Eventually Donald McLachlan, since he had been largely instrumental in Sir Bernard Pares's
visit, was persuaded to undertake it and formed, meeting twice a
week, a little extra-curricular group of half a dozen. This little
Russian group gradually flourished into activity, an enthusiasm
which even spread into the Shakespeare Reading Society to whom
Thompson gave a reading of Andrei in Chekhov's *Three Sisters*.
The *Wykehamist* reports him as making "a very inspiring though
not very competent speech in the Debating Society at which he
decried the evils of gambling declaring 'he had never seen anything
so gloomily unemotional as the West Ham Greyhound Stadium.
. . . Gambling was in fact the opiate of the masses and a disgustingly
cynical opiate. It was not a question of depriving the rich of
"innocent pleasures" but merely of protecting the working man and
still more his family from himself.' " In other debates he spoke in
favour of State interference: "It was only the second-rate artist who
was eccentric and who whined about State oppression for the true

artist was a normal human being." Even in the debate on National Service he spoke strongly in favour of compulsion, especially where physical fitness was concerned. Those who remember times between the wars will recognise the influence of pro-Communist Soviet propaganda running like an underlying current.

He was maintaining his knowledge of German. Taking advantage of the opportunities in those days of making 'pen pals', he began a correspondence with a German girl named Renate Rudolphi who called him *du* and gave him permission to address her as 'Natí', as she was called at home. He also noticed a Russian girl who advertised in *The Daily Worker*, but unfortunately the correspondence came to an abrupt end when Thompson began an argument that Brahms was as good as Tchaikovsky. "It is this dreadful new spirit of nationalism that is invading the Soviet," was his somewhat naïve comment.

Nevertheless he still flaunted a red jersey, tie, or shirt whenever he could. In his last game of Winchester football he appeared in a brilliant red shirt. There happened a long pause for one of the players to appear and much amusement was caused by the juniors chanting a ribald song, partly spontaneous, satirising his activities.

(ii) New College, Oxford

In March 1938 Frank Thompson left Winchester. Friendship and the family connections on Boar's Hill had been instrumental in obtaining letters of introduction from Sir Arthur Evans not only to the British School in Athens but to individual British archaeologists out there. Sir Arthur Evans reigned in Oxford as the grand old man of archaeology. Lawrence's patron, Dr Hogarth, had worked with him on the excavations in Crete and he still took the greatest interest in helping the young Oxford man towards archaeological work in the Middle East.

The early summer found him at 52 Odos Speusippou, the British School of Archaeology in Athens. Athens had in those days more than its quota of Russian exiles who had become band leaders, taxi drivers and housemaids. Frank Thompson seized the chance of getting Russian conversation practice with them whenever he could, as well as fossicking for some knowledge of modern Greek.

It was, of course, those introductions from Sir Arthur Evans that enabled him to meet the archaeologists at the British School. He was to acquire work on a dig at which his employment consisted in taking

charge of the pottery—the same sphere, strangely enough, as T. E.
Lawrence had filled long before at Carchemish. He had been in
Athens three weeks when, soon after meeting Mr and Mrs J. D. S.
Pendlebury, he was invited to help with their summer excavations
in Crete. Pendlebury had formerly been curator at Knossos and was
director of the excavations at Amurna, which was up in the hills
there. He now found himself supervising the locally recruited
labour, "the first real responsibility he had ever had apart from
being prefect at Winchester". Work began early, rising time being
six o'clock every morning. Frank Thompson's part of the dig
consisted of dusting, sorting and sticking labels on baskets of pot-
sherds, a drudgery that the uninitiated youngster hardly associated
with the magic of archaeology.

So the second week of June found him in Rome, returning home
"from the sunny valleys and snowy mountains of Crete". Reluctant
and repelled by the prevailing Fascism, he became enthralled with
the splendour of the Eternal City, "its gardens, fountains, a river
with bridges, a beautiful church in every street and quiet old houses
painted that wonderful faded gold—a colour which seems to have
been stolen from the setting sun at a time when it was too drowsy
to resent the robbery".

Having travelled across Europe away from his family, Frank
Thompson came back to Boar's Hill feeling very much a contemporary man. The lime trees and old buildings of Winchester were
farther away. From Boar's Hill he looked forward to a new life
within the stone walls of the university city. There was tennis with
Katharine Ross, walks around the south of Oxford from Boar's
Hill, tea with family friends, lazy, conventional summer days.

A cloud was over the Carritt family at Heath Barrows. The death
of Anthony (Bill) Carritt fighting the Fascist dictatorship in Spain
caused the family to feel intense hostility to the appeasement policies
of Chamberlain. Brian Carritt, his brother, was home from Eton and
politics took on a sterner reality. At Munich on 29th September 1938
Chamberlain accepted the terms of Hitler, which submerged Czecho-
slovakia. Russia, even after the withdrawal of France and England,
had still shown her willingness to aid the Czechs. Thompson and
his friends the Carritts felt this as keenly as anyone on Boar's Hill,
and in October when he came up to New College Thompson was
wearing the black tie by which they had agreed to mourn the disgrace, and he wrote, as it seemed to him then:

> Our last chance and that vanished. In the night
> A rumour like an east wind chilled the land,
> Of cowardly betrayal calmly planned.
> The pass was sold. It was no use to fight.

So it seemed to those young men, ignoring the crowds applauding in every cinema at the newsreel showing Chamberlain waving his scrap of paper. There was a by-election at Oxford that very October. Quintin Hogg, Conservative candidate, was supporting Chamberlain and the Munich agreement against Lindsay, Master of Balliol, the anti-Munich candidate. Frank Thompson joined the Oxford Labour Club, associated with the University Labour Federation, and, along with an enthusiastic group of friends in New College, threw himself wholeheartedly into the electioneering campaign to support Lindsay. (Another young undergraduate, Edward Heath, was canvassing for Quintin Hogg on the other side.) On his canvassing expeditions amongst the Oxford population he came up against the current admiration for 'Chamberlain the peace-bringer'. Arguments were useless and ended in apologetic distribution of Lindsay's campaign pamphlet. The triumph of Quintin Hogg shook and depressed him, politics and popular opinion seemed a farce, and for a time Fascists and Communists alike appeared to him murderers and persecutors.

He settled back into life at New College with a freshman's non-chalance. "Nobody expects me to get a good degree," he wrote, "so my old habits of idleness will soon have hardened irretrievably." He was expected to read the lesson on Thursday mornings, but, with rarely going to bed before 1 a.m. and his old habit of getting up late, had overslept the occasion in the third week. He played hockey for New College Second XI and had great fun joining the University Artillery, cynically enjoying the sergeant's lectures on the superiority of British military equipment and guns. "With a continental gun there's a two to one chance of it exploding. With our guns there's only a three to one chance!—I'm afraid that we shall have to fire them a great deal more than three times at Camp. It promises to be rather jolly!"

As one reads his letters and listens to the scrappy memories of those who knew him then, it is impossible not to hear, in this half-serious, half-mischievous attitude to military training echoes of that one-time member of the Oxford O.T.C., T. E. Lawrence.

Playing at soldiers, the frustration of politics, all turned him away from the conventionalities of the Labour Club which seemed artificial and "needlessly bohemian". A growing earnestness in his Russian reading, his friendship with the Carritt boys, and the Oxford example of Day Lewis, sent him hurrying to join the Communist Party, for which he energetically trailed his coat, appearing in the 1939 May Day procession. His schoolmaster, J. B. Brown, in a perceptive review later wrote,[1] summarising the motives that led so many young spirits this way: "He came to Communism by the roads

[1] *Draconian*, Summer 1947.

of intellectual conviction and frustration at what to him seemed the
helplessness of other political parties to deal effectively with the
problems of the time."

This earnest drift was expressed in a play written by Frank
Thompson in collaboration with his friend Leo Pliatzky entitled *It
Can Happen Here!* (a title claiming to be in advance of Sinclair
Lewis). In most melodramatic fashion a Fascist England was
imagined.

(iii) Undergraduates at War

English admirers of Soviet Russia had their first shock on the
occasion of the Nazi-Soviet Non-aggression Pact of 23rd August
1939, which was to be followed by the Soviet invasion of Finland
in December. Frank Thompson and his friends the Carritts were
staggered by this and needed all the dialectics of the *Daily Worker*
to recover balance. At the Declaration of War in September 1939
Thompson had volunteered for military service and was sent to the
Officers' Training Unit at Larkshill. He arrived at the same time as
David Wolfers, two years his senior at Oxford, and found there were
approximately forty in their batch almost entirely from Oxford
and Cambridge, though with a sprinkling of accountants and
engineers thrown in.

Wolfers and Thompson recalled the lecture they had attended
at Oxford the previous year when Sir Ronald Adam had predicted
that the major battles of the coming war would be fought in the
Balkans and in Spain and they often discussed the chances of
going up through Greece and Bulgaria to Romania. During that
bitterly cold winter of 1939–40 they found themselves in a rather
stark Nissen hut but in adjacent beds. Both were equally bad at
mathematics. Wolfers, an exhibitioner in modern history, and
Thompson, a classical scholar, had neither used log tables nor slide
rules since school—and these items were everyday tools of the
potential gunnery officer. This mutual deficiency linked them together towards the bottom of the group, despairing of top places
and only concerned with passing the qualifying examination for
their commissions; indeed, Frank Thompson seemed to spend
more time lying awake at night with classical verse than he ever
gave to mathematical calculations.

After the rather cloistered life of pre-war Oxford the introduction to the rawness of army life came as a shock. Battledress,
moderate institutional food, primitive conditions, caused some

members of the course to expand expressively, making up for paucity of adjectives with a continual spate of repetitive four-lettered expletives. Nevertheless the two friends managed to get away a great deal on the princely sum of 10s. 6d. a week as officer cadets. Saturdays were spent in Salisbury, where lunch at the 'Red Lion' cost about 7s. Sometimes also Frank Thompson went to Wolfer's house for weekends, and when the train fare allowed, they might both go to Boar's Hill.

That rare old character Colonel de la Haye was commanding officer at the 122 O.C.T.U. at the time. Unlike his conventional regular-soldier colleagues, he was outstanding for his progressive ideas; claimed a knowledge of Russian, having fought in the Archangel Campaign in 1919; and just before war broke out had been a Socialist candidate for Parliament. Lectures and exercises —in the autumn pleasant enough as maintenance signaller by farmsteads on the downs—in that bitter winter, became much tougher as when Thompson had to take duty as patrol officer with hands freezing on the controls of a motor-bicycle. But all worked into a routine that culminated in Frank Thompson being commissioned in the Royal Artillery in March 1940.

An officer now, he was posted to the Eastbourne district. From here he could sometimes come to London and meet his Oxford friends in the pubs of Fulham and Hammersmith. He would confide his bewilderment at the invasion of Finland, and his amazement to be taking part in an anti-Fascist war in which Russia had no share but apparently resented. How could he pursue this and be a true Communist? How was he to exist as an officer yet an opponent of class distinctions, in relation to his men? Even in meeting his former friends in the Hammersmith pubs he had to be conventionally discreet. Pliatzky recognised the inherent family earnestness here and gave up trying to reconcile the many conflicts it caused. In one respect the old Frank Thompson remained his former self, his irresponsible attitude to routine obligations unchanged—not lazy, not untidy, rather just careless, as on that occasion when, with only a few minutes in hand, he left his steel helmet behind in a crowded bar, perhaps infected with that Lawrentian tag, "Nothing matters."

In that first summer of the war the Royal Artillery were kept on the move with their 4·5 howitzers and old-fashioned cartwheels. From the early gorse and violets of Alfriston, Birling Gap and the chalk hills behind Eastbourne, Thompson's battery went to the Sussex woodlands by Northiam: later along by the Suffolk estuaries, hurrying down from Saxmundham to 'alerts' on that barren coast from Sizewell to Thorpeness in the misty dawn or relaxing on the ancient heathland, blackberrying and wondering at the multitude of pheasants and partridges there; then gradually hardening off from the bleaker Brecon Mountains and South Wales coast in October to winter manoeuvres, the artillery reinforced by an armoured division on the Yorkshire Moors in December.

London began to mean the Blitz from 1940 onwards and visits there presented to many their first experience of enemy action. Even leave times, which Thompson now spent at Bledlow, that lovely village below the Chiltern ridge, were not free from those nocturnal alarms.

In May 1940 his intensive work at modern languages had prompted him to apply successfully for the new G.H.Q. Liaison Regiment known as 'Phantoms', and by May 1941 the opportunity came to volunteer for service in Greece. By the time his draft reached the Mediterranean the disastrous campaign there was over, for the squadron had been destroyed while guarding the Corinth Canal. Accordingly he found himself in North Africa, engaged on more arduous training, an intelligence officer now and also responsible for maintenance transport.

With the Eighth Army, Frank Thompson's life was little different from all those others in the desert campaigns. He wrote home regularly and also to his friend Iris Murdoch. Through all his letters, always of course with regard for censorship, there runs unusual sympathy for the rank and file, together with a sense of duty to the post-war future. As patrol intelligence officer and M.T.O. he moved about a great deal on liaison duties for reports to G.H.Q.

On the morning of 22nd June 1941 the incredible news came to the Eighth Army that German forces had invaded the Soviet Union. Wonder and surprise changed to renewed enthusiasm. For Frank Thompson the war took on a new aspect. His Russian studies now supplanted his zest for Modern Greek and he began to hope that what he had learnt from Winchester days might be put to use.

Next week when he was leading his patrol on his motor-cycle, one of his trucks overturned on a desert track with severe injuries to the three occupants. On visiting them in Ismailia Hospital the day after, he himself collapsed with sandfly fever and found himself doomed to spend a month or so recovering in hospital. In September his detachment was posted to Syria, where he developed septicaemia and was again in hospital for two months. November found him back again in a cooler Cairo, at G.H.Q. Liaison Squadron M.E.F. with the Libyan Campaign to Benghazi and back. He saw the Western Desert and Cyrenaica in sand and dry scrub and again in the flower time of spring.

Then he found himself stationed in the land that had so often been the subject of discussion and debate in the gatherings at his home on Boar's Hill, the land of his father's campaign with the armies of Townshend and the unhappiness of Kut, the land of his mother's American missionary forebears and of which his maternal great-grandfather had written his autobiographical *Fifty-three Years in Syria*.

He had listened silently then with the respectful awe in which the young are expected to listen. Now, as he travelled from station to station in the fast-moving jeeps so characteristic of the 'Phantoms', a surge of admiration came to him for his father's account of the scene in World War I, its foreboding of the empty aftermath. And he began to understand the vacuum of human sensibility which Lawrence had penetrated in the desert and upon which the French had closed their unprogressive colonial grip. The Turks had gone, but what had replaced them? Was T. E. Lawrence a personal success but an international failure? For the Arabs, how were they better than in 1913?

Then from Iraq the 'Phantoms' returned to the Western Desert, to be transferred in August 1942 to Persia via Palestine re-crossing Iraq. Along the Persian roads it must really have seemed what Bickham Sweet-Escott refers to as 'Muddle East'. The many nationalities with their babel of languages—Russian, French, Arabic, Greek, Serbian, Croatian, Polish—all were to be heard on that surging wartime supply route across Iran to the Soviet Union, and in the vast organisation known as PAIFORCE Frank Thompsons' unit seemed small indeed.

He had time on his hands to study and enjoy the *Slavonic Year Book*, caricaturing "the solemnities of the Auden-Spender school",[1] 'and reading whatever Russian literature came to hand—even, when in hospital with jaundice, learning oral Russian from an Armenian wine merchant at 5s. an hour. Sometimes, like Mostyn Davies, he began to fret that fate kept him always so far from active combat: "I find myself," he wrote from Persia, "almost as far from the battlefield as England is, in point of time, perhaps farther. I joined this unit when it was represented, as it *still* is represented by the Press as something more dangerous than the normal line of country. In point of fact it has turned out to be a unit of uneven breaks . . ."[2]

Even the *Daily Worker* came out to the Middle East now, and this, with *Soviet War News* and Moscow radio, provided Thompson with enough material to inspire an exciting two-hour lecture to the squadron on "Occupied Europe". He mixed a great deal with the Polish exiles in Persia—Teheran being an escape route for Polish

---

[1] *There is a Spirit* (Gollancz, 1947), page 63.
[2] *ibid*, page 65.

refugees, women and children, coming out of Russia—and from one of them he was glad to learn that Bulgarian was an easy language. Sometimes he would pick up a Communist radio station talking to Bulgaria and urging resistance. Once he even dreamed of starting a one-man rose farm in Bulgaria after the war!

Men in North Africa were not destined to inaction, however. In the spring of 1943 Frank Thompson entirely recovered from his jaundice and found his squadron was to leave PAIFORCE to start training for the Sicilian landings. In May he was writing to Iris Murdoch from Alexandria, admiring what he termed the anti-Fascist character of the modern Greek and regretting that the Comintern had been wound up.

Admirers of the Soviet Union came right out into the open now in the various bars and restaurants from the Royal Artillery base depot at Almaza, Cairo, Alexandria and Port Said. K. J. Dover,[3] introduced by a Communist friend who was a 'fellow traveller' just then, came across Frank on several occasions but found him a rather cagey and chilly person compared with the usual set of such "young officers who wore their ids. on their sleeves and combined varying degrees of left wing political theory with a uniformly high degree of cultural and intellectual snobbery. I was vaguely aware", he afterwards recollected "that we did not impress Thompson so much as we impressed ourselves."

The outward shyness and reserve combined with inner fearlessness which K. J. Dover observed is clearly revealed by the published letter and diary sequence.[4] Frank Thompson diarised his training on the shores of the Red Sea, the sailing down the Gulf of Suez in June to the transit camp, the preparatory visit of Sir Edward Grigg on 23rd June and of Montgomery next day, the embarkation for Sicily, and the hazards of action in the desperate landing on 10th July, among the bloodshed, the blackberries and the lemon groves of Sicily, in one of the most vivid pieces of battle writing that exists, with characteristic reticence and understatement veiling his own efficient leadership—which brought his sea-barrow loaded with wireless sets into action.

He was attached to the Durham Brigade of the 50th (Northumbrian) Division, termed by the Germans the 'White Ghurkas' and described by the *Times Weekly* in their correspondent's contemporary summary of the campaign as "the sheet-anchor of the British Army".

---

[3] Professor K. J. Dover, University of St Andrews.
[4] *There is a Spirit*, pages 108–12.

4: Parachutist for 'Special Duties'

Signals in the Liaison Squadron ('Phantoms'), desperate action under mortar fire and every kind of anti-invasion bombardment, was a not unsuitable introduction for a future guerrilla fighter, for this had become the direction of Frank Thompson's ambition. As with so many, Greece lured him, and he was not sorry when the unit was withdrawn in July to Alexandria via Malta.

For a long time he had been offering himself for 'special duties', basing his claim to be selected on his knowledge of Modern Greek and his visit to that country. In Cairo, however, he had met other members of the Communist Party who looked more directly to the relief of Russia's difficulties by active intervention and whose interests were directed to Yugoslavia. And little wonder, for it was beginning to be realised in Cairo that, of forty Axis and satellite divisions in the Balkans, thirty-three were operating in Yugoslavia! One of the most active left-wingers he had met was James Klugman, whom Bickham Sweet-Escott[1] describes as "one cuckoo in the nest, one of the most efficient and hardworking men in the Yugoslav section, now a leading member of the Communist Party of Great Britain".

Not an Oxford man, Klugman had been secretary of the Communist Students' League at Cambridge and as early as 1942 had become intelligence officer to the Yugoslav Section of the S.O.E. with duties involving liaison with Tito's partisans. He confirmed to me that Thompson was able to go freely to him and seek opportunities for advice, quite apart from the friendly discussions they had together on Communist topics, on East European literature and their mutual admiration of Ehrenburg. (E. H. Cookridge in his book, *Inside S.O.E.*, Barker, 1966, page 56, notes rather cynically that "every volunteer for S.O.E. had to sign a declaration that he was neither a Communist nor Fascist").

In September, 1943 Frank Thompson was accepted for training in the Balkan section of the S.O.E. and found himself waiting in Shepheard's Hotel, Cairo. The secret organisation for obtaining information and making active warfare behind the enemy lines had always the reputation of working from the best hotels as bases, though the offices were now spreading from the large block of luxury flats known as Rustum Buildings near the Nile. S.O.E.

[1] *Baker Street Irregular*, Methuen, 1965, page 172.

had drawn west to Cairo those men held in Persia and Iraq ready to wage guerrilla warfare if in 1942 the Germans had broken through at Stalingrad and rushed on to invade the Orient. It was now making its own radio transmitters. Operational officers nevertheless were in short supply for both Greece and Yugoslavia because the S.O.E. was loth to allow officers who possessed much secret administrative knowledge to go into enemy territory.

The collapse of Italy, Churchill's visit to Cairo with Eden that November, rumours of a Second Front in the Balkans—such was the stir of events, some secret, some whispered in Cairo when Frank Thompson was recruited for Force 133. Monty Woodhouse who was in 'College' at Winchester with him, though far his senior, was deeply involved in the Greek section which seemed full of volunteers— almost a queue of aspirants. Hugh Seton-Watson of the Yugoslav section had been a fellow member with Frank in Donald McLachlan's Russian class, Sweet-Escott was a more senior Wykehamist. James Klugman, however, had progressive ideas more in common with Frank Thompson, who often sought him out. Klugman was deeply interested in events in Bulgaria. This was new ground and dangerous. It seemed to Klugman that by the time Maclean went in to Yugoslavia operations were comparatively easy as the preliminary work had all been done by the previous missions of Hudson and Jones and the following mission of Captain Deakin. Those early first parachutists had been dropped blind to make their own contacts, highly dangerous and full of risks—Atherton had been murdered and his gold taken—Captain Stuart, who was dropped with Deakin, for example, was killed shortly afterwards.

Bulgaria was a country which offered the same first-in-the-field appeal to the adventurer and the ideological type, of which Frank Thompson was a combination. Captain Klugman regarded this young Oxford man as the ideal officer whose sympathies with progressive anti-Fascist thought could lead to respect for partisan guerrillas in this new territory.

First there was the qualifying course through which volunteers for Force 133 had to pass. The S.O.E. sabotage school had been established on Mount Carmel near Haifa—known as Military Establishment No 102, it had been developed by Maxwell and Terence Airey for 'commando training' with a special view to wireless operations in the Balkans. After completing this strenuous routine, Frank Thompson presented himself on 22nd October at the parachute-training school which was close by at Ramath David.

He wrote in his diary: "It took more out of me than it should have done. Against this I have the comfort of knowing, as I knew before, that terror is not a paralysing thing—that whatever job comes my way in the future, fear at any rate will not prevent me from doing it."[2]

After 31st October, once qualified, back to Alexandria and then to Shepheard's Hotel, the waiting began. He knew he was to go to Yugoslavia to join an existing mission, but when? He lamented having spent so much time learning Modern Greek and applied himself to Serbo-Croat and Bulgarian with renewed zeal. He turned again to that little book of Marxist essays his brother had sent him last Christmas—*Studies in a Dying Culture*, by Christopher Caudwell.[3] The author had joined the International Brigade and was killed covering the retreat of his machine-gun section in the battle of the Jarama River, Spain, on 12th February 1937—and so was associated in death with Thompson's boyhood hero 'Bill' Carritt of Boar's Hill—but the book had much more than a personal appeal for Frank Thompson. To him it came as a vision of clarity, not merely to prove that the decline and demise of capitalism was just around the corner, but as an inspiration which threw the old giants of his youth in Winchester and Oxford into stark relief against the background of Marxist dialectic.

To Klugman and to Frank Thompson Caudwell's arguments, when applied to the great contemporary and philosophical figures of the West, had instant appeal; but the essay which moved Frank Thompson most was never discussed with Klugman. "The artificial light of present culture which had given the shadows of giants" to Shaw and Wells was one thing, but T. E. Lawrence had different connotations and this particular essay of Caudwell, "T. E. Lawrence, a Study in Heroism" had to be read and re-read.

Nor did Klugman himself, for all the long discussions they had together in Cairo, have the least glimmer of how Caudwell's interpretations were to shape his young friend's destiny.

In certain military circles around Cairo it had become the fashion to malign T. E. Lawrence. General Ironside, for example, was one of those conventional 'brass hats' to whom T. E. Lawrence was anathema and he wasted no opportunity of denigrating the popular idol when stationed in the Mediterranean. Even in 1939 he is on record as writing to Orde Wingate: "I had a good deal to do with that unfortunate charlatan Lawrence in the Rebellion in Iraq in 1920. He was such an impossible creature that I cannot understand how this wretched myth has sprung up around him. In the end, of course, he became egotistical and impossible. Had it not been for men like Liddell Hart he might have been forgotten."[4] So that

---

[2] *There is a Spirit*, page 154.
[3] Alias Christopher St John Sprigg, John Lane, 1938, pages 18-19.
[4] Christopher Sykes, *Orde Wingate*, Collins, 1959, page 209.

Caudwell's assessment had particular appeal to Frank Thompson as presenting a differing and Communist standpoint!

S.O.E. had now trained more operational officers than they had cypherines. Immediate coding and de-coding of wireless messages to and from the missions in the field was vital, and more F.A.N.Y.s had to be trained and brought out to Cairo. Life or death could depend on this when so many radio transmitters were scattered over the Balkans. (By October 1943 Sweet-Escott narrates that S.O.E. had succeeded in getting "something like eighty separate missions in the Balkans".)

By Christmas 1943 messages from Mostyn Davies had begun to come through regularly, and Seton-Watson and Klugman made arrangements for Frank Thompson to join him. Climatically November and December pass easily in Cairo, but not so in the Balkans. Not until the end of January was the combination of circumstances favourable for the Hudson plane to leave Cairo flying its eager little group with Frank Thompson *en route* to join the mission of Major Mostyn Davies.

5: With the Partisans in Macedonia

On 18th August 1943 an 'aerodrome', as the Macedonian partisans preferred to call dropping sites, had been established in the Slavej Planina, and here Tito's deputy, 'Tempo', with his commander-in-chief, General Apostolski, initiated the Mirče Asev Battalion. The Italian Firenze Division had collapsed at Dibra in the next valley across the mountains. For a brief while the long columns of Tempo's new battalion could cross that open basin in broad daylight, but not for long. The Royal Bulgarian Army swept in to occupy Ohrid and Brod, while the German Abwehr strengthened their barracks at Gostiva and Struga so that these four towns once again enclosed Tempo and his mountain men.

When in September 1943, the same month that the mission of Brigadier Fitzroy Maclean reached Tito's headquarters, Major Mostyn Davies landed by parachute at Tservena Voda, west of the wild fastnesses of the Kara Orman Mountains, he was accompanied by a small and select group with radio operator and explosives

Mostyn Davies at
Herringswell

Kenneth Syers (left) with
the C.O. of his Yugoslav
squadron

Frank Thompson

Kenneth Scott

expert. Eager guides led them from the dropping ground with their equipment to the headquarters of the Macedonian Liberation Army. They found this located above a typical Macedonian village, where the houses and the very mountain meadows hung on the eyebrows of the highest cliffs, secluded by the protection of the caves and beech forests along Stogovo's expansive shoulder northwards, while to the south only a narrow defile led to the levels before Ohrid Lake. Westwards stood the impassable heights on the other side of which the Black Drin hurls its rapids north, foaming white against the dark ravines. An old mountain railway used to run through the valley below Tservena Voda to Kičevo, but the partisans had blown up its tracks and tunnels. As for the steep road over Prešek, this was well protected.

Such was the chosen establishment of the chief of staff for Macedonia. Secret escape routes were always ready and sentries watched them night and day. After the tramp down from the 'aerodrome', there followed the typical Slav welcoming feast when Mostyn Davies met Tempo. The Bulgarian partisan, General Bojan Bulgaranov, was there, silent but with the disarming and acquiescent head-shake and the friendly open smile of his nation. Mostyn Davies was anxious to press forward towards the frontier. His mission was to obtain reports on Bulgarian resistance. Tempo, shrewd and calculating, was all for delays and preparations.

The way across Macedonia was sown with German garrisons. Rumour said there was another British mission close at hand with the Albanians. The Macedonian Albanians were anti-Fascist but the Ballist Albanians were treacherous and either sided with the Germans openly or became independent bandits. Mostyn Davies realised he was on sufferance, a kind of probation to be worked through in long discussions with Tempo. Good wine and roast lamb, melons and trout, the famous eels from Struga, laughter and songs were all very well but it was only as each got to know the other that Mostyn Davies came to know what was in Tempo's mind.

It was true the British were sending missions. Perhaps there were too many British missions. There was one reported as working with the Ballists that were Fascists. There was another with Enver Hoja in South Albania with the true partisans. There were three at least with the Greeks in South Macedonia. Who were the British supporting? Yes, he knew of the mission to Tito of Captain Deakin and he knew how Fitzroy Maclean had come out that very month. But a Brigadier Armstrong had gone also to Mihailović, and it was to Mihailović that the British sent supplies. What was the use of sending officers with radio stations to Tito's partisans when aircraft dropped tons of material to Mihailović to be used to kill the parti-

a

sans and destroy their villages? Tempo's shrewd face darkened with anger as he repeated "radio stations", and then, "We have had one Captain Hudson with us," he growled.

In that autumn of 1943, when Maclean was at Tito's headquarters and Mostyn Davies was with General Tempo in the south, British officers were comfortably stationed with *chetniks* and blanketed with ignorance, while close at hand partisans were ambushed[1] and driven out of villages;[2] Moslems were being massacred by Serbs as in the old Turkish wars.[3] What had made matters worse was that of the two Royal Yugoslav officers, Majors Ostojić and Lalatović, whom Hudson had brought with him in the British submarine, Major Ostojić had become Mihailović's chief of staff and that very spring had been with him at Foča commanding the *chetnik* forces who attempted to block the epic crossing of the Neretva by the partisans![4]

Mostyn Davies found it no easy task to avoid political discussion and at the same time preserve the sincerity of friendship. He was a soldier and not a politician. Tempo, however, was never lacking in eloquence or rhetoric. "It is I," he declared, "who wants the British mission. Tito says we must wait to see how the British will help Macedonia. Perhaps I am months behind what goes on at his headquarters, but what happened in Bosnia yesterday may happen in Macedonia tomorrow as we shall all see!" Tito had disarmed unaided, Tempo could declare, ten complete Italian divisions. True, the British might supply their automatic weapons, the best in the world, but when the German occupying divisions had all been killed, the Fascists might remain. They must not be left till the war was over! They must be destroyed at once!

The dark intense fury of Tempo prompted suspicion that weapons were needed first and foremost to destroy those enemies of Communism, the *chetniks*. Only with great difficulty could he be brought to accept that Balkan politics were incomprehensible to his English guests, and that Mostyn Davies was bound by the limitations of his mission as a soldier and could only operate accordingly. Periodically, sometimes for days at a time, Tempo disappeared from staff headquarters to make contacts, as he said, but on each return his cheerfulness and conviviality increased.

Svetozar Vukmanović (party name Tempo) was the most mysterious and dynamic of all Tito's followers. Born in 1912 in

[1] *Missfire,* Chatto, 1946, page 184.
[2] *ibid.,* page 192.   [3] *ibid.,* page 153.
[4] A.F.H.Q. Handbook, *The Chetniks* . . . Feb. 1943. Mihailović had exhorted the Montenegrin *chetniks:* "Now is the chance to beat the Communists to their knees."

Podgora, Montenegro, he went to school in Cetinje and then studied at the Department of Law in Belgrade. He joined the Communist Party of Yugoslavia in 1933. Soon after he finished his studies he became a professional revolutionary. For his political activities he had to answer to the Royal state courts, but he persisted with his objects and from 1937 to 1940 devoted himself to the task of strengthening the Party organisation in Serbia and Macedonia. Among his responsibilities was the leadership of technical studies in the Party. At the 1940 conference he was elected to the Communist Party Central Committee, and next year, 1941, became a member of the high command of the Partisan National Liberation Army, his duties also comprising leader of the staff for Bosnia and Herzegovina, and president of the Central Committe C.P.Y. for Bosnia.

In 1943 Tito, realising the impossibility of maintaining communications for immediate command of South Serbia and Macedonia, appointed Tempo as his delegate, and he arrived in February to become virtually the anonymous Tito of the south. Surely it is one of the most remarkable instances of devotion and loyalty that, soldier and politician in one, to this day he has preserved the same reticence, taking no personal credit but giving all to his leader and his party.

Everything in the south was complicated by the Macedonian problem, although never had the future of a free Macedonia seemed so far away. The old Bulgarian agitator 'Dada' (Georgi Dimitrov), who was Tito's contact in Moscow, had this ideal strongly in mind, but undoubtedly it was a Bulgarian free Macedonia he envisaged, and that is probably why Tito was always urging the most extreme caution upon Tempo. As for the British, the most recent documents indicate that they had no more conception of this Balkan endgame than in the earlier decades of this century! Mostyn Davies had only been provided with the routine instructions for British liaison officers to assist in the making of war, and they and their whole organisation of S.O.E. could make neither policy nor politics on any scale. S.O.E. in Cairo had promised him reinforcements, a linguist, a team with more radio sets, explosive experts and token gifts of military equipment for his hosts. His assignment was to move in the direction of the Bulgarian frontier, to contact Bulgarian resistance and report. General Bulgaranov asserted that Bulgarian soldiers were deserting from the Royal Bulgarian Army in large numbers; his officers were collecting them into a brigade. Mostyn Davies had yet to see evidence of them in any strength.

Quite apart from S.O.E. there was another British organisation working in the Balkans with the task of pure information-seeking, an organisation that never felt itself precluded from probing into politics. This department, sometimes referred to by Bickham Sweet-Escott as 'Z', had many channels and sources, and for its work in the Balkans had most of its traffic at Istanbul whence its complications went into Royal Bulgaria.[5] The German Reich had now presented Royal Bulgaria with an empire reminiscent of the best times of the Balkan wars, and emigration was being assisted to Bulgarise the newly occupied Macedonia. Alarmed by the example of Italy's fall, the Royal Bulgarian Government had now begun to intrigue to pull out of the war with its winnings and sent the banker Kouyoumdjeff to Istanbul to make the preliminary enquiries —a forlorn hope considering the isolation of Bulgaria and the tight grip of the German Abwehr, especially as all the enquiries presumed the retention of the ill-gotten gains. For both departments, S.O.E. and 'Z' alike, the only means of stirring something in Bulgaria was the mission of Mostyn Davies.

That September, 1943, a freedom parade was held in the liberated territory town of Kičevo with the Mirče Asev Battalion marching through the town in broad daylight to a tremendous welcome. Tempo addressed the crowd in the square from a balcony hung with placards and recruiting posters. Mostyn Davies and the British mission were on the balcony and prominently displayed to all. Albanians were present as well as Macedonians and some Bulgarians. All applauded as Tempo called for vengeance on collaborators with the enemy whom he designated not merely as Germans but Fascists and capitalists. This speech in the proud Ilinden town seemed a turning point for the future of Macedonia. Committees planned the opening of ten Macedonian language schools and cultural festivals of folk-lore and drama: the white caps of Albanians and berets of Macedonia went side by side in friendship. They even talked of opening up the mountain railway with a partisan train!

Autumn came, and the beech trees reddened as the mountain forests held the first nip of winter. Couriers came down the passes with the printed propaganda material drafted by Tempo. Since 1942 a secret press had been working near the town centre at Tetovo, hidden in the Moslem house where the Mulla Merta lived alone, his wife being in Belgrade. The house appeared secret enough, surrounded by high walls. A modern gestetner had been obtained from Tirana, and *Nedelen Bilten*, afterwards changed into a more frequent news-sheet, *Nedelen Vesnik*, had been consistently published by his little team of three. The printing was later resumed elsewhere in Tetovo with renewed vigour, to become firmly established as the *Gotse Delchev* when it was moved to the St Jovan

---

[5] *Baker Street Irregular.*

Bigorsky Monastery in the Bistra Mountains. Here there were natural caves and a spring of clear water, though one cave had to be carefully roofed to protect from water dropping when the snows melted. Besides the printing activity, the monastery became a secret refuge where couriers could rest, and pass and repass.

It gave Mostyn Davies no little surprise to find that printed proclamations, news-sheets and duplicated bulletins came down from the mountains to the base so regularly. From translations of what they contained he was able to form some appreciation of the dangerous hostilities into which his mission had jumped. Though they were within the new 'Demarcation Line', the old Bulgarian frontier was far away and there appeared no prospect but a long embroilment in bitter guerrilla skirmishes between the mountains and the great lakes Ohrid and Prespa.

Tempo and Apostolski, the high command of the Macedonian Liberation Army, now issued their manifesto in October 1943, seven pages neatly printed in Macedonian Cyrillic. On 29th November 1943 at Jajce was to be held the famous meeting of A.V.N.O.J. (Anti-Fascist People's Liberation Council) which in the thick of hostilities established the foundations of the new Yugoslavia. Later Mostyn Davies and the British Macedonian Mission were shocked to hear of the death of the two British officers there, Captain Donald Knight and Major Robin Wetherley, members of Fitzroy Maclean's mission, together with Lola Ribar and his colleagues. A German Henschel reconnaissance plane had dropped two bombs as it came flying low over a mountain just as they had been embarking for Italy in a captured Dornier 17.

Tempo's chief of command was the former regular Yugoslav soldier, Mihail Apostolski, a Macedonian born and bred, who had joined the pre-war Royal Yugoslav Army under the assumed name of Mitić and so obtained military training and promotion which would otherwise have been denied him, so great was the discrimination by the old Serbian military faction against Macedonians who were regarded as pseudo-Bulgarians. Apostolski guaranteed to to convey the British mission to the Bulgarian frontier, where in the district of Tserna Trava he said there were no chetniks, no Fascists, only good-hearted Communists and to which the Bulgarians came easily over the mountains. "They will be expecting you," he often repeated. "Couriers have told them you will be coming."

After the long discussions and the welcomings it was not surprising that news travelled elsewhere than to Tserna Trava. A German punitive division moved south and, in a battle lasting from the 1st until 9th November, succeeded in occupying Kičevo to command the approaches to Dibra; but the tracks were mined and the mountain railway had been blown up at Botun below the 'aerodrome' and headquarters at Tservena Voda, being also cut again above Strelsi, so that the valley began to seem quiet once more just when the beechwoods were deepest red and ablaze with colour after the sharp nips of winter frost.

The British mission anticipated a cold but pleasant suspense as the hard weather set in. Not so, decreed Tempo and Apostolski. The campaign begins, they declared. While the city soldiers of Germany and Bulgaria were shut in their barracks with camp stoves and petrol generators, the partisans were to move across the mountains, organise for the spring and give out rifles and military supplies.

Kičevo was lost for the time being as the centre of liberated territory, but a long march began in earnest by a route which developed through a chain of small raids and guerrilla battles in which the partisans fought and killed and vanished into the icy snow-covered fastnesses.

At dusk on 5th December 1943 Tempo and Apostolski, with Mostyn Davies and the British mission, moved right out of the Ilinden Valley, leading the newly formed First Macedonian Shock Brigade and having entrusted the continuance of resistance to the local guerrillas. Over the Ilinden *planinas* they went, keeping to the heights southwards to the forests that separate the beautiful lakes Ohrid and Prespa, whose waters glazed themselves bluer than ever against those winter snows.

Everywhere Mostyn Davies found a prepared welcome awaited him. The partisans and their womenfolk would crowd to every gathering and after an exhortation from Tempo and the local officers he would be required to give an address that was greeted with spontaneous applause. Always he found his words of encouragement were interpreted as lavish promises of supplies of food and stores of military equipment, but he had no illusions, and realised that Tempo was parading the military mission through South Macedonia to prove he had the backing of Great Britain and the Western allies. Tito's deputy needed to make the most of this one mission and its few British uniforms to offset the prestige given not only by those missions to Mihailović north of Nish, but those in Greece and Albania which he reckoned just as suspect.

Something of Demosthenes ran through Tempo's character, but Apostolski was the man of action rather than words, a typical soldier who organised, drilled and prepared battle formations in true Macedonian style. Here, at the hub of the Balkans, the crossroads of the ancient civilisations, he believed the people's war for freedom would be decided. It was from the south, in Berani (now Ivangrad), by open telegram that the first protest had been made against Prince Paul's acquiescence with Hitler. On 7th April 1941, the day after the Axis invasion, the Germans had rushed into Skopje. Even in July 1941 the resistance at Nish had become strong enough to put the Serbian-Bulgarian railway out of action for several days.[6] "At Tserna Trava, they are the people," Mostyn Davies was promised, "the true Communists who are still blocking the railways, and they will help you with the Bulgarians."

For thirteen days they marched along the southern frontiers of Yugoslav Macedonia, hurrying through the narrow neck of land that separates Prespa Lake from Little Prespa, passing north of Lerin to avoid the German regiment snugly wintering there, journeying through the Greek Macedonian villages until, passing far north of Edessa (also occupied by a German regiment), they arrived on 18th December at Fuštani in the Kožuv Mountains near Gevgelija.

Here in the open plain Tempo held another of his parades, On 20th December a motley crowd assembled to hear him. There were miners from the local mine, young men of many nationalities conscripted to forced labour but now freed by the partisans, and also Bulgarian soldiers who had deserted from frontier garrison posts. One company, influenced by working-class propaganda from the Fatherland Front, had deliberately left the Royal Bulgarian Army and had marched into Macedonia to form the famous Hristo Botev Battalion. All these Tempo grouped into the Second Macedonian Brigade in two divisions: the Bulgarians, Serbs and other Macedonians were to continue that strenuous winter march; the others to fight on the local territory.

On the 22nd there was another re-grouping: the Sveti Naum Battalion became the Third Macedonian Shock Brigade, and Trifun Balkanski took charge of the Bulgarian soldiers who became the nucleus of the First Sofia Brigade (one day destined to become the National Army of Bulgaria).

An 'aerodrome' was made on a secluded meadow north-west of Fuštani, and another dropping ground prepared on the high frontier of the Kožuv Mountain. As Cairo responded with supplies, it seemed to Mostyn Davies that he was nearer his objective—real contact with the Bulgarian nation. But for Tempo and Apostolski these were most anxious times, for on that 22nd December a congress was held at which 288 delegates assembled, the participants, made up from an extraordinarily complicated network, being the Communists from Albania, Greece, Serbia, Yugoslav Macedonia, Bulgarian Macedonia, and Bulgaria, some of whom had the cause of Macedonian autonomy deeper in their hearts than mere fighting with the Germans.

[6] *Wiener Tageblatt*, Hafas Ofi reporting from Sofia, 20th July 1941.

Intense national political feeling was causing the two Greek resistance organisations to look with hostility upon each other in spite of all their respective British military missions could do. That autumn, coupling their offensive with fierce propaganda lies asserting the British had ordered each to attack the other, E.A.M. and E.L.A.S. had begun their internecine struggle, made more treacherous in Greek Macedonia by the activities of the individualist semi-resistance leader, semi-bandit Gotseff. A baker and native of Florina, he was chiefly concerned with amassing arms and a band of guerrillas for some future Macedonian intrigue.

The winter snows were creeping lower down the mountainsides, but now north and south of the Vardar River the Royal Bulgarian columns of military and police began to penetrate the valleys. With them came the relentless, efficient German battalions such as the Eberloss Brigade, while the 91 Kotpusa came up from the Aegean to encircle Fuštani. Tempo, fulfilling his reputation of going through the enemy lines like a hot knife through butter, took his partisans, Apostolski's Macedonians and Trifun Balkanski's Bulgarians, in long black files over the highest snowfields, over the Tserna Reka on to Kozjak Mountains north-east of Skopje. To those hardy mountaineers as they turned north, Greek politics remained a mystery they were not sorry to leave. Tempo was later to comment on the situation in one of his extremely rare publications: "How and why the People's Liberation Struggle in Greece met with defeat."

But now he left these men and shook them off like the freezing snowflakes.

"Let us go into our own mountains and take you to Tserna Trava!" he said to Mostyn Davies. "We will warm ourselves in Apostolski's land with the South Moravans. They know whether slivovitz is better than ouzo! Let us take our rakia with the South Moravans and give them a parade in Tserna Trava!"

6: Tserna Trava: Topography of Resistance

West of the South Morava River there are deep valleys where, with each mill and church and store making a nucleus of habitation, the villages lie grouped below the forests. In Tserna Trava (Black

Valley), the deepest of those valleys, the bright sun comes down to reach the houses for a few hours only, sometimes in the morning but more often in the afternoon. Yet, unhedged except by wild forest, there are meadows above the beech woods upon which all day the sunlight falls in the best of Balkan summers. Upon such a meadow above Tserna Trava by Čemernik Mountain they had celebrated Ilinden Day.

It was the 2nd August 1942. The tracks up to the festival were full of folk coming and going in gay Slavonic embroidered costumes, walking in their bright best colours, the women with white laundered cloth splashed with red and multi-coloured needlework, the young men in russet brown with Serbian caps and the older folk in traditional black. The crowds were thickest where the markets were held. There was a short improvised play—*Joseph on Trial*, at which the audience reclined on carpets. One or two of the actors on stage, like Lela, were known partisans. The orchestra came from Todorvorac. People had come from all the villages and hamlets thereabouts from Stepenovac to Ruplje. Many photographs were being taken at the celebration and a casual observer would never guess from the crowd that this was in the middle of the war. Yet, in addition to the 300 villagers, there were seventy enrolled partisans openly enjoying the celebrations and taking part in all the dances, the kolo and the singing—the more daring because just the other side of Čemernik Mountain were the barracks of the German and Royal Bulgarian unit guarding the Maćkat mine.

Ilinden (*Ilin-den*=St Elias's Day) is the great symbol for Macedonia, marking the founding of the First Socialist State when on Sunday after market day, 2nd August 1903, the priests blessed the flag embroidered by the schoolmistresses of Bitola and the armed Macedonians marched secretly to surround the Turkish garrison at Smilevo. Then, as the Turkish bugle blew for the cry, "Long live the Sultan!", the Macedonians overwhelmed the garrison, shouting, "Death to the Sultan!" Such was the fervour that one revolutionary, had set his own house alight as a demonstration that he wanted Christian rights rather than worldly possessions. That night long ago revolutionary beacons and fires had blazed across the mountains, all too soon to be extinguished by massacres and executions.

Today on Čemernik there was a calmer atmosphere. The new aristocracy, the men who had possession of rifles, moved about easily and the committee met. On that Ilinden Sunday in August 1942 there were also a number of burly young men whom the Tserna Trava folk treated not just as good companions but with more than mere respect. They had crossed the mountain from Maćkat mine and on them depended much of the partisan enterprise. Most unobtrusive was the miner Bera. This celebration had provided the one chance of meeting his comrades in free territory. Among his miners he had organised a revolutionary cell whose tentacles spread right through the 5,000 people employed there. Maćkatica and Belo Polje were really two concentration camps into which not merely Serbian and Macedonian villagers had been forced but to which anyone not considered trustworthy in Bulgaria had been exiled. Bera had arranged a trickle of small sabotage actions in the mine—which really served as a nuisance to cover management of a secret underground gallery to which explosives, weapons and ammunition, first-aid stores, and every kind of war material could be diverted for transport to the partisans on Čemernik. Even the baker was enlisted and quantities of his bread went periodically up the mountain to mysterious destinations. Besides the secret tunnel for explosives, Bera had a covered pit for the propaganda newsheets and leaflets which came down the mountain in exchange for bread. Sometimes he could send news up to Čemernik on his own account for the revolutionary socialists of Sofia, the Fatherland Front, had members among internees in the concentration camps.

Contact with the Bulgarian mine workers developed more rapidly after Ilinden Day. Many deserted and went up Čemernik. Some deserters contacted private soldiers of the Royal Bulgarian Army, socialists themselves—and, sick of guard duties in that dreary winter, they also slipped away to form a separate group of Bulgarian partisans.

It was this nucleus of Bulgarian resistance fighters that caused Slavčo Trunski[1] to come out of Bulgaria on 1st November 1942. Then a student at Sofia and an active member of the Bulgarian Communist Party, he was imbued with hatred for the royalist cliques around the Coburgs. He had become hardened to the routine of repression in Sofia, with the uniformed gendarme lurking within sight of the black-coated political spy on the streets. Trunski was appalled, however, by what he saw in the hamlets around Tserna Trava. When he came to the Todorvorac hamlet he found no men there at all; every one of them had fled to the partisans. As he came dressed as a tourist, without rifle and carrying only a sports knife which he was very soon to give away as a present, he found himself faced, at the door of one apparently empty house, by three young women, two with rifles and one with a revolver and a couple of grenades. The latter proved to be Vasa Smajević. Her smooth healthy cheeks and her smile shone out in contrast to her dark hair and black embroidered clothes. A young graduate of Belgrade, she had come out on Party organisation work, and already she

[1] Slavčo Trunski, *Neotdavna*, Bulgarski Pisatel, 1965.

knew every village in the Tserna Trava district as well as everyone remaining there. She was able to conduct him to the Mirka Sotirović guerrilla band with whom he stayed seven days until Vasa was able to arrange for him to meet the Čemernik partisans.

He had come just in time for the celebration of the October Socialist Revolution which had been arranged to take place in Todorvorac itself. On that occasion the hamlet—yesterday deserted, in ruins and windowless—became a hive of activity. The men came down from the mountains to take part in spontaneous declamations of bellicosity with parades and demonstrations. There was singing, dancing and homemade plays, with the girls sparkling in their brightest folk costumes. Improvised anecdotes full of local, contemporary significance were acted while the old folk wandered round pipe-smoking and reminiscing over the Serbian Wars. Trunski was surprised how the girls had lost their pre-war reticence and reserve. Jovana Rašića's house, where the celebration was held, could scarcely be seen for the crowd around it. Both inside and out of doors the warm fires blazed, while from the open windows, specially to delight the Bulgarian partisan guests, came bellowing the stirring verses of Hristo Botev and Smirnenski, though the song that crowd took up most was the Haidouk revolutionary ballad: "Ah, see! The Kolo! Mother's Kolo, Mother's Rebel!"

Vasa and her friend Bera both interrupted the merry-making to give lectures on the October Revolution and Lenin! They then joined with Trunski to persuade the Bulgarians to re-group as a national Bulgarian unit.[2] Slavčo Trunski adopted the revolutionary code-name 'Kolo', and with the partisan songs still ringing in his ears returned to Bulgaria on 10th November to forge the first of the links that make up the story of this book.

The first big initial blow of the Tserna Trava partisans was that action on 13th January 1943, when an attack on the main railway to Greece succeeded in severing communication for ten days. The railway station, the stone road bridge over the South Morava River and the railway tunnel at Mominog Kamena were destroyed. One German railway train was completely wrecked together with explosive materials and military equipment. The explosives were loaded into a wagon which was forced into the tunnel entrance and detonated. Ten Bulgarians and Germans were killed. The partisans made off, but, heavily laden with weapons and plunder, including one precious machine-gun, their escape was hampered by a lagging trail of thirty captured Germans. However much it was

[2] The Slavčo Trunski Partisan Odred thus re-formed, and later developed into two brigades, with the Hristov Botev company already mentioned, eventually materialised into the Bulgarian National People's Army.

debated, no solution could be found to the problem, and as soon as news came that enemy troops were coming out of Vladičin Han in pursuit, all these prisoners were slaughtered.

Reprisals were severe. From the suspected villages on the right bank of the Morava, 200 peasants were taken out and shot. On 21st January an armed Royal Bulgarian detachment brought a group of villagers out of Bankovca and paraded them at the place between Brod and Ruplje called Vučja Rupa, where they tortured them to death in the open.

This was the beginning of the savage terror throughout the valleys. The Royal Bulgarian police garrison at Tserna Trava arrested twenty of the most quiet and respected peasants from the villages between there and the railway (Čuke to Brod) and began to attempt to force them to betray the partisans. The partisan *odred* involved was actually hiding on the mountain at Belo Polje and at once resolved to rescue the hostages.

With new weapons, laying the usual ambushes to block all the approach roads, they descended upon Tserna Trava from all sides. The Bulgarian garrison fled, abandoning hostages and making for the frontier by way of Strezimirovca. To their pleasure and surprise not only were munitions and weapons found in the empty garrison, but a complete radio installation. All the archives and incriminating documents were destroyed, in particular those of the hated Mika Moler, the mayor. At the burning of these papers and ledgers in front of the town hall there was a wild celebration with kolos danced round the fires and singing lasting far into the night. Commandant Alexander Vusija, who had led the attack, made a speech that rang across the square. He was beside himself with joy and joined in the enthusiasm, coming down and dancing kolos as heartily as anyone.

Next day Alexander Vusija led the *odred* away and marched them on to Mlačište. They moved in a leisurely way and felt secure, singing and loitering at the farmsteads they passed in order to boast of their victory. The rejoicing was as premature as the enemy's lull was deceptive, for 300 well-armed Royal Bulgarian troops had been detached from Mačkatica and these, obtaining the help of several traitors, came in hot pursuit and surrounded Mlačište village, which the partisans had chosen for a safe refuge in which to relax.

When the Royal Bulgarians came up, Mlačište was cloaked in thick mountain mist. The partisan sentries, shivering in the bitter cold, could see no more than a few steps ahead. They heard nothing until the Royal Bulgarian soldiers were at the open doors of the houses. A savage engagement began, with the fog aiding escape as much as victory—after which, though the partisans broke out of the net they found themselves dispersed and leaderless, for Alexander Vusija had been killed at the outset of the attack.

By February 1943 the chaos on the railway and the strength of the partisans had become more than a rumour throughout Macedonia. In this month Tempo paid one of his rapid visits to Tserna Trava. He was determined to give a dynamic military pattern to the rather improvised organisation which had sprung into existence. The loss of Alexander Vusija had been keenly felt and Tempo saw the need to weld the partisans into a more efficient guerrilla organisation, having regard to the *chetnik* intrigues going on in Eastern Serbia. From the time when Colonel S. W. Bailey had gone to Mihailović, it was feared other such British missions might go to the Homolje Mountains north of Nish. Partisan committee organisation was improved and in the higher hamlets radio stations and depots for couriers were established with a network of secret 'post-boxes' to collect or deliver mail, news or directions. Tempo gave detailed advice on the construction of 'earth-cabins' or secret dug-outs with concealed approaches away from the farmsteads where small first-aid posts could be prepared and typists work. Couriers were given special orders to go from village to village along what were termed by Tempo 'international routes', and if the way had to be sought— as when the Bulgarian Trifon Balkanski came out to Tserna Trava —no more was to be asked or given than the way to the next village. If any courier carried papers too big to swallow in emergency some means of burning them must be carried at the same time. After an address at a formal parade Tempo commanded that the brigade was now to be known as the Second South Moravan.

One misty early morning in March 1943, in Tserna Trava there was heard the noise of an aeroplane flying extremely low under Čemernik mountain. Suddenly the whirr of the motor changed to a loud explosion. The Stepanovca peasants ran to the spot in great excitement. Children were there first and were shocked to find corpses littering the meadows. Altogether they found a dozen and sent to tell the partisan commander. Aeroplane fuselage, cabin and wings had been thrown about in confusion. As partisans came on the scene to make a quick search, they snatched out two aircraft machine guns. These were hurried away to be hidden before the Royal Bulgarian authorities should appear. Family and dower chests were brought up on ponies so that the store of unexploded ammunition could be secretly stowed in reliable houses. Using wrenches and crowbars they levered away everything of military use and made sure that the wrecked cabin was completely demolished. When, with teams of commandeered ox-wagons, the party of some 160 Bulgarians arrived to carry the parts back to Sofia, there was nothing of significance left.

Quite casually someone arranged for an explosion that lit the hay in one crowded stable where, eating or drinking or half-asleep, some of the Bulgarian detachment were posted. Flaming tinder and straw fell across the doorway, blocking the exit of that old stone building. In the scramble and panic most of them, overcome by smoke, were burned to death.

On the 20th April the Royal Bulgarian civil representative with his officials came out to Donje Gare and began imposing fines in lieu of taxes, making a charge on every living head, requisitioning cattle and ponies out of their stalls and even requiring payment on the number of orchard trees and beehives. As soon as word came through, the partisan commander, Čićko, sent down a band which in one swoop killed the civil representative, the tax collector and their accompanying police escort.

Perplexed by their delay in returning, a military search party arrived in lorries. The corpses were soon found, for they had been left where they fell, none of the residents wishing to be implicated by disposing of them. The search party immediately posted guards. Donje Gare was blockaded. Reinforcements arrived and began to ransack the village. Seven of the most respected villagers thought to have partisan sympathies were arrested and taken to the school for interrogation under torture. After three days they were brought out into the school playground and made to dig one grave large enough for them all.

The petrified villagers gathered at the fence to watch in a dead silence. The very air seemed to freeze with horror as when the pit was waist deep the condemned men were pushed into line before the machine gun. Old Hrista Grujić suddenly began to shout at the Bulgarian officers. The crowd stepped away from him and he seemed entirely alone.

"Shoot me!" he cried. "Shoot me instead of my son! You only want heads! What difference to you—his or mine? It's all the same to you. Shoot me, I beg, and let him go!"

The Bulgarians stared at the old man and whispered together as he went on raging, "It's all the same! You will have your number. Take me!"

At last the colonel shrugged his shoulders. The son, limp from torture and the forced digging, was dragged away, while the farmer ran gladly to line up with the other six and died with a proud smile in full view of his friends and neighbours.

After the filling-in of that grave, the Royal Bulgarian colonel ordered all the villagers back to their houses with instructions to assemble at eight o'clock next morning on the road east of Donje Gare. Each was allowed to bring as many domestic necessities and possessions as could be carried and all were warned that anyone trying to escape the blockade would be shot.

Next day the inhabitants dragged themselves out on to the assembly place. Some who could not believe their ill fortune were pulled out and pushed along, with their women weeping and children crying, till the number amounted to some 1,300. In loud voices the Bulgarian police continued to shout that it would be worse for anyone who stayed hiding among the buildings. Then, after the count, to add terror to discipline, the Bulgarian colonel ordered all males over fourteen years old to come and line up away on one side. Machine guns were placed and preparations made for a mass execution.

On the stroke of the hour, a corporal came up and saluted to present a letter. The colonel took the document and made a great play of opening and reading it. The high command, he declared in a loud voice, had sent orders countermanding the execution. This gave him the opportunity not only to prove he was only 'acting under orders', but also to emphasise that if any partisans from the mountain had intercepted the message, or killed the courier, or even delayed him for a few minutes on his way, that village road would have run with a river of human blood, the blood of their own people.

As the line of villagers moved out of the valley towards forced labour in Bulgaria, they looked behind and saw their houses in flames. At the sight the womenfolk shrieked and wailed while their bewildered children set up a clamour of sobbing and crying. The guards ran up and down that long, straggling trail, firing shots menacingly over their heads, forcing them into a sullen silence, until, as they dragged on clutching their bundles of chattels, only the quarrelling and howls of the dogs and the cracking of whips accompanied that tragic procession.

Altogether 171 houses, 3 watermills and some 700 other buildings were destroyed. Even after the burning the blackened walls were pulled down in a search for weapons or charred remains of partisans.

About midsummer Slavčo Savov Trunski had come out of Bulgaria the second time, now with four Bulgarian companions. He joined in the attack on the Glavanovca dairy where a rapacious official named Tričkov had set up his requisitioning centre. With nine other police representatives he was directing local garrisons to demand supplies for the German eastern front. As usual the partisans made this attack at night, but in scrambling the fences they alarmed all the dogs, which set up such a terrifying clamour that the enemy police were the first to panic. Tričkov was captured and taken to the local district offices to be shot on the very premises where he had caused so much grief. The dairy was soaked with petrol and totally destroyed.

This action in which the Bulgarian partisans took the lead— Serbs, Macedonians, and Bulgarians fighting in unison—was used to give the lie to enemy divisive propaganda. After telephone wires had been cut, vigorous resistance graffiti were painted everywhere. Only one unfortunate happening marred the effect and that was the desertion of Modrohoj Beči after the action. Whether he was a spy or his defection due merely to cowardice—or did he meet his death in some unknown fashion—for the moment no one knew, but such an incident always gave rise to more anxiety than grief.

7: The British Mission Arrives: The Mountain Victory

Next Ilinden Day, 2nd August 1943, the folk of Macedonia and the partisans in the forested *planinas* heard the overpowering drone of Allied squadrons on their way to bomb the Romanian oilfields. To the lonely peasant leaning on his hayrick it verified rumour. The Allies were winning, the partisans would triumph! A German anti-aircraft gun at Belo Polje shot down one of the American planes. Four airmen escaped, including the pilot Henry Epom. They were collected at once by the partisans and, according to the wish they expressed, sent on from Jablanica to Tito's headquarters by selected courier escort, travelling mostly by night.

The *odred*, always re-forming and re-organising, retained its old headquarters by the Haidouk fountain at Ruplje. Here they had a hidden radio which gave them opportunities to hear the Free Yugoslavia, Moscow and London broadcasts. Such attacks as they planned now aimed at swift accomplishment, capturing weapons, burning archives and vanishing away.

On 28th August news came of the death of Boris, Czar of Bulgaria, news that was greeted with simple glee, though as Simeon II was but a little boy the regency that ruled for him soon became more repressive in a tighter German grip. Next month, the parti-

Tempo parading the British Mission with Mostyn Davies, on the balcony
at Kičevu, September 1943

Tserna Trava

Before the watermill, Tserna Trava

sans having begun to disarm Italians after their capitulation, there was more trouble with *chetniks* expanding from Barbarca; they came in a column supporting the Royal Bulgarians, only to be once again repulsed at Vlasotinca on the night of 15th September. The partisan command was now experienced and throughout that autumn its guerrillas seized quantities of foodstuffs as well as arms. Stores were established in the mountains close at hand to command-posts, where more substantial refreshment than water from the Haidouk well might be obtained and roasted over a brushwood fire!

On 7th November 1943, right in the heart of Tserna Trava, the celebration of the October Revolution was held. The new spirit in the resistance could be measured by the numbers attending, for it was said that 1,000 peasants came together with 700 partisans of the Second South Moravan Brigade. There were sixty partisans from Tserna Trava itself, not counting the sentries and look-outs posted in the surrounding mountains. Trunski was there with his Bulgarian *cheta*, now numbering forty.

Živojin Nikolić Berka and his commissar Vladimir Vujović Vuja, the leaders of the now reorganised *odred*, began the speeches. Trunksi was applauded when he declared that in Tserna Trava the partisan movement was not just the *odred*, for everybody, the whole people, made up the partisan revolution for freedom.

One or two things were only spoken of in whispers: everyone knew there was a typewriter, a duplicator and copying material, and it was rumoured there were as many as six radio sets spread across the *planinas*. The mysterious printing press with its founts of Cyrillic type was never mentioned and so well was the secret kept that its existence above Brod village was not discovered until the end of the war.

All autumn the new party organisers went through the villages, forming little committees and 'cells' for the liberation. Some of these begun among the higher farms were so naïve in pride of patriotism that they went about openly and posed for photographs, weapons in hand and grenades at their belts! 'Cells' of young people were also formed and lists made for the annals of the Communist Youth Union—records which still exist today. Yet in the middle of the Ruplje district falsified entries and forged lists were concocted, a mystery perhaps due to a belated anxiety to feature in history, or maybe from more sinister motives. Perhaps too many were admitted too casually into the ranks, for in spite of the assumed protection of partisan recruits, the heroine Stojanović Vusija, member of the district committee of Anti-fascist Women's Front (A.F.Ž.) and of the central committee of the Communist Party of Yugoslavia (K.P.J.), was surprised and taken in a Royal Bulgarian trap at

D

Vusa village. Unaware of anything untoward, the local watch not apparently being maintained, the other delegates gathered for the conference. The sentry on duty here suddenly deserted his post and ran away. The farmstead was easily surrounded and those within were actually caught wearing full partisan uniforms and with their incriminating documents upon them. The vicious Royal Bulgarian Captain Stojanov was soon on this scene with his cruel system of torture for interrogation, which he now employed to culminate in the barbarous Byzantine executions by impaling. After this disaster, there was a less enthusiastic system of enrolling. New additions were carefully sponsored and screened. One member, though without antecedents, was allowed to remain, attached to the Stručna band, and that was Micky, a tame squirrel He slept in the blouse pocket of Lazina by permission of the band leader, Stroković Vlad, the teacher from Leskovac. Everyone, however hungry, had always an ear of maize, a walnut or a hazel nut or two to spare for him. Even when the band was in hiding Micky would dash out, delighting the partisans by sorting away ears of corn to make his own little hoarding pantry, concealing them in the most secret places with burlesque gestures and somersaults like a born comedian!

Late that autumn Captain Kočo Stojanov led a punitive expedition of a squadron of mounted Bulgarian police with a military detachment into the valleys. Ten villages were simultaneously burned to the ground. All men under fifty years who were caught were transported to forced labour in Bulgaria. Those who had fled were condemned to death *in absentia* as partisans. Cattle were taken also and when the police left a pall of smoke and the stench of ashes hung in the valley.

Scrappy news came to Tserna Trava of the progress of Tempo with their own Second Moravan Brigade as the partisans were fighting their way from the Ilinden valley along the southern frontiers. But not till midwinter, when the forests were bare and the *planinas* snow-covered, did the Second Moravans come back with Apostolski and his Kosuv Brigade.

They were met with great wonder and unrepressed excitement, for accompanying them with bright new automatic rifles were the English soldiers, Major Mostyn Davies and his team, with the Canadian interpreter Nick. The Bulgarian partisans were particularly glad for they hoped to draw the mission to be specially attached to themselves as the source of supply for insurrection in Bulgaria. This, they argued, was the one thing needed to increase their numbers. Already because of their small enrolment they had not been strong enough to secure the one 'drop' of equipment allocated them and it had fallen into the hands of the Royal Bulgarians.

Vlado Tričkov came out from the secret headquarters of the Fatherland Front in Sofia to meet Mostyn Davies and press for this special mission to the partisans inside Bulgaria. There the resist-ance was the most persecuted in Europe and was the more depressed by being completely unknown to the West. Balkanski and Trunski joined in the appeal. By radio contact with Cairo, tentative suggestions were made for a real Bulgarian mission on the same scale as that in Yugoslavia if, and this was the essential condition, the preliminary resistance centres were prepared.

There was a more immediate difficulty for Major Mostyn Davies. It was now depth of winter. The partisans had vivid memories of the Allied planes going over in hordes for the pattern-bombing of the Romanian oil-fields. The sight of this team of Englishmen with neat packs, revolvers and binoculars kindled expectation of imme-date supplies raining down from above!

The British mission was lodged at the farmstead of Randgela Sinadinović, and at the first meeting of the central committee there Zivojin Nikolić angrily grumbled that the English had been seven days in Tserna Trava and none of the promised weapons had been given out. He became savage in his accusation. The enemy were only the other side of Orlovac mountain, and the battle was immi-nent. Without weapons? They had been waiting days to transport the equipment. It was not just that their lives would be lost. The Royal Bulgarians would triumph. The cause would be lost. Tserna Trava might cease to be 'free territory'.

Mostyn Davies needed all Nick's help to explain. He quoted his radio reports of the storms over the Mediterranean which had made air transport impossible. When the storms passed, and they were the usual midwinter storms, everything would be all right. Until then, nothing more could be done. Never had the Slav negative seemed so menacing as when *"Oruzja mema"*[1] echoed round that crowded farmhouse, and Mostyn Davies found his firm explanation unacceptable to his hosts.

Before the desperation of the partisans could push him into anger, he broke off his association with the meeting, promising to go straight to his radio and demand supplies from Cairo once again, but insisting that their own headquarters with Tito were as powerful as he. They should demand that Tito also ask for weapons. As he left the meeting amongst some embarrassment, he repeated, "Let Tito ask also! Send to Tito!"

For the English mission this was the most anxious time of all. They were hungry, their personal supplies were short. After that dangerous journey up from Central Macedonia, they had expected

[1] "There are no rifles".

to winter in a safe retreat in those wild mountains. They found themselves in the very jaws of a savage enemy offensive which was intended finally to Bulgarise Macedonia and exterminate any Serbian elements. Mostyn Davies now had some idea of the lavish expectations which had preceded the mission's arrival. It had indeed been regarded as the new mainstay of the resistance. The straight, sullen looks of those partisans told of disillusion and emphasised his own isolation. Back pages of *Vesti* (*News*), roughly typed duplicated news-sheets as they were, when translated by Nick clearly indicated these optimistic expectations were now dashed to the ground.

Mostyn Davies was too much of a Civil Service man to give any opinion even to his colleagues, but he had plenty of time to think about S.O.E. in Cairo during the next day or two when he made his routine journeys up to the dropping grounds. These were well chosen, wide meadows fenced only by the beech forests and lodged in the rolls of the *planinas*. If the fires were lit to signal a drop, nothing would be seen across the mountains, neither the garrison in Leskovac nor the military on the frontiers would notice a glimmer.

At last, on the afternoon of 19th December, the positive message came from Cairo. The mountain tracks all had sentries posted. At dusk Mostyn Davies and the shock troops went up through the deep frost and waited. The sky was clear and starlit. Late, not till towards midnight, as they waited by Pavlov's Mound, listening through the dark, did they hear the drone of the promised transport planes. Almost before the order, the partisans ran with petrol cans to ignite the fires.

The signal letter, all ablaze, came out perfectly. A wink of light in the sky blinked the first pilot's acceptance, Mostyn Davies shouted to bring the men back to the trees. Some came, others ran wild with joy under the very whistle of the canisters falling with the flap, flap of their diminutive parachutes. There were four planes altogether. The crump, crump of the intruding downfall as the canisters hit the hard snow or broke through the beeches with a crash of branches, taught everyone to take cover. The noise of the planes wheeling above the 'drop' was recognised by every peasant in the valley. Men and women jumped out of bed, dressed and came running up the mountain, caring nothing for the deep snow and the frost. Ordinary, peaceful folk caught the knack of finding the parachutes in the half-light of dawn. Ponies and donkeys seemed as keen and ready as the peasants. The whole supply was collected and scattered through the farmsteads to be hidden in rocks and secret earth-cabins.

Lights had begun to go up in the enemy barracks indicating they were aware something was afoot, but, two years of fighting the partisans having taught them not to venture along the ravines at night, they dared not stir outside their barbed wire.

Next day all the Tserna Trava district expected trouble, and, sure enough, the occupying enemy forces began to move from Orlovac. Villagers vanished into their earth-cabins, but many took heart and tried to join the partisans who were sharing out the new English rifles and ammunition. Ambushes were laid and plans for the defence of Tserna Trava put into operation. A wild renewal of enthusiasm seemed to breathe through every partisan patrol. The partisans chose to invest the forest of their favourite mountain, Čemernik. Here they awaited the enemy whose long columns wound in a great circling manoeuvre through all the valley roads.

There was now deep snow and the confusion of mist which carried the uproar of ambushes and the crackle of gunfire from far-away villages, making even distant conflicts seem close at hand. The main central enemy column came to Čemernik first, but, meeting fire from above, began to take cover and wait. The most relentless column came across from Trun in Bulgaria, burning and destroying cattle sheds and any houses still remaining, raping women who had stayed in their kitchens and plundering anything worth while.

Tserna Trava was empty. All the population had come on to the mountain to take a stand behind the rambling and uneven lines of the partisans that made a kind of defensive camp, as in the old Turkish days when they would so make ramparts and entrench against the Sultan's troops; and, just as then, they found themselves jobs, peeling potatoes, cutting bread, cooking maize and chestnuts. Even the children sorted and arranged ammunition or were detailed as messengers.

Not till later in the morning when the mist stole higher did firing break out on Čemernik itself and the enemy begin to attack in force. They were shocked at the volume of the fusillade that came down to meet them; at the new English automatics, the Bren guns and above all at the rapid burst of devastation from that great aeroplane machine cannon saved from the fallen American bombing plane. Village blacksmiths had repaired one of the two and mounted it upon a heavy iron stand, but until today fear of detection had prevented its being fired. Now it banged defiance and its shells exploded on the enemy's entrenched positions, causing panic and dismay, so that, though the fighting lasted all day, the Royal Bulgarians dared not come up the slope.

That night was bitterly cold and so frosty the trampled snow froze hard underfoot into block ice. Next morning, the mist had frozen away, making visibility sharp and clear upon cleaner white snow and hoar frost. As the sun climbed, the bright air seemed to betray every movement, especially that of the seasoned Kosuv detachment which had been held on the higher slopes to reinforce any weakness in the line of battle. Despite this, lines of communication were maintained, the wounded were sent out along pre-determined lanes of retreat, and good meals of hot potatoes stewed in the copper boilers were served out to everyone.

The enemy had fled from first positions and the partisans occupied their trenches, relying on the shells from the American aeroplane gun having long enough range to smash up their second line also. The more experienced partisans crept forward with grenades. The children carried up ammunition and refreshments while new recruits stayed in allotted places and picked off enemies who showed themselves. The Kosov Brigade came towards the centre like a wedge. Before it the enemy suddenly weakened, breaking line as the Royal Bulgarian police took to their heels, causing either wing to retreat in panic, fearing to be encircled. With wild yells of triumph the partisans gave chase, shooting into the backs of their enemies who dashed down to escape along the stream. As for the aeroplane gun, the crew, anxious to join the pursuit, looked madly round, and in fierce enthusiasm let go a couple of cannon shells into the air above both pursued and pursuers, adding to the panic. Children caught in the excitement of victory ran downhill screaming and snatching up rifles abandoned by the wounded who lay mangled in that now dirty and bloodstained snow.

A hundred and twenty-seven enemy dead were counted and forty wounded. Thirty captured men were taken away. What could the partisans in their desperation do with either wounded or captured? Nobody asked. Clothing was valuable that winter; belongings, any possessions at all, were useful to those burned-out peasants. Bodies were stripped, as in the medieval ways of war.

Mostyn Davies and his team were present at the reckoning and checked the military booty. As the equipment was being collected, news arrived of the successful ambushes which had held back enemy reinforcements along the narrow approach valleys. The enemy were retiring towards the frontier and re-grouping on the higher ground across the wide bogs of Vlasina (where the great lake is today). The Second Moravan partisans hurried up the valley and attacked them here in the night, but they were tired now whereas the enemy was in strength, so they contented themselves with plundering stores under cover of the dark and came back to rest.

News of the defeat at Čemernik and the unexpected fire power of the partisans caused a German division to be hurried into the mountains to take over from the Royal Bulgarians. These Germans came up with the Second South Moravans who were relaxing at

Baince. Despising 'peasant rebels' they recklessly charged into the village to find themselves cut down by rapid fire from English tommy-guns out of the small windows of those old stone houses. Twenty-eight were killed. A machine-gun crew of six Germans who led the action was captured together with the machine-gun, automatic rifles and much ammunition. These six Germans were curiosities to be sent on alive to the Central Committee headquarters as (officially) the first Germans taken at Tserna Trava.

On 23rd December Mostyn Davies attended the meeting at the partisan headquarters at Ruplje and next day went to Dobro Polje to consider a better place for a dropping ground. Dobro Polje is one of the historic places in modern Balkan history, for here, on 16th September 1918, the Bulgarian troops at Raina mutinied, abandoned their trenches and careered back to Sofia to demand the abdication of Czar Ferdinand. The river spreads out at Dobro Polje through a wide, flat valley, and high on the dome-shaped mountains are long natural runways of greensward.

Rumours came in of the Royal Bulgarian divisions being withdrawn. The German division replacing them was beginning, as the partisans complained, without regard to the 'international laws of soldiers' a campaign of torture, execution and plundering the villagers.

Christmas was spent by the British team in the pleasant village of Brod, down below Tserna Trava. Here there could be a brief reprieve from the anxious discussions of the certainty of reprisals, of speculating which village would be burned first and who should be brought up to the mountains. Tase Nikolića's coffee house was in the square, and was warm and comfortable. Here the British mission was close to the secret radio station from which, besides the message to Tito, a hearty message which was more than seasonal went out to Cairo. The mission had now redeemed its popularity, its purpose was recognised. S.O.E. had backed up its men in the nick of time and its emissaries were now harbingers of victory to all Macedonians, Serbs and Bulgarian partisans.

8: Enemy Reprisals

After the new year opened Mostyn Davies realised that, quite apart from reprisals as a deterrent, the Germans were conducting a systematic search to locate his mission. This was the more serious

because S.O.E. were arranging to augment his staff and help him
satisfy the Bulgarian partisans who now regarded it as a matter of
national honour to press for a British mission specially for them.
The Fatherland Front was sending more representatives from Sofia.
The 'aerodrome' at Dobro Polje was ready and Captain Frank
Thompson and his men were waiting to be brought over when the
weather was right. They should have come earlier, but the urgency
for military supplies had had priority, so no men were dropped that
night before the Čemernik battle. He smiled grimly as he reflected
how difficult it would have been with another half dozen Englishmen
in the mountains and no largesse of weapons. Yet they would have
came down that night safely. As it was, the heaps of brushwood
at Dobro Polje, the petrol cans secretly arranged at this new dropping
ground—all might be discovered!

On 5th January the Royal Bulgarian army came up from Skopje,
their armoured trucks in force coming through the lightly-held
entrance to the valley, searching for any traces of the British equipment, and their technicians tracking especially for the radio station
which they supposed had communicated with the transport planes.
Up on inaccessible trees near Tservenkovci hamlet, right under
Čemernik, they found two English parachute balloons—nothing
else, but enough to excite their suspicions. They turned the little
cluster of cottages inside out and shot five villagers one after the
other in the broad winter daylight.

Then, in the cottage of Mileva Sinadinović, something seemed to
excite suspicion. Mostyn Davies's radio station had been there at
the end of December, and there was also a cache of the British
war supplies concealed near by. They searched again and again
and would not pass on. Mileva stood there watching them with a
proud smile and denying their suggestions. She was seized and held
by the soldiers who threatened to burn the house unless she gave
them the secret of the radio station. Brushwood was piled up ready.
Mileva went stiff and tightened her lips, prepared to see her home
in ashes.

"We can make you talk," said the police official. "We can make
everybody talk. You can talk now or after suffering."

Slowly and with expectant pauses, the flogging began. The little
knot of old women and children who had been dragged from their
shelters, muttered as they watched. Kept at bay by rifle butts and
bayonets, they froze with horror as the beatings turned to torture.
Mileva's nails were plucked out. She could no longer stand, and, as
they began to cut off her fingers one by one, with the intervals for
slow, calm, persuasive questioning between each amputation, the
sky swung before her eyes. She cast a look upon her son, seven-

year-old Peru. A soldier was holding him and his torture had
begun.

The vital strength of madness came upon her. In the power of
frenzy she brushed aside the burly soldiers pinioning her arms.
With her blood-dripping hands she seized the rifle that was threatening her son and drove its fixed bayonet through his heart. The
soldiers recoiled as she stared down at the dead body of her tortured child, waving her tormented arms and screaming, "Fly, my
child! Out of here! Away from vampires, fascists and scum! The
day shall dawn ..."

The swing of a rifle butt cut her words away and she fell. Ten
soldiers ran together to add their blows where she lay on the slushy
snow, spreading her arms and mouthing words of defiance which
she could no longer utter. The policemen with the petrol lit the fire
and the blaze wrapped the house. Without an order or any instructions, they caught up her living body with bayonets on an upturned
table which they held into the flames till she was burned alive. Sick
and stunned, the little crowd of peasants was hustled away with
rough threats, except for poor old Velimir, one of the oldest small-
holders there, who was dragged away and after a cruel beating left
dying in the snow by the roadside.

The secret knowledge of the radio station and the cache of
British arms had been burned with Mileva and her little son. Though
the punitive column went on through the villages around the ruins
of Tserna Trava and did to death, some say, as many as one
hundred people and came as near to its location as Ruplje and
Brod, no one was ever found to betray it.

The news of this bestial terror came up the mountain to Mostyn
Davies and filled the liaison mission not just with indignation but
with a great deal of concern akin to guilt. The bitterness of the
Balkan midwinter in war time, the starving peasants deprived of their
young men on forced labour in Bulgaria, was bad enough without
fomenting this local war and its atrocious reprisals.

"Once you follow the road of such thinking," the British signals
sergeant grumbled, "you get on to the same ground as Mihailović,
and where does that lead?"

Nick, who was free of the language with all the partisans, knew
in any case of many such tragic incidents that had happened before
the British had arrived.

The roofless cottages were real enough, however, and now a
watch-tower had been built by the enemy on the *planina* above Kačar
Forest. The partisans through binoculars showed to Mostyn Davies
the sentry peering out across the slopes, unwittingly thinking he too

could see through those woods and valleys. The whiter the snow, they said, the less he will see into the forest shadows.

The blackened ruin of the lonely farm just below them near Kačar had its own story. In the previous March the partisan *cheta* had come out of the forest and taken shelter there from the deep snow and bitter frost. The husband on that farm was interned in Bulgaria and the wife had three young children, yet she shared her food and made the partisans warm and welcome. At about ten o'clock she got up to give the youngest child the breast. Sitting by the window she happened to glance towards the forest. Keeping quite calm, she shouted, "Get your rifles, comrades! The Bulgarians are here!"

Before the farm could be surrounded, the partisans had jumped through the windows and fought their way back into the forest. In condemnation for sheltering partisans, the Royal Bulgarians burned the house down and she was killed on the very threshold, her children left in the snow. "The baby is adopted and growing well, and as for the other two, you can see them playing in Ruplje village, pretending to be partisans!" concluded Nick, with a touch of realism.

Any movements were always made at night. The wounded, laid up in earth-cabins or ruined cattle stalls, could be visited then, and supplies of potatoes, wheat and cornflour brought from less impoverished districts to be shared out. That winter was the worst for any wounded partisan. There were no doctors, men had to depend on the bravery of women and on their own natural healing powers and ability to lie secret underground.

Mostyn Davies kept sending immediate requests for medical supplies, though when they actually arrived he was more concerned as to how they would be used. Natural healing was better than 'kill or cure' by inexpert hands. Discovery of any traces of British pharmaceutical wrappings or remedies could lead to extreme penalties for the amateur nurses, but the plight of many young men seemed appalling as they lay injured in the earth-cabins, hourly expecting discovery and relying on healing by plum brandy and rags. The few selected barns like that at Todorovca were only temporarily safe.

It was not only the condition of the wounded that was the worry that January. The accumulated weapons hidden in the secret dumps could be discovered. Lying under the snow they were certainly deteriorating. The captured Italian and German equipment now made that little district the most heavily armed of the Serbian Macedonian borders, for there was also access to the explosives stolen by the Mačkat miners. He knew the presence of the mission must be known to the enemy and felt the pressing need to move away from the valley and be no longer the cause of the peasants suffering police interrogation.

During the next conference Mostyn Davies promised that as soon as they shared out the surplus arms, still more and even better ones would come from Cairo. Cairo, however, did not sanction his moving out. He was to keep stationed near the dropping ground to arrange for a subsidiary mission to make contact with the Bulgarian partisans who were impatiently waiting under their leader, Vlado Tričkov. A considerable quantity of arms was to go to the Kosuv and South Moravan partisans with Tempo, but it was agreed to send the main share to the Bulgarian bands along the frontier, now referred to as the 'Demarcation Line'.

Six strong ponies were seized from the valley farms and loaded with twenty-eight boxes of ammunition and as many rifles and items of military equipment as they could carry. Fourteen picked men, each a walking arsenal, set off in the afternoon, led by Ćira Drumski and the pre-war army sergeant, Voja Milovanović. Rakić Stanka was jumping for joy beside the ponies, hoping at Jablanica to see his partisan brother from whom he had been separated for a whole year. Mostyn Davies watched them go with some trepidation. They were so lighthearted. Singing as they went along, they could have been going to a wedding festival.

It was a January winter afternoon, the light soon faded and the little column trudged on through the snow, traversing those dark *planinas* until they came to the frontier and hid away to await their couriers. These had sped on a fourteen-hour race before them to make the necessary contacts. Punctually they came out to bring them in and conduct them safely through the gloom of early morning into Lapotinca village of Jablanica region. As soon as the first of the ammunition boxes was brought in and opened, the partisans ran their fingers through the thousands of brass cartridges as if they were gold or silver coins. Lapotinca village went wild with delight. About a hundred rifles were shared out there and then. The fourteen partisans were fêted from house to house. Reeling with rakija, men and women danced in the street as if the war was over. Only the deep snowdrifts protected the village from certain discovery during three days of joyful uproar.

Perhaps this was really why all the fourteen declared the journey back difficult and toilsome. They grumbled that they had to make many detours to by-pass villages where *chetniks* and informers lived, and as for Rakić Stanka, he did not meet his brother. Yet every one of them returned successfully at seven o'clock on the morning when the Second Moravan Brigade made their first New Year thrust against the return of the enemy.

The first sign of that enemy offensive was a plane from Leskovac, which on a clear day flew over the farmsteads dropping leaflets. Printed in a muddled Serbo-Macedonian dialect, Cyrillic type of course, and also in Bulgarian, the pamphlets commanded all men between eighteen and fifty years of age to report immediately to the nearest Bulgarian barracks, failing which they would be deemed rebels and executed as such. The committee, who had seen such edicts before, acted at once to put into practice their civil defence plan. Mostyn Davies and his team realised that the leaflet amounted to an extermination decree and could only marvel at the cool fatalism with which it was received.

Messages and couriers were sent to Tempo. Meeting after meeting was held. Many men were recruited directly into the Liberation Army and took the oath. Others were given special advice on refuges, and on concealing earth-cabins—not easy between the snowstorms; in fact a successful long-term hide in an earth-cabin depended most on reliable women and children.

Tempo advised an attack on Kriva Palanka where, in a huge concentration camp, some hundreds of peasants had already been penned up. In a determined advance through the dead of a January night his partisans swept up and slaughtered the garrison, destroyed the post and freed the starving prisoners who came back on to the mountains in dire need of clothing, boots and food, to say nothing of rifles.

Never a meeting went by without some activist making an urgent appeal to Mostyn Davies to radio the Allies for direct supplies in greater quantity. As the skirmishes resulting from each ambush became more bitter, once again the tension increased and once again he felt that sense of impotent responsibility. There were now squads of men drilling without arms who could only hide when hostilities began. During the day, leaving the radio operator, he would take a party of boys to work on the dropping ground, covering the store of brushwood to keep it dry, and marking the bases with stones where the fires would start to light up the signal letters. One or two dummy dropping grounds were made, just for luck.

True to signals, in the second January week the airfield proved itself. Almost to the hour the British planes came over. Every fire blazed along the letters and down came the canisters. The young partisans were in charge. Everything had to be carried on their backs this time, for there were no ponies available. The early morning search was more thorough than after that first drop on Čemernik;

every parachute and marker balloon was found and taken away to be hidden. Besides the rifles there were precious boots, clothing, medical supplies, food and grain for the spring sowing of the peasants.

Shortly after this came a tragic incident involving one of the young pioneers, the most active and vivacious of the partisan youth brigade. As the Fifth Royal Bulgarian Army with its Fourteenth and Seventeenth Infantry Divisions moved slowly up from the Skopje roads, some of their N.C.O.s noticed that one lad was constantly appearing and re-appearing, sometimes after several hours. Always he would be busy on some innocuous peasant task, gathering sticks, or repairing a stone wall, but on many different properties. Twelve-year-old Tomislav Stojanović Vuzija, on his own initiative, was keeping a daring watch on the enemy and reporting back, even hoping to get news by overhearing conversations.

Since boys generally ran away and disappeared, his hardihood was unusual and attracted attention. He was seized and questioned. At first he was prodded with knives. As he continued to refuse information, the police began torture, passing him through their vicious stages as if he were an adult. Though he knew the whereabouts of the partisan headquarters and the hiding places of the cache of papers, even the printing press and typewriter, he betrayed nothing and was shot.

The Serbian forces of Nedić and Mihailović's *chetniks*, which followed the Royal Bulgarian Army like jackals, did not come far up the valley. When their leader Ćora was severely wounded after a few skirmishes they faltered and lost heart. The main Bulgarian Army and the Germans, however, were preparing their most ruthless spring offensive. Every partisan meeting gloomily insisted this would intensify as the snows melted.

Now and again Bulgarian deserters would find their way into the mountains to be kept apart from the partisan *odred* and handed over to Tričkov and Trunski. These Bulgarian freedom fighters continued to insist that they too should have a separate military mission with British liaison officers so that they could march into Bulgaria. That prospect began to seem remote to Mostyn Davies, tied down as he was and surrounded by enemy forces. Nevertheless the promise had been made, and the Bulgarians expected the new mission with confident enthusiasm.

9: The Augmented Mission of 'Mulligatawny'

After one or two disappointments the authorities at Cairo considered that the night of 27th January was favourable. Mostyn Davies, the partisan leaders from the *odred* and the Bulgarian representatives went up to the dropping ground and waited. The roar of the planes seemed the loudest yet. The fires blazed and the signal winked. The transports came in, flying low. Even today in the mountains, they say twenty-four planes made that enormous drop. Actually, down came the canisters and the planes wheeled round again, and once more, to dump all the cargo, then the last plane almost hovering in a penetrating whistle; but as it left the white of parachutes patched the night sky, falling determinedly, becoming larger and bearing up men.

Again it was the young boys who found the newcomers, tearing along after the parachutes, jumping upon them and holding them firm, shouting in whispers. Captain Frank Thompson and his team from the sunshine of Cairo had come to augment the mission on the snowfields of that Balkan night. A Bulgarian partisan was the first to encounter the young English captain, who surprised him with "*Narodni partisani?*" and welcoming phrases in real Bulgarian!

Neither Frank Thompson nor Mostyn Davies had met before they shook hands on that dropping ground, making themselves into a reception committee for the rest of the team, and at the same time encouraging the great scramble to retrieve all the equipment. Everyone had come down safely. The parachute material had now become immediately essential, much too valuable to bury or hide away. The neat uniforms of the newcomers gave Mostyn Davies a shock.

"Straight from the bar at Shepheard's Hotel!" he exclaimed with a grim smile, and taking out his silver whisky flask, "Try our Tserna Trava cocktails?"

Then, remembering his rank and seniority and buttoning down his flask, "So they do know about us then," he continued gruffly.

The motley throng of partisans, men, women, boys and girls, wrapped in bundles of rags with here and there a military uniform —German or Italian—sown up and with the rents that had slain the previous owner mended, were well enough protected against the cold and glowed as they ran about in the moonlight, their very shadows appearing to steam on the snow.

The first essential was to clear the dropping ground and get everything away. There was more material than had been anticipated, but though there were yet no ponies for transport, even the smallest boys were quite desperate in begging to take the largest loads. As they wound down to the river, other parties hurried up to help, carrying poles and canvas for makeshift litters. An hour or so at dawn was all the time they could use. After that, the morning mist might lift and the enemy move in, perhaps calling up a reconnaissance plane from Leskovac.

Mostyn Davies found the new arrivals had been well briefed on conditions, but as far as their operational future was concerned knew as little as he.

"To make contact, to bring down weapons and equipment out of the sky, and report and report," summarised Captain Thompson dryly, pulling at his pipe.

"And never to be caught," added Mostyn Davies.

Mostyn Davies knew safety depended in being on the move and also on the mission being very small. It was now a larger team and there were no definite orders about dividing it or apportioning any of the mission to the Bulgarian partisans. He guessed Cairo wanted the newcomer to be seasoned first, but that meant remaining in one place. The mission had already been in Tserna Trava too long. He wished Tempo would arrive and set things moving.

Whereas Mostyn Davies kept to strict B.L.O. rules and avoided definite political expression and never gave any indication of commitment, Frank Thompson made no secret of his sympathies in this war for the freedom of all the peoples. "Boyish frankness and high spirits!" thought Major Mostyn Davies, consoling himself that, even when boasting of his ultra-left affiliations, such a colleague was more acceptable to the partisans. Acceptable Frank Thompson undoubtedly was, to the Bulgarians especially. He had already some knowledge of Bulgarian, and as he worked to improve this the Fatherland Front representatives began to claim him as theirs exclusively.

There was a contrast between the two Englishmen that under any other conditions than active service would have made for a clash. Major Mostyn Davies believed in and was experienced in exercising authority, he achieved discipline not just by seniority but by the reticence and impersonality of rigid devotion to that routine which some call duty and which is preserved by rank. His young captain, an idealist with the missionary tradition of giving confidence in order to obtain trust, expanded and revealed his own personality with a

frank abandon that worried his major. His blind faith in these
partisans was unmilitary.

February came. The expected search and punitive campaign by
the enemy did not materialise. The partisans grew gay, light-hearted
and thirsty for celebrations. A great meeting was called for 4th
February. Word went along the valleys and into the highest mountain hamlets, rumours of a magnificent share-out of weapons, clothing, equipment and, best of all, corn for the spring sowing. The
partisan army protected the roadways in a demonstration of strength.
Long columns of peasants came down the mountain tracks, accor-
dions playing and clarinets blowing: girls were in the brightest
folk costumes, old men in Serbian caps and velveted breeches.
Everyone who could perform brought out some old-fashioned
Serbian instrument to play his friends down to Jabukovik meadows,
where townsman and peasant gathered as if at the biggest market
of the century. But nothing here was bought or sold. For patriots
everything was free, and the trade was in hearty friendship, singing
and dancing, and the declamation of partisan ballads.

About eleven o'clock the trumpets began to blow. The partisans
lined up before the people, the lucky ones holding bright new
weapons and using cartridges as ornaments and decorations. Unused
to such crowds since war began, it seemed to the folk of Jabukovik
as if thousands and thousands were assembled as they welcomed
friends to their burned-out, ruined houses. The rooks whirled disconsolate overhead, taking no shelter in the trees, and the magpies
clattered angrily, driven away to the forest fringes, but the sky was
clear and the white snow on the surrounding mountains seemed to
pour sunshine down upon the valley meadow, making it like a
summer day. Even the many women wearing mourning grew cheerful and chattered with hope.

The representatives of the partisan high command were there,
self-conscious and important, and also Major Mostyn Davies and
Captain Frank Thompson with the English mission, for this great
occasion, thanks to the supply of British weapons, was to be the
establishment of the new Fifth South Moravan Brigade. After the
usual preliminary military movements of men and weapons to orders,
the trumpets blew again, and the delegates made their addresses about
the meaning of that day, the purpose of the struggle and the certainty
of victory. With a dramatic flourish the representative of the central
committee and the high command showed the document which established the staff of the new brigade and read its contents to the people,
naming as commandant, Ćura Zlatković Milić, and deputy, Radoslav
Mitrović Šumadinac, with Denovski Dinko Zare as political commissar.

General Apostolski, Major Mostyn Davies, General Tempo (copy of a photograph found on Mostyn Davies at Dobro Polje)

Captain Stoyanov's headquarters, the school at Gorni Bogrov

The Bulgarian soldier deserters forming the Hristo Botev partisans

This was Tempo's policy, the proliferation of brigades. No sooner was one formation of his partisans shattered or dispersed, than he held a meeting, gathered the remnants with promises of ultimate victory, appointed commanders, issued a new banner and proclaimed a new brigade. The Abwehr itself was astonished at this extraordinary multiplication of brigades, which puzzled them at first and then by its vigour and persistence excited their envy.

Every speaker instanced the British mission as an emblem of victory. Future attacks on Darkovačke and Gradski, along the river or the valley, all would end in triumph for the partisans! Each speaker conjured spontaneous cheers and shouts of approval, and each round of applause culminated in a tribute to their friends the Allies, the Soviet Union, and the British mission they had received as guests.

Major Mostyn Davies was called upon to speak. With the Canadian, Nick, at his side to interpret, the pauses in translation gave him time to compose the encouragement his listeners needed. As he stood on the rough platform, his clear English voice rang out mysteriously across the heads of the people towards the high snowfields, probably the first English military voice there since crusading times.

His words, as upon Nick's Canadian-Slav tongue they changed into Serbian, gave unbounded pleasure. With another enthusiastic cheer the partisan formation disbanded in laughter and jocularity and the merriment began. Smells of potatoes cooking and roasting corn cobs drifted along with the semi-oriental music as some tuned and some played while the women made up the wood-burning fires. Partisan songs were taken up by many over-vociferous groups. The sentiments of these were provocative enough to cause the more volatile men to look for their rifles and fire them off, first in the direction of the enemy barracks at Svodge, then wildly into the air. And especially when the dance circle of the kolo began to revolve, wilder spirits ran round the ring firing as madly as in the oriental times when the Turkish regiments ruled: "Just to show we have a military brigade!" "An invitation to where the Germans lie in the bunkers!" "Our bullets are invitation cards!" "Let them come as guests!" "Come Fascist swine! Come and join the kolo!"

Every young man had a joke to crack which needed punctuating, an exclamation mark made by the crack of a rifle bullet. The *planinas* of Tumbi echoed and re-echoed against the wild shooting. As he smoked his pipe, Frank Thompson was bewildered. He strolled about with Mostyn Davies, who was a little more used to this effervescence.

E

"They don't allow for any love-making in the shrubbery!" he commented, as a volley shot across the hillside.

"We can't stop them," replied the Major. "We're only spectators. For all that, I wonder what G.H.Q. would think!"

They protested mildly at first to the partisan staff, and then with more exasperation. As the extravagance of ammunition began to seem limitless, the leaders went through the excited groups remonstrating, achieving a partial success which only made the sudden, unexpected crack of a close-at-hand gunshot the more disturbing. As the afternoon wore on it seemed to Mostyn Davies a whole battle had been fired away, if not fought. The cartridges were the price of goodwill, however, so he contented himself with strolling around smiling and dropping the comment in Serbian, "They are not blanks, you know! Kill a German, not a partisan!" a remark which had no effect except to provoke hilarity.

Late in the mid-afternoon, as soon as the sun disappeared, the cold wind blew down from the snow on the mountains. The potatoes had been eaten with bits of sausage, black bread and tough burnt mutton. The bugles blew and the partisans formed up to march in a long column out of the Jabukovik meadows. They went up in their usual single file over the snow, blowing hand kisses back to the thrown kisses of the women. There were no shots now, for they were going towards the enemy and no longer felt as secure as down among those ruined roofless houses, though they left with boisterous rhetorical shouts: "Here come the Foresters!" "Remember the Fifth Brigade, the Adventurers' Brigade!" "Onward the shock *cheta*!"

That evening more arms were distributed at Pusta Reka to the untried men who had none and wisely, as it turned out, for the celebration had not gone without notice, and the retaliation it was bound to provoke was soon on the way. The Royal Bulgarians met them at Mlačišta village and were driven back by Lužnica in the direction of the barracks at Svodge, from where they were reinforced until, over 200 strong in numbers, they moved towards Kozila and Rakov Dol. The unexpected armed strength of the partisans combined with the treacherous snowdrifts to defeat them, however, and they withdrew from all their outposts.

The British mission were out of these skirmishes, having gone straight back to Dobro Polje, where news came in of how, when cutting once again the Belgrade railway between Skopje and Nish, the partisans had been opposed on the slopes of Ruja mountain by the Fourth Chetnik Brigade of Draža Mihailović on 10th February. The Second South Moravan partisans with the Macedonian 'Shepherds' Battalion had killed 70, wounded 40 and taken 136 prisoners, to say nothing of a great deal of booty. This had been the signal for the partisans to clean their 'free territory' of some such groups of military bandits fighting with the red star on their hats. Mostyn Davies and Frank Thompson listened to this news that February with concern. They remembered the B.B.C. homage to Mihailović and knew of the B.L.O.s stationed with him. The bad weather that ensued gave the mission time to prepare for contacts with the Bulgarians. Frank Thompson was finding his Russian an easy stepping stone to the Bulgarian language and found an intelligent Bulgarian, Gočo Gopin, with whom he arranged an exchange of language lessons. Gočo already had a good smattering of English, though not as much as Vlado Tričkov. Mostyn Davies also spent some time in gaining the conversational essentials, though he found his Spanish very little help and the Bulgarian post-positive article confusing.

10: Spring Offensive

On 16th December 1943, after a surprise action on the frontier, sixty Royal Bulgarian soldiers with horses and full equipment had deserted. They had heard of the freedom movements in the Sredna Gora mountains. Georgi Dimitrov's voice had come to them over the Russian radio, and the Fatherland Front had made its contacts among them. On 19th December, at Fuštani on the slopes of Kožuv *planina*, they had paraded and declared their allegiance to the National Liberation Struggle, naming themselves the Hristo Botev Battalion after the Bulgarian poet-hero of the nineteenth century. Tempo had welcomed them with enthusiasm. The Trun Bulgarian partisan division now came down to winter at Dobro Polje and renamed itself the Vasil Levski Battalion after their famous revolutionary martyr.

They held a great celebration near Tserna Trava at the beginning of March, less ebullient than that on the Jabukovik meadows. With the Bulgarian soldiers neatly arranged, their horses still with them, making a parade of showy military manoeuvres, there was the usual interlude for inflammatory speeches, the worker revolutionaries of the Vasil Levski partisans being more verbose, with that delightful shake of the head that makes a Bulgarian positive affirmation. There was no random firing of bullets on the occasion of this celebration. Across the frontier they knew every cartridge would be needed to free Bulgaria, where as yet there were no dropping grounds.

They were internationally minded, these Bulgarians, and welcomed even the party of Italian ex-soldiers. These had been disarmed by the German garrison at the capitulation of Italy on 8th September, treated like slaves and impressed for forced labour at the Mačkat mine. They had escaped in a body and were now proving themselves good comrades and, after all their disillusionment, eager Communists. Mostyn Davies found several among them who knew Spanish and had been to Spain even before the Civil War.

Much of the talk between Mostyn Davies and Frank Thompson speculated on the future of the mission. S.O.E. apparently only wanted to know what was going on inside Bulgaria. 'Contact and report'—the old formula without precise objectives. But the Bulgarians, Vlado Tričkov and Trifon Balkanski, demanded action, the same treatment as for Tito, two missions at least! Let only dropping grounds for arms be arranged and the whole nation would rise from Varna to Sofia! S.O.E. was about to move from Cairo to Bari. It was still midwinter and the weather was atrocious. The wireless stations were working well, both the partisan set at Brod and that of the mission at Dobro Polje. They had now to await the arrival of Tempo from his operations in the Kozjak *planina*.

Any danger to Dobro Polje would come up the valley from the direction of Leskovac, where there was an airfield in addition to the German barracks. Also the road through Vlasotinci-Babusnica-Priot made the boundary of Mihailović's *chetnik* region. The little township of Vlasotinci held the entrance to the valley, so in early March the partisans decided to occupy it in order to test whether the people there were still Mihailović inclined; also Vlasotinci could give early warning and hold up any spring offensive.

After the usual formalities of cutting telephone wires and blocking roads, a brisk attack was launched against the enemy positions. At once there broke out the most deafening clamour. All the church bells rang, out of time and tune, some cracked as if hit with hammers, sirens screamed and steam engines blared out their whistles loud enough to warn the railway along the Morava River. This was *chetnik* resistance without a doubt and would have brought up the enemy garrison from Svodge as well as Leskovac. After blowing up as many installations as possible, the partisans discreetly withdrew. Next day the Nedić Press was able to report a brave victory by the citizens of Vlasotinci against an army of 2,000 partisans equipped with modern weapons!

The enemy now determined to probe the real strength of the

liberation army. News came to Dobro Polje that the village of Gornja Bistric was being attacked by a police column who had blockaded every exit and were conducting one of their punitive enterprises, torturing and executing villagers, pillaging and burning houses, carrying off the cattle. In the preliminary skirmish Veljović Svetomir was killed and his friend Stefanović Milorad wounded. The partisans came secretly up from Dobro Polje in two scissor-like columns along the main road and down the slopes of Čorbanca mountain. There was a dark winter cloud of freezing fog which went reeling everywhere. They intercepted the police column at Lopušnje, taking it completely by surprise and fighting all through the afternoon in a heavy driving snowstorm until the enemy fled, abandoning everything, cattle, food and equipment.

Major Mostyn Davies and his captain had found the official scheme of B.L.O.s—to stay on guarded stations and vanish at the enemy's approach—was impossible in these hard mid-Balkan conditions. They both more and more identified themselves with the partisans, sharing not just their hospitality in seclusion but their struggle and privations, whether the dreary howl of the wolves through the winter dusk or the rattle of enemy automatic rifles.

In the first week of March, Tempo arrived. He came like an old friend to Mostyn Davies, but regarded his young captain with curiosity, laughing with good humour when Thompson insisted in chatting in one of the Slavonic languages, only to pass hastily from Serbian into Russian. The partisan leader, very conscious of being Tito's representative, could infuse a passionate national hatred just as easily as good humour. The British mission saw this clearly demonstrated when he addressed the partisans to form the Sixth South Moravan Brigade on 8th March at Tergovišta out of 400 assembled men. One or two eager hands had stretched out for weapons then.

"Get your own!" cried Tempo. "The mountains are full of German and Bulgarian Fascist weapons. Take your own and leave the corpses behind!"

His rhetoric had its effect, for when the brigade went into action as he planned at Kriva Feja they captured eleven machine guns and nineteen automatic rifles, to say nothing of ammunition and other supplies. The British mission rejoiced, hoping this was a symptom for the coming spring and claiming it was their own supplies of modern automatics that had set the ball rolling.

Frank Thompson had spent much time with the Bulgarian partisans and continually expressed his keenness to work in Bulgaria, but Tempo gave an enigmatic smile to his eagerness.

"You must remember," he cautioned, "this is like Macedonia—

a problem for us all. You English neither know or understand this country Macedonia! It is not on your maps. In Bulgaria everything is different. You talk of resistance in Bulgaria. And I say, 'Where is the resistance, the Bulgarian resistance?' It is here in Tserna Trava with us now! With Vlado Tričkov, Trunski and Balkanski! What more is there?"

Tempo had a busy and anxious time during those first weeks of March, for his couriers were bringing in news of the enemy's preparations for a spring offensive. Would the Western allies invade the Balkans via the Adriatic? Major Mostyn Davies could only shrug his shoulders at the question. Certainly the number of troops concentrating along the great Balkan highroad from Nish to Skopje and that ancient military road, the Via Egnatia, indicated that the German High Command were insuring against it. The British mission, the quantity of arms supplied, and indeed Tempo's own almost superhuman efforts had made them alert to the probability.

The commandant of the Royal Bulgarian Fifth Army, General Bojdev, had set up his headquarters at Vranje. Colonel Nedev was in command of the Fourteenth Infantry Division from Skopje. An operation under the code-name 'Radan' had been worked out so as to bring motorised and infantry divisions in a gigantic sweep up all the valleys converging upon Tserna Trava. The number of troops to be employed, according to Yugoslav sources, seems to have been overwhelming—some records mentioning 453 aircraft (!) others two squadrons and as many as 10,000 Royal Bulgarian soldiers and 3,000 police, an artillery regiment with fifty lorries, an armoured division and a mountain cavalry regiment. Nearer the frontier, as if to intimidate these Royal Bulgarian troops, there were the 600 Germans in their barracks at Surdulica and Belo Polje with some tanks and anti-aircraft batteries. The Fascist operations were to be brief and to last five days, commencing on 15th March.

On 14th March there had been another big arms drop on the Dobro Polje field, this one specially scheduled to be divided between the National Liberation Army of Yugoslavia and the Bulgarian partisans. Frank Thompson was particularly delighted. He had begun to identify himself more and more with the Bulgarians' own peculiar sympathies, relishing their humour and idiosyncrasies quite different from the more Serbian aspect of the Liberation Army. They gave allegiance to their central committee in Sofia, and referred to Georgi Dimitrov in Moscow, extolling their 'army' in the Sredna Gora, which they hoped to join and march upon the capital, while Serbs and Macedonians had Tito's name always upon their lips, worshipping him from afar.

Tempo found it necessary to drive his men hard. He was beset by the absolute necessity to get all the military material away and dispersed. Every courier, every scrap of news made him certain the offensive would begin at any moment. He requisitioned sixteen pack horses for the British mission. Mostyn Davies had all the Bulgarian share loaded up and, under armed guard, the supply column made a desperate journey across the *planinas* to where the Hristo Botev and Vasil Levski headquarters had been established at Kalna. Risks were taken to gain time, but the column actually succeeded in arriving on 17th March, transporting among the large supply of equipment and ammunition, four machine guns and seventy new rifles, eight automatics and boxes of grenades. As they shared them into ready hands, they shared also the latest news of the enemy's movements.

Actually the great offensive commenced on 18th March. General Bojdev gave the following order to all the Royal Bulgarian troops: "Immediately execute anyone found outside his village boundary. Ransack every village, hamlet, farmstead, and cattle byre. Any person who seems at all suspicious must be handed over to the police. Burn any cottage or hut of which you have the least suspicion. Any inhabitant who does not submit to your instructions must be shot where he stands. For everyone killed, for every building burned, for every partisan taken alive or dead, a good bonus will be awarded."[1]

When the offensive began, no partisan was taken by surprise. Tempo and the Macedonian staff had rejoined the Sixth Moravan and the Third Macedonian brigades with the local detachments in the Kozjak region. The British mission at Dobro Polje made themselves mobile and hid unnecessary equipment. At first dawn on the 18th the enemy began a simultaneous sweep up all the valleys from every point of the compass, even coming over the frontier from Bulgaria via Kalna; and once again, following them like jackals, the *chetniks* came down from the north, from the new frontier line and from the Moravan valley.

Couriers brought in the news to the H.Q. at Dobro Polje where spirits were high. There was deep snow on the *planinas* and the partisans knew the routes by which the enemy must move. Ambushes had been prepared. Recollections of the victory on Čemernik kindled optimism of greater successes. The commander at Dobro Polje was now Danilo Jovanović Radjica and his commissar, Kosta Ivanović Kole. He placed thirty trained partisans and ten armed and robust workers at the village of Vus as the headquarters security guard. Suddenly the British mission found itself protected as if important

[1] Trunski, *Neotdavna*, Bulgarski Pisatel, 1965, page 445.

political non-combatants. "You are our guests," came the smiling reassurance to Frank Thompson's protests. "We shall take care of you!" Mostyn Davies, with his mature experience, was able to take a more serene view. "This is how they always do it," he explained. "We have to go along; after all, we are a supply mission and our job is only to liaise and report."

The British mission soon realised there were others who came in to be protected. As in the earlier Čemernik battle, a host of refugees —'the flight'—began to arrive. Every loyal civilian, old man, woman or child, who feared the invader sought shelter behind the partisan lines, following the centuries-old Balkan tradition by which the peasants evaded slavery through camping with the Haidouks till the Turkish invaders had left their mountains. Major Mostyn Davies began to share his captain's anxiety as it became obvious how the refugees outnumbered the combatant partisans.

Every available weapon was distributed. The command headquarters had two machine guns, three Bren guns, and three automatic rifles: every partisan there had ample grenades and small arms ammunition. As the enemy made their expected advance from Svodge, word came in of the three hostile columns also moving in to blockade the Bulgarian frontier. It was hardly light when the enemy vanguard of sixty soldiers led by the hated Stojanov, moving to encircle from another direction, came into the defile at Vidnje just outside Vus. They met a staggering burst of partisan fire in a resistance which lasted four hours, until at last their armoured reinforcements blundered through and came to Gornje Gare, converging with several columns hoping to capture the partisan command. They were disappointed, for the headquarters location was never permanent and had been quickly transferred to Garskog graveyard.

Gornje Gare was destroyed, houses were set on fire and blown up. A great column of smoke, the first of many such during the next week, rose and hovered, black against the snowy *planinas*; solitary cattle lowed and bellowed from their burning stalls. The few villagers who could be found were assembled in front of the armoured trucks. Some were shot, or tortured according to their answers to Stojanov's questions.

The tattered, beaten crowd of peasants fled up the valley to carry Stojanov's message of terror to confuse the higher villages, emptying them before the enemy advance and swelling the numbers in 'the flight' behind the partisan forces.

Although the partisans had clear evidence now of the overwhelming strength matched against them, far outweighing anything in earlier battles, they clung to their old strategy and moved to the higher hamlets, making for a battle stand on beloved Čemernik, reckoning that the enemy's aim was as before to capture and take the men into forced labour in Bulgaria. This concept was the fatal mistake of the defence that March.

11: Defence in Balkan Style

Meanwhile at Kalna nearer the frontier, even women and children had taken arms and were fighting in the woods and among the ruins and ancient walls, firing and escaping, blazing away and vanishing. Although forty Royal Bulgarians were killed here, including the commandant of the unit, the armoured column lumbered on regardless of losses, broke into Kalna, burned the village and executed the five men and two women they found hiding there. They then came straight on by Plane towards Rupska River. Other columns came up the valleys by Ruplje and Preslap.

In the dusk the partisan H.Q. had moved again. Not chancing to employ horses, they moved their equipment up from Dobro Polje using the reserve of ten brawny labourers. All the people of Ruplje and Brod came along, hurrying to join the folk of Tserna Trava in their position on Čemernik. Mostyn Davies and the British mission went with them, travelling by the pony tracks high along the verges of the snowfields. From time to time the enemy investing the valleys could just be seen by the mission with the aid of binoculars.

Lying up there, watching the arrival of partisans and refugees, the British mission knew they were in the midst of the most cruel of all guerrilla struggles. It was not a campaign like Tito's, where resolute columns marched on and on, from Montenegro to Bosnia to Serbia, campaigning for liberation as military strategy decided. Here on Čemernik were men fighting in the ancient warfare of Macedonia, milling round and round on the mountain top of their homeland, returning and returning to fight the invaders in the bravest of all guerrilla fighting, a contest of piercing ever-closing circles.

Mostyn Davies watched through his binoculars the gathering weight of the enemy forces massing in the valleys. In that twilight the partisans grouping along the great forest so high above seemed like a dream of freedom, a cloud floating above earthly dross through which the dimmed headlights of enemy lorries moving up against the partisans crawled in an ugly threat. The partisans showed no lights and formed a line from Kozaračka Meadow to Pavlov's Mound as far as Ceverljanka, the mission's first dropping ground.

There was no attack up the slopes that night, though rockets and star-shells lit up the *planina* and from time to time the crackle of gunfire would burst out from some nervous sentry, showing that the enemy expected to be attacked. As night wore on, the bitter Balkan wind dropped and a freezing cloud came down from the height. Towards dawn this hardened into a powdery snow which changed to a fierce snowstorm. Children began to cry with the intensity of the cold. Women and old men among the refugees dug out better shelters.

After dawn the partisans realised they were not going to be attacked. Enormous forces had massed against them with the one purpose—encirclement and total destruction. The enemy's intentions had been underestimated. Down below the camp stoves and ovens began to steam and smoke. The enemy columns marshalled for breakfast.

In the bitter cold of that icy winter morning, hours seemed endless. Patrols confirmed the strength of the enemy forces. Every valley was invested. For safety they mustered the refugees and formed three divisions. The first shock division was to attempt to force a penetrating wedge into a weak point, which, when discovered and pierced, would be reinforced by the Tserna Trava battalion so that the third division, the headquarters command, and the British mission with the refugees, could pass through.

News came that the band of Bulgarian partisans were prepared as a diversion to make an onslaught and fight their own way through with head-on collisions if necessary. This column of forty experienced ex-Royal Bulgarian soldiers faced the enemy in Plane and actually fought on towards Lužnica, keeping military formation and driving all before it till they reached safety along the Demarcation Line on the Bulgarian border.

The First Division decided to attempt a penetration through the dip between Great and Little Čemernik where the ski hut is situated. There were heavy drifts here but the surprise was effective. They burst through and fought their way against strong opposition towards Vranje. Unfortunately the enemy was not only in depth but mobile. When the Tserna Trava Division came up to possess the gap, the snow cloud cleared to reveal the enemy reinforced in strength. Only with intense fighting and considerable losses did they succeed in escaping from what had now become a three-fold circle. At last the advancing detonations of rockets and grenades told of their success.

Calculations, however, had gone astray. The Third Division of the partisans found that their two predecessors had only drawn away the two first detachments of enemy opposition, and a third remained to oppose them. The British mission, as they pushed blindly on, carrying heavy packs, the radio station and the reserve ammunition chests, knew from the savage ambuscade closing in ahead that the plan had failed. The partisans faced a dilemma—to use their mobility to secure victory, or to keep formation to protect their women and children. They chose the latter and fought their way forward in a wild expenditure of ammunition. For them there was no other way than this narrow pass at 1,500 metres through the snow. At the critical moment the clouds came down, sweeping an oblivion before all who knew not the paths of Čemernik. Using bayonets now, the partisans drove the enemy towards Baincke River. The partisan left wing pressed on to the village of Mlačište before the clouds changed into impenetrable fog. Now they knew they could not get over the mountain and, closing formation, they came slowly back to find their first positions at dusk.

Nobody counted the losses that night. Now and again there would be hopes that unanswering names had survived to escape in the fog. Avoiding thought of their own missing comrades, everyone was shocked to hear how the nine-year-old son of Milenković Vlajko from Brod had run straight into that machine gun at Mlačište graveyard. He had warned the partisans of the ambush, but at the cost of his life, for though his father had now hidden him in an earth-cabin, there was very little hope: they said bullets fell out of him as he was carried away.

On the night of the 19th the partisans held their old positions in closer formation. The fog made star-shells useless, ammunition was scarcer so the dark seemed more quiet. It became clear the move to avoid encirclement had been thwarted, that their leaders were hesitating, the whole expedition was in a panic of indecision. Optimism had gone; hunger and cold and despair for the morrow spread a fatal readiness for tragedy, a doubt of victory. Only the young seemed to be alive in the cold of that night. Alexander Sinadinović, the youth leader, gathered a band of his friends—girls and young women, who dared to go through the fog, working till far into the dark to bring up food and cooked potatoes. Regardless of stray bullets, they made up relays to go down to the rocks for the caches of ammunition. They helped secure the machine-gun posts and carried cans of soup to fighters and old people as well. Whenever the units came into a position where supplies were needed, these young women were ready and went up to the bitter front line as nonchalantly as if gathering sticks or working in the summer hayfields.

As time came to midnight spirits began to revive. Wherever possible women and children were urged to get into earth-cabins. The huge rabble known to the partisans as 'the flight' numbered 1,000 refugees, all of whom had lost hope by now. Through clinging to the fighting detachments they had begun to realise they kept closer proximity to the firing line and to death. Soon they required little persuasion to take to the deeper woods and search for concealment in rocky gullies—pathetic alternative as it was, it presented them with at least a modicum of hope.

At midnight the command of the Tserna Trava battalion decided to move towards Jovanovca hamlet, hoping to get food from the cottages there and proceed on to the frontier via Novo Selo, but at Obradovca they lost somewhere the link to the main headquarters command with the British mission and fell into despair. The enemy soon sensed there was this considerable movement taking place somewhere out in the dark. Rocket flares and starshells began to light up all the peaks, making nowhere safe except in the woods and compelling the battalion to shelter. At about three o'clock, as the frost deepened, everything became quiet. Then towards dawn these lost partisans had the intuition to divide into smaller groups and go down to the Rupska River, keeping in the defile, crossing the just passable summit of Del.[1]

At the same time the main unit guarding the headquarters command and the British mission, having secreted a large proportion of their refugees in hiding places across Čemernik, was beginning to push forward following the Rupska River but keeping high above river and road. As it grew light, the long file of partisans plodded on, the British mission beside them. 'The flight' of peasants was now reduced to about 100 women and older men, but it contained some forty Italians who were serving practically as camp followers, for they had no rifles and were unarmed. In the stronger light all were startled to perceive another file lower down on the opposite bank of the river but making in the same direction as themselves. They halted and watched anxiously until it emerged to traverse an open glade in the forest. It was the Tserna Trava battalion with the Kosov detachment who had not been able to pierce through the Čemernik Pass after all!

Recognition of friends instead of enemies, even though it betokened failure, was heartily welcome. A glad cheer went up and either file pressed on to unite at Stojmirova just below Ruplje, by now in the broad light of early morning. They had come back almost to the very place from which the campaign had started, but, though just as determined as ever, were shorter of ammunition

[1] Milivoje Perović, *Južna Serbia, Beograd*, page 358.

and hungry, dragged down by the fatigue of bitter cold and sleep-lessness.

In that bright morning light the blue uniforms of the Royal Bulgarian soldiery could be clearly seen against the black forest and white snow, moving in little, widely-flung squads of thirty to fifty men. Watching them disappear into the mountain slopes, the partisan command realised how tactics had altered. The enemy were not advancing as an army to drive towards some decisive battle. They were investing the district, laying series of ambushes in depth, hiding their machine-gun posts and relying on surprise manoeuvres similar to the guerrillas who opposed them. Far from continuing to unite their columns, the partisans quickly appreciated the immediate necessity was for smaller dispersed bands, and began to move along Rupska River on either bank in smaller re-grouped companies.

As they came out on the exposed road from Kačar forest, they met the first enemy ambush. Mortar and artillery fire from the heights tore open their ranks. When they re-formed and advanced, a rain of machine-gun bullets mowed them down. Not till ten o'clock did the partisans on the left bank break through to Novo Selo and Dadinica, 100 in all with the British mission. Here, when they should have been clean through the enemy lines, they were ambushed again by combined *chetniks* and Royal Bulgarians. Forty partisans were slain besides many nameless, unarmed folk who had staked their lives in partisan company. Even as they re-grouped below Rupska River with the British mission, they could hear the main party with headquarters meeting another ambush in the woods towards Stojmirova Hamlet. This column that was now grouped round headquarters command also had those forty unarmed Italians.

Every attempted penetration seemed to face a new ambush. It was said that corpses lay every fifteen metres. Retreat towards Ostrozub, fighting a rearguard action, was inevitable. All the route back these corpses showed the way, yet even here they could not break out to Bankovca village. In Ostrozub valley it was apparent they were completely encircled. Headquarters command divided the partisans into bands as small as ten soldiers, but when they plunged into the forest they found the woods full of enemy riflemen and the steeper glades covered by machine-gun posts. In such a trap towards Rajčetina all forty Italians perished, mown down together as they ran across an open glade. At the clearing called Selište, by the Roman cemetery, twenty-six partisans were killed and as many wounded, while under Ostrozub, by the meadows called 'Broad Ploughland', thirteen partisans were shot down. In attempts to demoralise the partisans, the enemy paraded captives so as to give

the impression that by surrender men could remain alive. The commissar of the Terenski battalion attempted once again to go over
Čemernik via Stojmirov, but a *cheta* came in from the watermill
in Kačar forest to declare that way was still impassable. The whole
headquarters staff was completely encircled, and any escape must be
fought every inch of the way.

Novak took command of headquarters and formed a shock group
of the youngest partisans determined to break through Kačar at
any cost. As they went on in batches, they seemed only to increase
the numbers of corpses lying in the forest, where under the heavy
fusillade even the branches were shattered down upon them. Without hope of survival they persisted till they won through and held
the track over the rocks to the river. That road from Ruplje to
Novo Selo, which used to take only some forty minutes to walk,
was fought out by those hungry, tired men over half a day. Even
the route down from Rupska River canyon had its traps, for
machine-gun fire ricocheting made splinters from the rocks as men
crept under the trees and cliffs, the only safe way being to wade
in the ice-cold water, waist deep.

Now at this critical stage the British mission became a problem
to the partisans. They held up progress, being townsmen unaccus-
timed to such extremities of cold, fatigue and hunger. Major
Mostyn Davies urged that they be left to fight their own way
through. He had maps and he knew the lie of the land. Novak
would not allow any such thing. Tempo would kill him if harm came
to his guests. Reluctantly Mostyn Davies agreed to dispose of their
heavy equipment. Despite the anxiety of their wireless operator,
Božilo Kovac with Dragan Dordević helped them to bury their radio
station at the opening of the Novo Selo valley beside the Rupska
River, camouflaging it hastily so that the enemy would not find it.
The mission could now fend for themselves better, especially as the
Liberation Army had splintered into close bands of comrades prob-
ing to escape, some towards the frontier, others towards the South
Morava.

The immediate way for Major Mostyn Davies and Captain
Thompson was down the icy Rupska River. The British team split
up into pairs, except for the wireless operator, whom Mostyn
Davies insisted must stay with him. Down under those banks
corpses were caught up in the roots of trees whilst beside them,
hiding under tree trunks and old walls, were refugees scarcely
more alive than they. About 100 metres from Bučje hamlet they
made for two cottages on the right bank, only to discover those
riverside cliffs hid another fierce ambush. They got by, wading
waist-deep again, creeping almost under the flood water. Frank

Thompson was for stealing away and hiding in some earth-cabin to be made on high ground, but Mostyn Davies, greatly to his signals sergeant's satisfaction, declared they could perish from exposure and must find shelter by nightfall. They were able to dodge the machine-gun post in Bučje by creeping along an overgrown brook whose tangled bushes and tree stumps provided cover.

The constant need to hide lost them any news of the others in the British team. Near Novo Selo they crept out of the brook into a hayrick, a little band of eight partisans in filthy garb and three British no better in tattered, dirty military uniforms. Even then they were not safe. Their sentry, a man of the Kosov brigade, cried through the dusk, "Comrades! Throw a grenade! Quick, or the Bulgarians will pitch us back into the river."

A little squad in blue Bulgarian uniforms was coming along the track by the brook as if making for that very hayrick. Those not destroyed by the burst of automatic fire that followed the hand grenade disappeared like silent wraiths without returning a shot.

That night the vital warmth from the hay, a dry internal heat, kindled and dried the damp from wet clothes as the soldiers, partisans and British, huddled together, itching with the stirring of the old inheritance of Balkan lice as their bodies packed close—the biting lice that caused men to move and curse through the dark, that sent the blood irritating away to fight against the frost until eyes could close at last and even the sentries drew deeper into the hay and fell asleep.

When the hayrick moved it was broad daylight, though the sun had not yet climbed above the eastern *planinas*. The wireless sergeant declared his legs were 'blocked', but a few exercises and a couple of cigarettes soon put them to rights. The party was staggered to see fires still burning on the hillside. The fresh sods of new-cut trenches could be noticed where an enemy column had spent the night just above them! They also learned how another column had been at the Novo Selo school that night and, guessing this column had gone down to the river, they decided to go up the slope past the trenches, over the hill until on the sheer side of the next slope they stopped at the first of two solitary farmsteads before which a woman stood, holding children in both her arms like white flags of truce.

"Are there Bulgarians in your village?" the partisan leader demanded.

She turned her head and waved her smaller child towards the crest by which they had just crossed. A detail of Royal Bulgarians filed along the top, rifles looming large against the sky-line. Two exhausted partisans could go no further. They begged to let them hide in her stackyard. It took a brief minute to hollow the stack and close it.

The diminished band fled on, moving faster towards Leskov Palina cottages. In the bright glare of midday, with the sun bursting on white snowfields, they knew, however fast they moved, German binoculars could pick them out miles away. Two aeroplanes had already appeared that morning. Above that diminutive group of cottages, they decided to hide at one lonely farmhouse before making a dash to the frontier. Mostyn Davies was sure the Hristo Botev partisans were there somewhere and would have contacts across the Demarcation Line. Only the sergeant, the wireless operator, demurred. It was time they were on the air. What use would they be in Bulgaria or anywhere without the radio set? Surely they must drop back to pick it up?

They had, except for the drying-out in the hayrick, been on the move continuously since 17th March, and every one of them, after a drink of plum brandy and a bite of black bread, fell fast asleep in that dry room at the back with its shutters drawn and faggots against the door.

Fog had come down again on that 21st March when at ten o'clock they moved towards the frontier, going through the night, avoiding the open snowfields and keeping parallel with, but above, roads and byways until just before dawn at Palojca they approached a house and woke the landlord to ask what was happening in the village. His reticence confused the partisans, who pressed inside. He ran out, thought better of it and came in again. He was a wealthy farmer and had two cottages attached to his farm. Nobody would say if the Royal Bulgarians were along the frontier or not.

The village stretched along a glen down which a stream flowed. As they looked at the silent and shuttered houses that lined the valley going higher and higher to the border, they saw the new watch-tower on the ridge, dominating road, village and frontier. Were there Bulgarians in the tower? No-one had broken the order to stay within doors since the offensive began, so no-one could say. From the glances the shivering inhabitants gave at the partisans' weapons it was clear they were terrified. Each of the little band took turns, one guard to mark the watch-tower and one to make sure no-one left the house, while the landlord brought food and made them comfortable, though not welcome.

At dusk a cripple knocked at the door as if he had been sent for. The landlord, trembling with anxiety beside the sentry, asked him in and brought him at once face to face with the partisans, who greeted him with the levelled barrels of their weapons. He was neither informer nor spy, but a partisan courier who hobbled

Tempo addressing his partisans in the snow, February 1944

The road to the frontier above Tserna Trava in summer

'The Long March': British soldiers marching with the Second Sofia Brigade, May 1944 (Sergeant Kenneth Scott leading, Major Frank Thompson third from right)

regularly to that end of the village in case he should be needed. The sight of the drawn revolvers astonished him, giving as it did the immediate impression of *chetniks*. As he handed out Bulgarian cigarettes, even the landlord relaxed. All the watch-towers he asserted, were manned with Royal Bulgarian soldiers and across the frontier every village had troops and armoured vehicles. His own house was 600 metres from the 'Demarcation Line' and even he could not cross it safely. Bojišina hamlet between the two watch-towers was by no means safe in the day.

There was nothing for it but to travel on, keeping, as he advised, along the mountain tops, avoiding every road. *Chetniks* were the danger now, he warned Mostyn Davies and Thompson ominously; while the Royal Bulgarian soldiers and police kept to the roads, the *chetniks* were coming into the forest for plunder like wolves looking for corpses. When it was really dark and they moved away, the courier came with them a mile or so before going back to the frontier. As he advised, partisan stars were taken off uniforms, and no one was to declare whether he were partisan or *chetnik*. Mostyn Davies and his colleagues were to keep strict verbal silence.

They made their way towards Delina Bara. Here, as they approached a house to ask for information, the partisan who crept to the back to prevent anyone running out to betray them, stepped on the rotten boards of a well covering. He shouted as he went down and the peasants came out. In the alarm of fetching a ladder and the chatter of the women, no one let slip that the group was partisan. Only the wireless operator forgot himself in a fit of humour as he whispered, "Fell down the well, he did! The well is the way to hell!"

"There are worse places with rotten boards round these back-yards!" commented Thompson grimly.

"Better shut up, or that's where we'll finish!" commanded Mostyn Davies.

Safely indoors, the unfortunate got dry clothes and a warm drink, the little battle group being received as *chetniks*. The children, perhaps more daring, were the most suspicious, though the partisan leader turned the tables on them by the challenge: "I know you boys are partisans, though you keep saying you are *chetniks*!"

Next night after this accident they were very glad to push on towards Kozaračkoj, and at about eleven o'clock in the morning they waylaid a solitary traveller as he crept stealthily across their path near Dadinca. The three Britishers tightened their lips as they heard him describe how *chetniks* on the previous day had laid an ambush at Dadinačka graveyard and slaughtered the squad of partisans guarding a remnant of the refugees, amongst whom were

F

two members of the British mission. There was no news of the rest of their team, who had not come to Dadinačka nor been seen anywhere thereabouts. *Chetnik* ambushes were everywhere. The Royal Bulgarian soldiers were re-forming and the police with them.

"The Bulgarians, they are fat," remarked the peasant, with a wry smile, "and they like to warm themselves to eat. But the *chetniks*, they are as hungry as we."

He drew his finger across his throat. "And they move in the dark as we do!" he emphasised, croaking hoarsely.

The peasant did not wish to join them, but later in the afternoon was allowed to go on. The partisans were anxious to press on to regain their unit. Frank Thompson was for going with them, relying on their good fortune so far, but Mostyn Davies insisted they could now be as safe in a house as in the open. A house could be fortified and guarded. Dodging ambushes was not a game that could be played for ever, not with so many *chetniks* in the forest. The wireless operator was desperate to retrieve his set. He reckoned they had been off the air for a week at least. The apparatus might get damp under the melting snow. They could recover it next morning and locate it somewhere better, perhaps in a shed or stable.

Reluctantly, the partisans agreed, and after sunset they all came down to Novo Selo. The way down was sickening. No one had moved the corpses. Some seemed to shine in the dusk. They passed the first cottages in Novo Selo and reached the watermill on the Rupska River. The partisans were uneasy.

They waited outside for a while. The mill house proved empty and really deserted. They fixed the shutters and jammed the door. The partisans posted a sentry and went down to look at the cottages. Frank Thompson was ill at ease and uncomfortable. As they lit a fire he tried the windows and slipped outside through the rear window.

"I'm watching for the well!" he remarked with a grin to his sergeant.

Not so far up in the forest came a dismal howl. A wolf, perhaps, or the abandoned dogs of the deserted village. There was something uncanny about the houses higher up. Not a chink of light to be seen. An unfastened door somewhere slammed on its hinges and slammed again. A wisp of white smoke shot up from the mill chimney. There was no smoke from the cottages. Pitch dark came like the drop of a cloth.

"We can put the radio set under the granary," the wireless operator was saying when he returned. "The great floor-boards are loose and come up easily. "We can be on the air tomorrow once we dig up the set." The fire crackled its warmth into the shadows. Mostyn Davies passed round his silver flask. There was dry straw and sacks. The sentry came in and stretched out his hands. Suddenly a heavy boot crashed, tripping on the step outside. There was a scramble by the door. A rifle-butt battered on the shutters. Frank Thompson was up and vaulting through the window at the back. Mostyn Davies sprang to follow, unfastening his revolver. A grenade hurtled through the broken shutters and burst as he reached the window. He felt the savage blows on his back and heard the groan of his sergeant and the clamouring voice of the partisan sentry; yet before he knew he was wounded he found himself astride the window-sill, where a spurt of machine-gun fire cut him down.

Frank Thompson waited in the trees some thirty yards away, listening to the breaking-down of the door and the gunfire. Suddenly the detonations ceased. After the bursting of the grenade, the snapping of wood and the explosions, deep impenetrable silence came on the night, so intense that for some long minutes he dared not move.

Nobody came from the watermill. Realising gradually that though he was alone he would surely be hunted, he fled through the trees to the higher slopes, higher and higher towards the snow.

Next day as the command headquarters were coming along the Rupska River with their partisan remnant, moving stealthily before dawn, they found Major Mostyn Davies, heavily wounded, but still doggedly surviving beside his dead sergeant wireless operator. They brought him on a rough litter, carrying him all the way to Dadinca wherever they went, until he died in the ravine at Gerdelička, near Ruplje, where he lies to this day in the grave they made for him.

And they tell of him still, from Dobro Polje by Rupska River to Čemernik, how he smiled and had the golden ring upon his finger. And the silver flask from which he tasted rakija is kept to this day somewhere up there in the *mahalas* of Kačar forest not far from the Haidouk fountain.

12: Extrication

As he hurried up through the forest and the night, Frank Thompson paused continually. Nothing else was moving. He heard no gunfire and saw no lights. Higher still, where the tall trees gave way to scrub and meadows just below the snow, he made himself a shelter, digging out the soil where it seemed dryer against the rocks. He pulled himself deeper into his coat, seeming to get intrinsic heat out of the earth as he crouched through the worst hours before dawn, and he broke open his emergency pack for rations against the bitter frost. Even in peacetime night closes everything up on the Balkan highlands, windows are shuttered and nobody stirs abroad; but in that frost even the military stoves in the distant valley simmered out and gave never a blink of light.

Next morning, all through the early hours, he expected soldiers to come searching for him. Once a reconnaissance plane flew over the empty slope. Only when a shepherd passed below, obviously making nothing but a routine journey, did he believe his escape unnoticed. As the man came back, he called to him softly, *"Partisan! Dobre došerl!"*

The shepherd hesitated, stopped, but went on. Thompson called again, "Help a partisan!"

The man turned as if looking for something but never stopping, seemed to linger, walking to and fro, until he asked, "Are you wounded?"

"No," replied the fugitive, keeping low in his little cave. "Where are my comrades?"

Fumbling with his leather bag, the shepherd dropped some bread and cooked potatoes on the ground, picking the handful up and replacing it in case the fugitive should not see.

"I will tell them," he said.

"Tell them I am the Englishman!" said Thompson.

The shepherd looked startled, forgot his caution and came closer to see this foreigner upon his sheep-walk. He raised his hand to his old Serb cap. "I will tell them," he repeated. "They will come! They will come!" and glancing anxiously around, he made off down the mountain.

Frank Thompson slipped out of his hiding place and seized the bread and potatoes, which were still warm with the crumbling crusty smell of baking on them. As he ate skin, dirt and all, and ground his teeth on the flat cake of black bread, he wondered, repeating the Serbian, "They will come!" The food was delicious and filling, making the very lice upon his body stir into new activity. But who would come? Who would they be? He checked his revolver hopelessly, remembering the automatic fusillade of last night. The day passed slowly in old intellectual exercises to relieve monotony—classical memories, the virtues of shepherds, pastoral joys, tags of Pushkin, attempts at verse, yet all seemed to provoke uncertainty.

At the shadows of sundown he feared to be surrounded and captured in the dark, for his hiding place was known, at least to one person. He crept higher in the dusk and found a better, where animals had undermined the boulders making a rough cave underneath. Sheep had often sheltered there. He could now peep down into the valley and also survey his old refuge. A little scraping, and he had blocked some of the entrance.

Though he had resolved to listen throughout the night, this new shelter proved so comfortable that he slept unwittingly and awoke next morning to the hoarse sound of a Serbian folk song coming up the valley. When he peered down the slope, the shepherd had already passed the lower hiding place. He crawled out and crept down towards him.

"Partisans!" he called softly.

The shepherd shuffled towards him indirectly, as if on part of his journey, stopped, and put down some food and milk in a tin can.

"They will come!" he said, with a smile this time. "They will come tonight, after first dark. Do not you move! The police are on the roads. It is all in blockade. And there are *chetniks*!"

His slow and deliberate words seemed too precious to interrupt with thanks, but he touched his forehead to Thompson's Serbian, muttering as he walked on, "They will come, yes, they will come!"

And come they did, an hour after dark, locating him by the low singing of that folk song, a little squad of five, armed to the teeth, with grenades at their belts. Headquarters command had sent them. There was to be a '*pokret*'[1] through the night.

They knew about the disaster at the watermill and they thought one of the other Englishmen had been captured after the dispersal at Rupska River. Watermills were unlucky places, they all agreed. Two brothers, Danilo and Steven, had concealed themselves within the mill-wheel at Milinčina watermill. The Fascists suspected someone was there and closed the sluices to make the wheel turn. As the water came to move the wheel they shot the struggling lads and left the mill still turning on their bodies.

When Frank Thompson climbed into the snow with his escort that night, he was appalled to hear of the slaughter which had come upon those quiet villages. The refugees on the mountain had been mown down. Villagers who had stayed indoors had been dragged out, shot and their children left to die. Even the accompanying Bulgarian aeroplane had amused itself by firing rockets down upon peaceful villages like Pavličina. The entire Brod district below them was in blockade and the enemy were now concentrating on Dejićevo,

[1] Sudden guerrilla march.

where one of the dropping grounds had been, interrogating by torture everyone they could catch, in a determined effort to locate the British radio station.

Both the Bulgarian police and the military had made a great show of withdrawing from Brod. As soon as the villagers trickled back from their earth-cabins and forest shelters to the warmth of their houses, the blockade was set up and the inhabitants dragged out into the snow to face machine guns and the questions, "Where are the parachutes? Where is the radio station?"

Some, like the first victim Tihomir, had been shot in front of the shivering crowd; another, Ljuba Milenković, took off her marriage coin, a big golden ducat, and just managed to give it to her six-year-old son before she was killed in front of him. Finally they tied others in front of their houses and publicly burned them alive. A few Italians who had survived there were taken into cellars and tortured in secrecy before being shot. Some knew the answers, most did not, but the silence of all had increased the frustration of the police who might soon go on to other villages.

The partisans, mostly younger men than Thompson, stumbled on through the dark, leaving the snowfields now; for, travelling westwards, one descends into forests, then along glades to sheep-walks and meadows. Here they caught sight of houses below them, and whispered in great relief, "Dobrotina Village!"

The leader broke a stick and cracked it against a tree. They listened and came nearer the village. Once again they clapped the stick against a tree trunk in a harsh staccato, a set rhythm. They listened, paused some minutes and tried again. Down below came the sound of an axe chopping wood. "*Vodič!*"[2] the partisans whispered expectantly.

As the chopping halted, once again they tapped the stick, then hurried down to where an old man chopped logs from his wood-pile, just outside the first house in Dobrotina.

"Is it wood?" he challenged them.

"No, we have none," came the password. "It is stone!"

For the rest of that night the old man conducted the escorts so as to avoid the *chetnik* columns that were still hunting along the way to Dadinca. At about four o'clock in the morning they came to a watermill by the South Morava River. With the old man leading the way into the ice-cold water, they waded across, sometimes waist-deep in the swollen flood. The railway and the Belgrade-Skopje road follows the river here, and as they were crossing they were shaken to see an enemy armoured wagon patrolling down the track. The German occupants were half asleep, huddled together

_____
[2] Guide!

from the cold, and although it was dawn-light, saw nothing of the bedraggled group below, whose bodies and limbs were so chilled they could hardly have fired one shot between them.

Once on the other side of the Morava, passing the first village, they discovered that Bela Breg was occupied by Nedić riflemen, so it was necessary to take to the woods above and make the most arduous journey of all to Tula village, close to the predetermined rallying post on the slope of Kukavica Mountain.

Here was the luxury of a safe house, with the warmth of its blazing hearth to stir together body-lice and bugs and human souls. The smell of food cooking, the bravery of friendship was framed in a security which contrasted so vividly with that anxiety of householders on the other side of the South Morava, where the rattle of sub-machine guns and the odour of burning rafters had made peasants glad to get back to their cold earth-cabins, and partisans restless to march on across the snow.

Scarcely had a day passed before a courier came with the news that two other members of the mission, Sergeants Walker and Monroe, had escaped and been brought to the secret partisan head-quarters at Bistrica.

Once again Frank Thompson found himself crossing the Morava River with his little band of guards, not through the snow this time, but along the lower slopes north of Predejane to the thick forest overlooking the River Vlasina. The snow was lower on these northern slopes, and, coming right into the forest, had hardly begun to melt. Up on the far edge of the woods over the crest to the southern side and not so far from Dobro Polje Mahala, in a little farmstead which hid from all the terrors, Frank Thompson regained his comrades. They knew already of Mostyn Davies's death, and had gloomily reconciled themselves to their captain having shared the same fate.

Mutual joy at re-uniting was short lived in the realisation that their wireless set had disappeared! Gloom descended on that trio of survivors. The snows were melting. Perhaps the partisans needed more time, more security, in order to locate it, perhaps indeed the enemy had discovered such a hastily concealed cache. Frank Thompson understood the importance of this loss more than the partisans and impetuously pointed out to them the insignificance of the mission without it, but they insisted emphatically it could not be found. They knew the place. It was not there.

The sang-froid of the folk at Bistrica irritated Frank Thompson. Tempo had a secret station, they insisted, and the partisans could send out the mission's messages to the allies, so nothing was altered, nothing at all.

13: At Tempo's Headquarters: Partisan Warfare: Ambushes and Reprisals

Other British missions operating in the Balkans, quite apart from and indeed sometimes not in very friendly relationship with S.O.E., had duties more akin to intelligence than to the actual waging of war. Some were secret information—finding missions responsible primarily for reporting. The function of the S.O.E., so well explained by Mostyn Davies's colleague, Bickham Sweet-Escott,[1] was a military one, to promote and develop hostilities against the enemy and to assist the winning of the war. Some missions, however, remained more secret and more sensitive, travelling to collect information and search out the truth, with a responsibility to remain unnoticed and above all undetected.

An active gatherer of such intelligence was Kenneth Syers, an astute and versatile journalist whose success can be measured by the anonymity with which he has surrounded his work. He himself, in the uniform of an R.A.F. flight lieutenant from the military intelligence branch of the British General Headquarters Middle East Command, had been parachuted to replace Captain W. F. Stuart after the latter had been killed by a bomb at Tito's headquarters. He had thus, in the summer of 1943, joined the first mission to Tito, the British mission with the code name 'Typical', which, with Captain F. W. Deakin as its leader, had preceded Fitzroy Maclean.

In the spring of 1944, Kenneth Syers, with the rank of squadron leader in the R.A.F., was about to return to Serbia from his base at Bari, in order to head another mission to the Serbian partisans, when Tempo's Macedonian partisans managed to get a message through to Cairo to report the disaster at Tserna Trava, the death of Mostyn Davies and several of his team. This had caused the greatest disappointment at S.O.E. headquarters, for the interesting reports sent in had raised expectations of contact with the Bulgarian partisans. The Fatherland Front, the Agrarians, and the followers of Dr G. M. Dimitrov, seemed to be simmering and ready to make a flourishing resistance. Moreover, news had reached the British H.Q. of the first Bulgarian approaches to withdraw from hostilities.[2] The Bulgarian banker Kouyoumdjeff had left Sofia and reached

---

[1] *Baker Street Irregular.*
[2] Bickham Sweet-Escott, *Baker Street Irregular*, page 194.

Istanbul to make a tentative approach to the United States O.S.S. representatives there. Though General Donovan, the O.S.S. chief, was tardy in letting S.O.E. know about this, the news of the Bulgarian anxieties highlighted the importance of Captain Thompson and the remnant of his mission that survived.

It was immediately arranged that Kenneth Syers should be diverted from Serbia and should drop to partisan headquarters in Macedonia with a new wireless set, a fresh briefing, positive encouragement and news of home, and only thereafter should he resume his assignment to Serbia. This was a fortunate choice as not only was Syers both a resourceful and sympathetic officer, but he had a family link, having known Frank Thompson's father.

In the meantime the survivors of Mostyn Davies's mission, still clinging to their code name 'Mulligatawny', were making their way south, crossing the fatal Rupska River and guided in the dark along the *planina* tops to Čemernik. Their guides knew of the blockade of Kalna, which had been surrounded on all four sides. This could have been the greatest catastrophe, for in that village were the Seventh Moravan and the Bulgarian Sofia brigades together with the partisan headquarters command, including Tempo, Vidojan Smilevski, Berka, Slavčo Trunski, Bagra Ivanov, and other leaders.

By chance in the night the lad Kalančanin Pavlović Velisav happened to go outside his shepherd's hut to look to the fastening of hurdles round the sheepfold. He found they were secure. Pausing to rest, he heard far down below the sheep-walk a tramp of heavy boots and knew the noise was made by Fascist soldiers coming up the valley. Without going indoors, he ran on barefoot as he was to warn the headquarters at Kovačev Mahala, just giving them time to pull out the partisan army and take up the best positions on the heights before the fog came down.

Through the dark and the cloud the enemy marched into a wall of fire. Bugles blew from the scattered outposts and created the illusion that the enemy was outnumbered as well as surrounded. Some 600 of them were captured, immediately 'tried' and executed, and it was reckoned that only about 150 succeeded in escaping to the frontier.

On the more western *planinas* of the Tserna Trava district the Nedić forces and *chetnik* bands were astir for massacre and plunder. Isolated columns of partisans still moved along the higher villages with their little groups of refugees in a state of desperate fatigue and hunger, finding everywhere burned-out farmsteads, ruins and blood-stained snow. Djokić Dragoslav led eight partisans with Italians and refugees to shelter at Dadinca, not knowing that the mayor here was in league with the *chetniks*. This so-called 'friend'

gave them bread and then excused himself, leaving quickly in order
to inform against them. Next day the eight partisans and the thirty
Italians with them were brought before a *chetnik* court martial.
The *chetnik* leader Ahil decided they should be executed. First he
ordered the Italians to dig two large graves in the Stamenkov plum
orchard, above which there stretches the old corner fringe of the
oak forest.

Seventeen Italians, including four officer doctors, were executed
to fall into the graves with the partisans. Before the execution the
partisans clamoured that their youngest member, the teenage only
son of his mother Vitomira Ilić, should be spared. The *chetniks* therefore shot him first before them all, though the partisans cried out
that names were taken and known, and they should answer for their
crimes. Nothing made any difference, for all were shot. Ahil and
his companions, however, now took especial care the graves should
be concealed.

It was this group of *chetniks* which went along the forest firing
shots to prevent the partisans trickling through either across the
Morava or to Bistrica, though by so doing they only warned their
nocturnal enemies of their whereabouts and certainly did not deter
any native partisans.

During those last days of March and early April there was deep
snow on the heights of Čemernik. The third battalion of the Ninth
'Banger' Brigade of partisans, all armed with rifles, were now
marching into the Tserna Trava district when they found Frank
Thompson and his little band cramped in on Čemernik by detailed
squads of the enemy. These had spread out in scattered pockets,
maintaining the semblance of ambushes but really keeping themselves
warm at the military stoves which their lorries kept replenished.
Collecting the Englishmen and their guards, the Ninth 'Banger'
Brigade made rendezvous with Tempo at Ostrozub and took over
the duty of conducting him with the partisan headquarters command south to Jablanica and on to his more permanent headquarters
at Radovnica.

Tempo left Čemernik and Tserna Trava with a heavy heart. This
township, astride the most vulnerable way into Bulgaria other than
the fortified Dragoman Pass, had been punished by a pogrom
beyond any military necessity. The Bulgarian Fascist commander,
Colonel Bačinski, had decreed that every farmstead in Brod and
Tserna Trava, in fact all the Vlasina valley, should be burnt and
utterly destroyed. The First and Second Battalions of the 45th
Royal Bulgarian Infantry were brought up from Prilep and Bitola
to carry this out with the help of the garrison from the Mačkat
mine and the police divisions. In two days they had filled the valley

with smoke, slaying cattle in their stalls, destroying even worn-out horses, and driving women and children through the snow into the woods.

In Brod the number of houses, watermills, barns and cattle byres destroyed was counted as 256. In that pocket-like valley at Tserna Trava where the houses group around the town square, the heat was so intense that no one could remain. Spectators hiding in the forest above still tell of the dark silhouettes of the black uniforms of that punitive expedition. The school and all its practical rooms, the shops, the coffee-houses and the bake-house, all were blazing. A cloud of smoke and cinders rose and hung in the cold air above, loitering as if to warn the partisans as they crossed to the Vardenik mountains on their southward way to Radovnica. Though the campaign seemed to have reached the utter depths of despair, the partisans began to write down names for retribution against the dawn of that victory which all their propaganda and Comrade Tito himself had promised them.

Tempo wrote from his headquarters at Radovnica-Tergovište to his colleague Peter Stambolić: "The devastation at Tserna Trava is frightful and despairing. We need to get food at once to our people and evacuate the burned out families to Jablanica, for our own soldiers must not leave this centre of battle."[3] Nevertheless, despite the *chetniks* in the north and Royal Bulgarian reinforcements across the frontier, his partisans broke through across the *planinas* and kept the way open for evacuees to Jablanica.

From late 1943 to the beginning of 1944 the German High Command was consolidating its experience in combating guerrilla warfare in Eastern Europe. The old system of attack in the pamphlet "Battle Instructions for the Fight against Bands in the East", dated 11th November 1942, was superseded by a more calculated method, later expressed on 1st April 1944, in the high command treatise, "Warfare against Bands". This involved a more direct employment of *Jagdkommandos* for harassment and on the other hand a battle technique of encirclement, forcing the partisans into a cauldron to be annihilated by *battue* shooting (the 'Spider's Web' or the 'Partridge Drive'). Techniques of cleaning up the cauldron by splitting into sub-cauldrons and driving in wedges by shock groups were worked up—the whole aided by a more vigorous intelligence system and aerial reconnaissance. This proved an aggressive development from former tactics which began to be employed against Tempo's forces with only as much increased efficiency as the German regiments could put into their colleagues in the Royal Bulgarian Army.

The agitation at Cairo and Bari over the tragedy of Mostyn

[3] Archives CK KPS, letter No 5777.

Davies had set things moving quickly, so that on 1st April Kenneth Syers and his little team of five men were flying through the night across the Adriatic. Major Dugmore was now British liaison officer in charge of the British mission to Tempo's Macedonian headquarters at Radovnica and his messages had stressed the urgency of swift action to renew contacts with the Bulgarian partisans.

Unfortunately, as Kenneth Syers was about to drive out to the Bari airfield, he learned that John Ennals had taken away for another job the special man earmarked as wireless tuner for the new mission and they had both been involved in a motor accident, on one of the treacherous South Italian roads. This was serious. Training for special duties such as radio operators involved a six-month course for men selected as being already highly proficient. The plane, a D.C.6, was loaded up, and rather than wait another week for the next allocation, the party left without one of its most essential members, the radio operator.

On this night the D.C.6 met the the usual anti-aircraft fire as it crossed the Adriatic coast, flying high, and continued towards Macedonia, being on a scheduled two-hours flight to make sure of crossing and re-crossing the coast in the dark and arranging to be back by three o'clock, well before dawn.

Major Dugmore had come up to the dropping ground at Radovnica and he personally supervised the lay-out of the flares in the shape of the chosen letter of the Romic alphabet. Tempo came later and through the night the little party waited with two men standing alert by the flares, which were placed at the standard twenty yards apart. The pilot had to navigate to a pin-point with nothing to see until, over the dropping ground, he could make a circle, not too wide, but enough to be identified. Radio silence was always the rule on these occasions and no ground-to-air communition was advisable.

At the signal the two men beside the flares threw their cans of petrol at the piles of brushwood and scrambled back from the clearing into the woods. The flames leapt and the great letter lit up the night. Nothing came down at first, for the plane circled lower while the pilot, co-operating with his bomber, prepared himself to take responsibility for the drop. He had never any way of judging the ground wind, for the flames told only location.

Suddenly the containers began to come down, whistling as they pierced their direct passage through the cold air. The men had been trained to drop at very nearly 500 feet. Too high a drop meant difficulties and perhaps drifting parachutes, but too low presented obvious dangers for both men and the aeroplane. The whistle of the dropping stores stopped and the plane circled once more. Then the pilot winked his lights going away as a goodbye signal, while the engine noise faded into a distant drone, through which the gentle flapping of parachutes overhead began to penetrate. Partisans ran out to dowse the fires. The mission was coming down out of the night.

As he struggled with his parachute harness Kenneth Syers found himself seized and wildly kissed by a figure in the dark who waved his partisan card in one hand and his revolver in the other. His comrades ran up to take possession of the parachute. Embraced, kissed again, and half dragged half carried he was brought before the tall, lean figure of Tempo to receive a more diplomatic welcome. Major Dugmore next came, shouldering his way into the group with the traditional English handshake and friendly grin, and with him Frank Thompson, rather anxious but smiling and fumbling with his unlit pipe as if waiting to go out to tennis.

English summers were far away, and the bitter cold of the hours before dawn seemed to cut that clearing in the woods wide open around the gathering of uniformed Englishmen and embattled partisans. The peasants had brought out the mules and a couple of donkeys were already loaded up. Most of the containers had been collected. Frank Thompson was rummaging amongst them, scrutinising the markings. Suddenly he gave a joyful yell. "There's a set in the containers!" he shouted, rushing back to congratulate Syers once again.

Leaving the rest of the party to go on searching for parachutes and dropping stores, Tempo and his guest hurried through the pickets set to guard every access. Though the track was downhill all the way, dawn was almost breaking as they came to the command headquarters.

There were letters, food packs, news from home which gave special delight to Walker and Monroe, but Frank Thompson made for the container over which he had watched so carefully on the way down, and, nearly weeping with delight, took out the attache case with its compact short-wave transmitter. The other essential apparatus had also arrived, the generator with its stock of already-charged batteries and sets of spare radio parts, but Syers had to break the news about the loss of the wireless operator in the Italian car accident. As Sergeant Walker was really an explosives expert, his colleague Monroe being their interpreter, Frank Thompson's mission was still almost as far from being launched as ever!

During the three days Kenneth Syers spent at Radovnica, Thompson, now with the temporary rank of major and nominally in charge of his own mission, poured out his heart. The briefing Kenneth Syers had brought authorised him to make liaison with the

Bulgarians and act as British Liaison Officer to the Sofia Partisan Brigade; in short, the initiative of developing the command and work of Mostyn Davies was entrusted entirely to him. He rejoiced at the responsibility with all the impulse, the impetuosity of youth. He was critical of Mostyn Davies's military attitude and caution. Months seemed to have passed away in which 'Mulligatawny' under Mostyn Davies had been continually on the run. Yet what had they actually accomplished? A battalion of 200 Bulgarian partisans, most of them, he insisted, former trained regular soldiers, were looking to the British mission for help. Moreover, they had been promised it.

Kenneth Syers pointed out how for the greater part of February and March the weather had made parachute drops impossible, and, as for Tempo, of course, he had his hands so full with the Fascist spring offensive that he could not be expected to enthuse on the far-off hope of chance Bulgarian resistance.

As an intelligence officer, Kenneth Syers, with his keen and perceptive information-seeking motives, was quick to sense Frank Thompson's lack of accord with Tempo. Perhaps the latter also was colder, reserving his warmth for the memory of Mostyn Davies, with whose military attitude he himself, as a regular soldier, had more in common.

The sheer dominance of Tempo made him seem almost a diabolic figure in those days. He had unbounded energy akin to genius, and a capacity for inspiring hate and fanatic bitterness to the death against Fascism. This was more than a matter of that mere rhetoric in which he excelled, it was a dominant motive, giving his tall, lean figure that unbounded courage which took him through the enemy lines like a phantom and brought him into the thick of the most perilous danger spots at the critical moment. Comrade Tito might be far away from Macedonia, but every partisan had reason to worship the right-hand man who conjured in his name.

Frank Thompson found the pervasive authority behind his enigmatic smile exasperating and pursued Kenneth Syers expounding his discontent during the latter's three-days brief stay. He had become so restless that he hardly accepted the possibility of Bari providing another wireless operator.

On 4th April Kenneth Syers left him, promising to return. The little group of Englishmen banded in their new code name of 'Claridges' seemed really forlorn, for they had everything except power to operate. Without their sergeant of signals they were entirely dependent upon Tempo and Major Dugmore's mission, which had no significance for their Bulgarian liaison. Tempo himself, a diplomat as well as a soldier, tended to keep the Bulgarians away from his own men.

14: Retrospective Biography III
Sergeant of Signals:
Kenneth Scott

Frank Thompson need not have been so concerned when Kenneth Syers departed, for S.O.E. had already chosen the best man they possessed for this key post: Kenneth A. V. Scott, an experienced sergeant of the Royal Corps of Signals, a Londoner with that typical sense of humour and stolid direct efficiency wrapped in adroit adaptability so characteristic of the British wartime non-commissioned officer. Educated at Dulwich College, he had been a keen rugger player and an enthusiast at squash. When he left school he had become Assistant Scoutmaster 'Roebuck' of the Fifth Beckenham Troop and joined the Territorials (The Rangers). He was promptly mobilised in August 1939, while at camp, and soon found himself a signal sergeant in the K.R.R.C.

Adventure had always appealed to him, and he volunteered for special duties at the first opportunity, to find himself transferred to the Royal Corps of Signals and allocated to a mysterious course of training which would involve becoming an efficient parachutist.

Eventually Kenneth Scott found himself at one of the most important finishing schools of the war: S.O.E. Middle East Training School for Wireless Operators. Men here had been selected (after volunteering) from every type of unit, and anticipated being sent to work behind the enemy lines with partisans in the Balkans, or on small Allied craft in enemy waters—anywhere, in fact, where danger was greatest and communication most vital. It mattered not what their previous military experience had been, for it was this that united them—the consciousness that they had left unit and regiment behind, and all belonged to the same firm; and this indeed was the cognomen for their outfit: the 'Firm', Force 133 of S.O.E.

After training there came that feature which no-one really looked forward to, the parachute course at the airport close at hand, Ramat David. There was a physical-training programme, the drill ground for which, possibly for psychological reasons, gave a glimpse of parachutists descending—not always so morale-boosting as intended. On Kenneth Scott's first day he just caught sight of a Greek soldier, only a glimpse from the corner of his eye. The poor fellow was plummeting down three times as fast as all his companions! He lived, for the parachute had partly opened, but the sight, and worse still the recollection, was chilling. Possibly stuck with the memory of this, one of the men in Scott's night jump developed a 'shake' and crawled over everyone till he got to the end of the 'stick' so as to be the last to jump. In doing so he caught Kenneth Scott's webbing so that as Scott jumped his left shoulder strap fell down to his waist. Quicker than thought Scott braced it back, tightening the buckle only just before the 'chute opened to give him a very nasty clip across the ear.

This course lasted ten days only. Entrants qualified after four daylight jumps followed by one in the night.

A day or two later the call came. At four o'clock in the morning Kenneth Scott was hastily awakened, told to dress and pack immediately. A fast, powerful car was waiting to take him at once to Cairo. At Cairo some hitch occurred—why, or how, he never knew. After a tense couple of days, he was told the assignment was cancelled; he was to remain, pending further orders, in the S.O.E. flat he already occupied—unbelievable luxury for one transferred from an army camp and "the nearest to civvy street the army could muster!"

Secreted in privileged districts of Cairo, selected officers and other ranks relaxed in these S.O.E. surroundings, rarely more than three per room and enjoying not just comfortable furnishings but attendance by Arab waiters, cooks and houseboys.

The months went easily, lazily by towards early summer. Living in these extraordinary circumstances, three months altogether, inured Scott to boredom and to complete inertia. Then, suddenly at midday on 5th April 1944, orders arrived. "Pack! Obtain everything you need. The 'Firm' will pay. Catch the night plane to Bari, Italy!"

A scramble into action and gathering of possessions, abbreviating instant farewells, and together with others whom he describes as "a few odd Brass Hats", he just caught the plane en route for Benghazi and Malta to arrive at Bari at 1800 hours on 6th April. Here he found himself a person of consequence quite apart from the 'Brass Hats'. A special, exclusive car awaited to whirl him away to the H.Q. of the 'Firm' where a reception team had gathered to brief him on his particular mission and entrust him with further orders, codes and secret equipment before making sure he had a good meal and a comfortable, isolated and protected billet to enjoy a good night's rest.

Next day at a not too early an hour, he was awakened and brought out to be again given a more detailed briefing. He was taken to draw his parachute and to complete his full inventory from S.O.E. stores, being swept along in a whirl of activity by

assiduous and careful organisers whose kind cheerful attention went
to such extremes of consideration for the non-commissioned officer
as might have seemed ominous had they not kept Scott going on a
veritable fury of preparations until, at 1700 hours, he was standing
by at the aerodrome. At 2130 hours the plane took off and headed
due east from Bari.

Scott put aside the realisation that he was alone, that he would be
dropping solo, for, to his complete amazement afterwards, as he
settled comfortably in his seat the motion of the plane, the warm
and comfortable surroundings, sent him into a deep sleep from
which he was roughly wakened by the aircraftman at 2330 hours.

"Here we are, sergeant!" said the voice, half apologetically, half
in a desperate effort to be cheerful.

The plane was circling. Far down below a group of fires were
burning right on the top of a Balkan mountain. Then suddenly,
fully and immediately, did Kenneth Scott realise he was making
the drop absolutely alone. He groped for his half-pint flask of army
rum and began to take an occasional swig. Five times the plane
circled and each time, as it crossed above the fires, the heavy
bundles of arms and equipment were released through the bomb
doors. The sixth circle was the final and Scott sat in the hole ready.

> I look down, [he said, himself describing that vital moment] and
> even in the circumstances I cannot help wondering at the wild, cold
> beauty of those hills slowly sliding away below.—We're running in!
> The Red Light! "Action Stations!" "Go!!" I heave myself—then
> the hole—and plunge down to God knows what. The 'chute opens
> and I widen my legs to get the leg straps more comfortable, when
> from under the ground mist comes a faint cry: "Get your feet and
> legs together!"—the good old paratroopers' cry! Soon I land, scarcely
> a few feet from the fires, and am shaking hands with a couple of
> English lads, Major Dugmore and Sergeant Rogers. They take me
> down to the house, where I offer my rum flask, only to find that
> I've already emptied it!

Not till next day did Kenneth Scott realise he had actually
dropped to 'Entanglement Pin Point Radovnica' at 2355 hours on
Good Friday. Dugmore and Rogers spent the day acquainting him
with local conditions and listening in return to gossip about Cairo.
Late in the afternoon the mission, his mission, arrived in a condition
entirely belying the code name 'Claridges'. Major Thompson and
Sergeants Walker and Monroe had come down from their latest
trek over the mountains to the north. They were tired and quite
drawn with fatigue, very, very dirty, unshaven and hungry. They
spoke of heavy fighting ambushes and occupied villages, but the sight
of the new wireless operator was as great a tonic for Frank Thomp-

G

son as were for his famished companions those gastronomic delicacies brought by Kenneth Scott's own 'air mail'.

Kenneth Scott had the radio station for 'Claridges' operating at
once. He presided there like a benevolent magician, sending out his
coded signals, in answer to which night after night Dakota loads
of guns, ammunition, explosives, clothing and staple foodstuffs
came down to those fires on the mountain top. Every drop would
also plummet one container full of cigarettes, chocolate, tinned
fruit, sugar and a skilful variety of other delicacies.

15: Out of the Soup
into 'Claridges'

Major Frank Thompson was now commander in the field of the
mission with its full complement, charged with maintaining contact
and encouraging Bulgarian resistance. This was no easy matter. The
Bulgarian partisans were on the other mountain towards Kalna,
and after the confusion caused by the enemy spring offensive, the
punitive burning of Tserna Trava had filled all the mountains with
horror as well as fury.

'Claridges' under Major Thompson prided itself as a separate
identity from that of Major Dugmore, whose rather more traditional
eyebrows had often cause to lift at the revolutionary attitudes under
which its leader worked. In Thompson's mission there was no such
thing as rank. Though Frank Thompson existed as the 'Boss', he
undertook equal share of every duty with his men, including all the
odd jobs, cooking, making fires, sweeping, and clearing up, not to
mention checking and storing supplies from the aerodrome drops.

The Englishmen had come down from Radovnica to Tergovište,
and here on his second visit Kenneth Syers found them all, a cheerful little group, the sergeants contented and living in luxury. The
assembly of the three missions, well fed and happy, made a photograph such as might have been taken in some camp on the Sussex
Downs!

As far as Frank Thompson was concerned, the satisfaction was
superficial. He was inspired with a deep consciousness of purpose
which transcended military routine. He admitted he did not get on
with Major Dugmore, whose policy and methods were very much
akin to those of Mostyn Davies. Often he lamented that his mission

had accomplished nothing. The Bulgarian leaders, Georgi Chankov and his wife Jordanka, and also Vlado Tričkov, had visited him. Slavčo Savov Trunski had also made contact. Their Levski battalion had delegated an escort to guard the mission, and one of them Gočo Gopin, detailed as interpreter, was exchanging English lessons with Frank Thompson, who was relishing new progress in the language. The picture his Bulgarian friends painted of their country under Fascist repression caught his romantic spirit.

"I have done nothing yet," he complained to Syers, "except scuttle around the countryside here. I am bored with doing nothing! In Macedonia the peasants must fight. They are forced by events because the situation is intolerable, the alternative is for them to lie down and die. In Bulgaria they will rise and fight for an ideal!"

When Syers enquired, "But where is the Bulgarian resistance?" Frank Thompson argued that the whole country would rise together, of their own accord, not by being asked by propaganda or radio, but by example of the partisans.

"You can't ever teach the people *en masse*," he persisted. "You don't know anything to teach in the first place. They aren't teachable in the second. Only example, active intervention will teach, and my mission can provide that."

Both Kenneth Syers and Frank Thompson had read deeply on the subject of the Russian Revolution and had much in common. Syers was amazed at the correspondence Thompson had had with left-wing and Communist political figures and idealists. At the same time, while admiring his friend's practical turn of cleverness, Syers was mystified by what he sensed, seeing in him an amateurish attitude to revolution rather than the ruthless qualities of a leader.

Thompson desperately blamed the authorities at Bari for not giving him full commitments to act, and he thought Major Dugmore should have backed him to force the S.O.E. authorities there. Nobody knew the significance of these missions. Nobody knew whether the Balkans or Greece were to be invaded by the Allies. They had the right to know if they were the precursors of such an onslaught. At any rate he distrusted 'Brass Hats' always. His faith and trust above all were in the peasant, the Bulgarian peasant, to whom example would give freedom. One rising would prove the world was with the Bulgarian people. And when Syers interjected, "But there is no rising!" Thompson persisted, "Because they don't realise how numerous they are! The potential strength of the Bulgarian Resistance is underestimated by themselves as much as by us at Bari. Only their own Czarist authorities take it seriously. Relying on tough repression, they reckon they can stamp out the trickle to the woods. What these Fascists don't realise is how

WANDSWORTH PUBLIC LIBRARY

much they are hated, nor the potential growth of that hatred."

That spring there came out to Tempo's headquarters one of the
most spectacular drops of the war. There was the heavy droning of
Liberator planes, the signal fires blazed, the containers whistled
down and the parachutes floated gently through the night. The
green containers were larger; the team that descended was different.
In Tergovište those visitors are still remembered for the uniforms
they wore—"Beautiful, beautiful clothes from the cinemas!" The
containers had the finest saddles ever seen thereabouts.

It was a team of United States journalists and photographers,
so they said, doing publicity for *Life* magazine! The marvellous
equipment and cameras, the unused and polished weapons, seemed
to Sergeant Scott straight from the best of Hollywood. But the
saddles! They were far too magnificent for any poor little ponies
and mules that could be provided. There was no cowboy cavalry
in Macedonia. The whole team moved in splendour. They were
lodged in the best house, but the radio sergeants all wondered
whether the lice appreciated such a change of diet. They took their
photographs and held their interviews with handshakes and back-
slappings, distributing gifts and robust humour before trotting
heavily away on their astonished mounts towards Albania. It was
as if deliberately intended to advertise the Allied intention to open
a second front in the Balkans, and puzzled everyone.

On 21st April Tempo came in person to the farmhouse which
was the headquarters of the British mission. He had received hard
intelligence that the enemy were planning to encircle Tergovište
in much the same style as at Tserna Trava, intent on avenging
the more recent reverses. Tempo declared also that the presence of
the British missions indicated that the Western powers would invade
the Balkans via Greece and the Adriatic. The Germans had determined that the missions must be wiped out.

"It was not the partisans they were after at Tserna Trava so
much," he said, looking grimly at Frank Thompson. "It was you
and your comrades. And now!" he added with a wry wave of his
hand to the group of Britishers in the background, "It is your
turn! If you are caught"—and he made the well-known Balkan
gesture. "But you are my guests," he continued reassuringly. "We
have to move, but you shall stay with us and you shall be safe."

Major Frank Thompson pointed out that he was now associated
with the Bulgarians and would go with them.

"You will be safe with us to wait for a better time. Be our
guests," Tempo urged.

But Frank Thompson's enthusiasm would have no delay or
hesitation. His orders were to stay with the Bulgarian general

staff. He had promised Bulgaranov and Chankov. General Dobri Terpeshev in Bulgaria was relying on his mission. Procrastination for any reason would be fatal.

"How can I refuse you?" replied Tempo. "But it is your decision, not mine. Everywhere is bad news, and danger. All I say is: we get out! And in the early morning!"

Everybody shook hands, and when Tempo had gone Dugmore turned to Kenneth Syers.

"Well," he said. "No problem with you, at least!"

"No problem with me!" echoed Syers, who up to this point had been a silent spectator. "I can tell you, it's one big problem with me. I'm not supposed to be here, in the first place. I'm nothing to do with this side of the 'Firm'. I have to get out to Serbia at once!"

"Serbia?" remarked Thompson, pulling at his pipe. "And I have to put up my wireless set in the middle of Bulgaria!"

That night the partisan leaders came in to discuss strategy and plan the campaign against the latest information of the enemy advance. Majors Dugmore and Thompson sent along a joint invitation to the chiefs of staff to attend a farewell dinner. This was cordially accepted, to the consternation of Sergeants Rogers and Scott who were expected to perform as chief cooks. Supplies were dwindling. A search through stores could only furnish a menu consisting of sardines on local bread (toasted), followed by hot chocolate and bread and treacle. This was weighed down with a form of appetising porridge for which Kenneth Scott took responsibility.

There were congratulatory speeches, rhetorical speeches interspersed with fine inflammatory partisan songs (which Scott and Rogers mistook for sentimental love ballads) and a typical anti-Fascist denunciation by Tempo which would not have left even a deaf mute in much doubt of its flavour. The festivities were not prolonged, for tomorrow's action seemed to hover over them all. With exchanges of photographs, insignificant small token gifts and embraces, the partisans hurried away to pack and seize a few hours sleep.[1]

Kenneth Syers went to Thompson to say farewell, for he had arranged to leave before daybreak. Thompson confessed to being depressed. Tempo's lack of enthusiasm for his departure coupled with Dugmore's hints at caution gave him a feeling of frustration. "Nobody knows anything about my opportunities," he insisted.

---

[1] This was probably the meal so much quoted in the Traicho Kostov trial when the prosecution strove to attach significance to Tempo's words when he left, replying to a Bulgarian who asked where he had been, "I have been with those who feed us!"

There was no connection between Yugoslav resistance and the Bulgarian underground except by remnants of the Comintern via Moscow. The connection with the central committee of the Communist Party at Sofia was so slight. What could Tempo know? Syers pointed out that James Klugman and Hugh Seton Watson at S.O.E., who were responsible for the mission, had good information about Bulgaria and they were backing him. Frank Thompson was restless. Action was something he hoped for, not to spend more months running away with a wireless set. To go on the run for dear life! Again? This was a blow, a spoiled moment for him! His pent-up feelings burst out.

"Here we are going round and round the mountain when a whole nation across the frontier is waiting for the signal to rise for Freedom! I think myself, I have often thought it these last months—to hell with the job I was sent out to do! Better do something positive now! The whole Bulgarian issue needs a complete reappraisal at Middle East H.Q."

Kenneth Syers could only listen. He realised that the rejection of Tempo's offer was quite in accord with S.O.E. instructions to liaise with the Bulgarian general staff, yet he felt Frank Thompson had developed a political approach quite out of character with requirements of British Liaison Officers, who were in the field as guests purely and simply, and this could lead to a non-military enthusiasm in situations which, though politically and poetically ideal, could be very wrong from a military point of view.

Next morning Kenneth Syers had accepted his escort and left, going mainly by road north via Stajovica to Bresovica. Frank Thompson's wavelength was suitable for them to contact each other and they had worked out details to listen at set times twice a week. Both missions were on the run, however, and it was seven days before Syers's wireless operator could make the attempt to raise Thompson's radio station without avail.

16: On the Run across Encirclement

In the meantime the Bulgarian partisans were being rounded up out of their billets in peasant houses. The mission to Tempo, Major Dugmore and his team, with Sergeant Rogers, left the farmhouse taking almost no kit with them, for their route necessitated going straight into the enemy lines and creeping through. At the last moment Major Dugmore had a search made for a vicious pair of dentist's forceps and stowed them away carefully. He had a raging toothache and reckoned on commanding Sergeant Rogers to pull out the offending molar at some proscrastinated moment on their march.

The bright moon was still shining as the Bulgarian partisan column led the way up the *planina* with Major Thompson and his team in the rear. The couple of hundred men wound their way onwards in long single file through the trees and beyond to the snow-covered meadows. Moonlight silhouetted them against the snow and flung their long, hazy shadows across the white expanses. They went up to the *planina* in deepest silence, snow cushioning every footfall. No one sang, no one laughed, lest the sound should fall into the valley where the enemy might be only half asleep. The mission had just then two donkeys which kept well in step with the column as if they knew closeness meant both food and safety. Thompson went ahead, but his men never went out of arms' reach of those donkeys, which carried the precious radio transmitter, the charging set and batteries, sleeping bags and as much food and stores as could be.

The column made for the villages south of Čemernik, intending to pass above Tserna Trava and stay at Dobro Polje to take up a position with the other Bulgarian partisans at Kalna. They had information that the punitive columns had moved and they aimed at infiltrating behind them to make their southward advance pointless, a subtle guerrilla strategy so often successful. The Royal Bulgarians under General Bojdev with German detachments were manoeuvring to occupy a line from Kumanovo–Kriva Palanka–Vranje to Vladičin Han, but also closing in an ominous northern half-circle from Trun to Pirot. Every partisan knew that safety and military advantage rested in keeping to the mountain tops. The column took roughly ten days to reach its destination on 30th April–1st May. They saw Tserna Trava beneath them, reduced to ashes and crumbled walls. Only the higher and more scattered hamlets of Dobro Polje survived.

Generally the column spent each day hiding in the open, but if ever a house were found the partisans would set it aside for the mission's use. One such to which they were billeted was unusually large and had the most ancient of Balkan refinements, a three-walled toilet chamber projecting over the cliff so that refuse dropped through a specific hole in its floor straight into the pig sties for instant consumption. Whilst the mission was at this house, a mother left her hidden earth-cabin in the forest to come and ask help for her daughter. The little girl was in great pain for she had outgrown the ring upon her finger, into which severe cold had penetrated, causing the finger to swell to more than twice its size. Discolouration had begun ominously. She was cold, distressed and weak, and so pitiable as to give the three British sergeants as great a concern as any they had encountered. Sergeant Walker tackled the problem, but it took him half an hour of gentle, coaxing effort before he succeeded in breaking the ring with a couple of pairs of pliers taken from his explosives kit.

Two days later, the local doctor called in. His practice, if so it could be called, consisted of five villages with all the neighbouring farms, to say nothing of the earth-cabins in which wounded partisans were sometimes laid up. He planned his work on a circuit, using all the tracks and short cuts across the forest and *planinas*, but found himself more on the move than any partisan column. He knew how the two loyal friends of Slavčo Trunski, Stefan and Ilija, had escaped from the Rupska River disaster, although Stefan was wounded across the throat and Ilija in both legs. They had been carried off by peasants from Dejićeva and then taken out of the village house to a secret shelter. Here they survived ten days until the suspicious Bulgarian police cut down the entire wood and exposed the hiding place. The two wounded partisans were butchered and all the women living near that cottage were beaten with spade ends and left naked in the snow—though, as was grimly added like an epitaph, the names of the police were known and entered in the black books of the partisans.

Great care was taken up to keep 'Claridges' and its equipment as far from the centre of hostilities as possible, but as they came near Čemernik, 'free territory' as the partisans called it even now, Frank Thompson knew they were well within the combat area.

At one of the last villages in which the mission dared stay they found themselves in the middle of a typhus plague. 'Claridges' had established itself in the house adjacent to the church. Funerals were too numerous to be carried out only on traditional evening occasions. Several times a day there would be the ominous tolling of the bell to announce a procession up from the village. There were no young men residing with their families now, so the priest was followed by a group of elderly men carrying the corpse on an open tarpaulin. The women came last, traditionally dressed in mourning rags with ashes on their faces, weeping and wailing to display distress in the age-old manner. Despite the food shortage, usually there would be a feast after the ceremony, sometimes a lamb being slaughtered and roasted on a spit at the graveside.

Standing back from their windows, the mission watched with horror the groups of relations squatting and feasting by the new graves. Scott especially was glad when the order came to move on, for he realised he had been due for an anti-typhus inoculation booster, but had left Cairo in too great a hurry to get one. Moving on was no real escape from this danger for at that house the members of the mission picked up another new quota of lice which took no exception to Scott's company, though perhaps he, as a newcomer, had cause to work harder to exterminate his share of them.

Once in the Kalna district, great precautions were taken by extending guards and pickets to make sure that the British mission was secure in its refuges. Fighting was taking place all along the fringes of that so called 'free territory'. At the end of April the snow had been changing to sleet, and sometimes in May this was superseded by thick mist and cloud which rarely moved and gave the partisans the advantage in hand-to-hand combat. On fine days Trunski's outlying couriers reported more and more lorries and military transport of General Bojdev's army moving in from Sofia.

In the valleys the plum and cherry blossom had come into bloom in that long-extended Balkan flowering time which stretches the season of spring slowly towards the highest mountain slopes. News had come of the Red Army's successes. The liberation of Odessa on 10th April, the siege of Sevastopol, and now the Soviet progress into Romania promised to bring the Russians to the very doorsteps of Bulgaria. The invasion by the Western powers through Greece into the Balkans seemed a logical sequence after the collapse of Italy. The British missions in Yugoslavia and Albania were the obvious heralds of this. The fierce enemy May offensive against Macedonia was launched to clear them out before the anticipated invasion. The Tserna Trava district bristled with danger, for besides imperilling road and rail communications, it provided a perch on which the Bulgarian partisans assembled, roosting like hawks to menace the Bulgarian capital, Sofia.

As the offensive began, there were two days of heavy snow on Čemernik, after which the crisis of the battle developed into an intense series of skirmishes, this time unhampered by the traditional camps of refugees. Once again the enemy garrison from the Mačkat mine was brought into action, while all the fords and bridges across the Morava were occupied to prevent partisan escape towards Serbia, the intention being to encircle the partisans and squeeze them into a narrowing circle around Tserna Trava. Fierce winds and the variable weather of the Balkan spring made reconnaissance difficult for the enemy aeroplanes from Leskovac, but a new and unpleasant feature was the presence of mobile artillery. Nevertheless the partisans drove the Mačkat garrison off Čemernik Mountain, where the enemy left thirty dead and abandoned two heavy machine guns and a quantity of automatic weapons. This success enabled General Apostolski, who had come up with his Macedonian Brigade, and Tempo, to withdraw to Dobro Polje and give the partisans a rest.

The First Sofia Brigade of Bulgarian partisans had marched the thirty kilometres from Kalna, crossing above Tserna Trava to arrive at Dobro Polje on the 2nd May. Here the vital meeting of all the Bulgarian partisans took place. The resistance agitators from the interior of Bulgaria met their partisan army and asked the crucial questions: "Why are you fighting in Macedonia? Why do you not advance into Bulgaria and free your own Fatherland?"

These political agitators had for long conducted a terrorist assassination campaign in Sofia. German officials, Gestapo, and Royal Bulgarian collaborators had been cut down publicly in street and theatre. Successful as these blows were, they had provoked reprisals[1] which terrified well-wishers amongst the population who were also resentful of the Allied air-raids on their capital.

The Bulgarian resistance therefore moved headquarters from Sofia to that historic location of past centuries of insurgence, the Sredna Gora Mountains north of Plovdiv, Terpeshev had escaped from prison and he, with Anton Yugov, Tsola Dragoicheva and the Politbureau, planned from there to rouse the peasants and spread armed rebellion across the land. They had sent Chankov and his wife, Nacho Ivanov and his wife, and Vlado Tričkov to the meeting with the sole purpose of bringing the Bulgarian partisans back into Bulgaria where the great revolt would begin.

Nothing could have been more welcome to Frank Thompson. As an ardent Communist, he was thoroughly in sympathy with all that the newcomers urged and he promised lavish arms and equipment. His sergeants, with an eager force of young peasant labour, made ready the old dropping ground above Dobro Polje. Hopes went high. The Bulgarians lamented they had 1,000 men unarmed. On 5th May the squads went up to accept the drop. All night long they waited, but nothing arrived, not even the drone of a plane was heard.

---

[1] Some indication of this repression is given by the available data (Ministry of Justice Letter No. 2816, item 407):
By military courts martial . . .
   Death sentences passed on persons present: 405
   Death sentences passed on persons absent: 1185.

This was a set-back. Frank Thompson inwardly cursed his over-optimism and, as he went about crestfallen and worried, could not conceal his severe disappointment. Why had S.O.E. headquarters failed him? Why had no signal come through postponing that drop?

Even today the reasons are not clear. Perhaps S.O.E. had ominous memories associating Dobro Polje with the disaster to 'Mulligatawny' and Mostyn Davies, or some explanation may attach itself to the remarks by Bickham Sweet-Escott in his memoirs,[2] when he explains how by this time the number of British Liaison Officers in the field exceeded the capacity of the girl cypherines to decode their messages, so that very serious delays did occur in responding to some wireless telegrams.

Frank Thompson's anger and frustration resolved itself into a fury of messages to S.O.E., as the result of which in the second week of May several assignments were dropped and apportioned to the Bulgarian partisans. It was not enough, however, to supply the peasant and soldier deserters who were now trickling over the frontier hoping to receive weapons, especially to possess a new English rifle or automatic.

As the penetration of the enemy into the Tserna Trava district intensified, Tempo and Apostolski began to insist on immediate application of their first principles of Yugoslav partisan warfare —never to stay more than a day in one place, never to remain in the house of a village, never to concentrate forces but to keep on the mountain and move at night through the enemy lines like wolves through the forest.

Faced with the insistent demands of the Bulgarians for arms and equipment, coupled with the pressure of Vlado Tričkov, Dencho Znepolski and the Poltibureau agitators for their 'armies' to return and rouse the whole nation, Frank Thompson put forward a grandiose plan to move the Bulgarian partisans across the interior in a gigantic air-lift. When he outlined the scheme there was excited jubilation at the meeting. The Bulgarian partisans had seen the huge squadrons of Allied bombers passing overhead, and easily imagined themselves transported in the brief space of an hour or so to become freedom fighters in their own mountains. Disappointment at the slow trickle of arms from the parachute drops vanished and exhilarated preparations were made.

Frank Thompson foresaw no difficulties. The major part of the Bulgarian brigade could be transported by an airlift working a shuttle service in the day. Trunski could take the Bulgarian mounted cavalry in by traversing the Rila Mountains at the same time.

[2] *Baker Street Irregular.*

The face of Kenneth Scott as he glumly brought in the replies from S.O.E. was not reassuring. Questions and doubts and delays meant hours of de-coding, until the peremptory and definite order that thoughts of such a plan must be shelved. Thompson did not know, but the numbers of Liberator planes at that moment were not even enough to supply the missions adequately, and S.O.E. headquarters could never stake them all in one such venture. He could only make the best of poor explanations to his Bulgarian comrades.

Now, at this critical time, Tempo and General Apostolski had completed their plans to take their own brigades out of the enemy circle, and it became clear that the Bulgarians must make the decision either to go with Tempo or obey the new messenger, Rusi Hristolov, who had arrived with detailed instructions from the Poltibureau at Plovdiv.

Both Tempo and Apostolski assured them they were welcome to stay and continue the fight side by side as of old, but as he watched their faces, Tempo knew they had another destiny. To Frank Thompson also he renewed his promise of hospitality. "It is your own decision," he insisted significantly. "I want you as comrades, not just for your gifts. You will be safe with me!"

Frank Thompson returned to his billet that evening full of gratitude for the fashion in which the Bulgarians had accepted his explanation that the air-lift had been cancelled. Like hungry children, they had received with trusting glee his guarantee of more arms equipment as an alternative, actually cheering as if they would rather have the latter. Yet after giving Scott the text of his next appeal to S.O.E. at Bari, all his old discontent and resentment returned.

Did S.O.E. expect him to stay in Tserna Trava, moving from hide-out to hide-out as Mostyn Davies had been content to do? Or did they expect he would now fall in with Tempo and ally his mission where Major Dugmore would be his senior?

He had an army at his disposal, a secret army, ready at his beck and call to invade and raise a revolt that would bring a whole nation to the side of the Allies just as the Second Front was preparing. He suspected S.O.E. were holding him back. All the old chagrin he had expressed to Kenneth Syers came back. The wasted opportunities because of bureaucratic indecision, of imprecise and over-cautious instructions were now more obvious to him.

He had no definite orders. So much the better; he could decide and act on his own initiative. Was he not in the same position as T. E. Lawrence had been? Only here, in partisan warfare, events were too quick and much too fast-moving for disillusionment. He reflected on Caudwell's comments on the failure of Lawrence as "a might have been, a pathetic figure". Of course, that essay was only a peg for Caudwell's own philosophy of Communism in a bourgeois world, but here among the partisans there were no bourgeois, only men who could dominate and mould their environment—heroes, in fact. It was only S.O.E. and H.Q. that seemed an intrusion of bourgeois officialism.

T. E. Lawrence had freed Arabia, but for what? Here was the prospect of freeing Bulgaria for life in a new Europe, in a new world. To hell with S.O.E. Like all the bourgeois, they would turn and bow to success. Could he not take the Bulgarians into Sofia just as Lawrence had led the Arabs into Damascus? Only he would go, not as a leader but as an equal, a comrade among comrades.

Alas, there indeed lay the kernel of disaster. For T. E. Lawrence dealt with Feisal, one dynamic leader, but Frank Thompson had to deal with Communist committees, structures much more debilitating than even democratic ones. So, unknown to him, while Sergeant Scott worked his radio station, the wireless of the Bulgarian partisans was communicating with Georgi Dimitrov in Moscow as well as with the Politbureau near Plovdiv. Even while Frank Thompson slept, his motives and situation were debated by the Bulgarian committee, the commissar and the commandants, none of whom had any power except in joint agreement.

Sergeant Scott and the British team listened to Major Thompson's political enthusiasms respectfully, for they reckoned he knew what his plans were, though they were wistful about parting with Tempo for it would have been pleasant to have joined up alongside Dugmore's team to renew old times. The great point of their training had been to eschew Balkan politics and Balkan women— both had been represented as equally disastrous on such campaigns. Major Thompson to them was unique, for he renounced rank and was one of them. They worked as a team without a boss, conditions which made their major entitled to any philosophy he needed to get off his chest.

In a series of further meetings new plans were made for the Bulgarians to march out of the enemy circle; Trunski to take his men, the First Sofia Brigade, across the Rila Mountains; and a new brigade, the Second Sofia, which the emissaries of the Politbureau and the British mission should lead, to invade north of Sofia to make a headquarters brigade for the national resistance centre in the Sredna Gora, linking up with the Chavdar partisans there. Vlado Tričkov was its commander, while Trifon Balkanski, Načo Ivanov and his wife Vera Načeva, Dencho, Blagoi Ivanov,

Delčo and Gočo Gopin, all held office in the new brigade, an amalgamation from the Hristo Botev and the Vasil Levski battalions detached from the Trunski Sofia Brigade with the addition of new recruits and emigrés from Bulgaria.

A solemn ceremony of swearing the partisan oath was held before the new banner of the brigade, sewn from British parachute cloth, a tricolour in green with the letters O.F.[3] in the centre applied in white cotton. This was the banner's first appearance. For the past fortnight Jordanka Nikolova had been making banners with her little team of seamstresses.

The brigade was drawn up in four columns. Though so many were raw recruits, men and women, all were dressed in as much military uniform as possible, the men being well-shaven with neat hair-cuts. They took the partisan oath, declaring altogether: "We are offspring of a heroic nation. We are ready to give our lives for its freedom!"

In his deep voice Vlado Tričkov addressed them with a warmth and enthusiasm which was to remain in their hearts throughout the many privations that lay ahead, and concluded, "I am happy that upon me has fallen the honour to announce the name of this newly-formed regiment that was once only part of the First Sofia Brigade, and now becomes the Second Sofia. May our new formation, the Second Sofia Brigade be first in the battle with the enemy!"

After a pause and raising his clenched fist Vlado Tričkov cried, "Death to Fascists!"

And the reply came in a great shout, "Freedom for the People!"[4]

Thompson and the British mission renewed their radio messages appealing for supplies to equip the new formation, while Načo Ivanov and his wife Vera were allocated to stay with them and take charge as their hosts.

In the meantime the other Sofia brigade, the First, prepared to take the southern direction into Bulgaria, down the River Struma towards Kustendil and the Rila Mountains eventually to link up with the partisans in the Rhodopes. Thus they would menace another railway from Greece in preparation for the expected Second Front of the Western allies. Its battalions and *chetas* were also organised in Red Army fashion; Slavčo Trunski was commander, Ninko Stefanov his commissar, and it went without a British mission. As they began their long arduous march into Pirin Macedonia, they commenced singing the Botev song: "He who falls in the battle for Freedom does never die!" words that lived with

---

[3] *Otečestven Front* (Fatherland Front).
[4] Trunski, *Neotdavna*, Bulgarski Pisatel, 1965, page 557.

them from the first difficult days on Tumbi and Čemernik Mountains till the end.

That march over Tumbi was the first crisis from which they emerged by application of the strategy they had learned from Tempo—constant movement and sudden strike. Hopes were high that they would all meet again when they left the Second Sofia Brigade and the British mission and they quoted the old Bulgarian proverb: "Mountain does not meet mountain, nor river come to meet river, but man with man may meet!"

Perhaps their feet dragged a little as they came out of the homely village of Kalna on a spring day with the sun shining, reluctant to leave the friends in the cottages there, grateful for the kindness and hospitality, fearful of what might happen now their rifles no longer protected the patched-up white walls set in the bright green meadows of that secret mountain valley.

These marches of the two Bulgarian partisan brigades upset the Fascist plan, and in the confusion General Apostolski was able to release his forces and escape encirclement. He now fought his way through, defeating the enemy cavalry and drawing his own Macedonian brigade southwards so that as the enemy closed their circle they found only a vacuum, whereupon the Royal Bulgarians and Germans took revenge by burning Preslap village, the smoke of which was seen far across the mountains. Now that the leaves of spring had begun to thicken the forests not even the aeroplanes from Leskovac could be of much use. One Messerschmitt, for example, had descended so low over the trees at Tservena Jabuka that a partisan climbed into a beech tree to meet its next dive with his sub-machine gun. The plane burst like a bomb down to the tree, killing with its fall the gunner who had brought it down.

Instead of the new Bulgarian partisan banners waving over Tumbi Mountain, the long streamers of smoking reprisals spread across the sky, and as the men of the two Sofia brigades looked back and thought of the desolate ruins and cinders they left behind, fierce anger replaced their nostalgia for Kalna village and put renewed defiance into the singing of the Botev song.

Tempo himself had set the example his strategy required and on 11th May had successfully slipped through the enemy lines and crossed the Morava River, travelling west to the little partisan centre where, between the mountain of Radan and Kukavica, Kenneth Syers had arrived and established his own secret mission.

17: A Parallel Mission: Kenneth Syers

Syers had come to Bregovica on 22nd April with an escort of about 120 men of the Vranski and Ogrenski partisans whose leaders were 'first fighters', i.e. partisans from 1941. The rank and file included students, peasants, miners and even ex-*chetniks*. On the 23rd his escort took him on across country to Klisurica. He was able to travel through the rather poor villages in broad daylight without enemy interference. In spite of the season these villagers brought out food, of which they seemed to have plenty, and made no doubt of an open-hearted welcome, always, in traditional partisan custom, providing a guide to conduct the party on to the next village. After only a short rest, he travelled on through the night of 23rd April and on again by a forced march which scarcely allowed a stop.

The party went on foot, all five ponies being used for transporting the radio gear and stores. Somehow they crossed the Morava at Priboj bridge. Here they had to run the gauntlet of three Royal Bulgarian pill-boxes containing fifty men and two machine guns. The railway level-crossing was another hazard, guarded by six Serbs of the Nedić Army, but this was also crossed without incident. The partisans in the escort amused themselves by cracking jokes about the notoriously slack discipline of the Royal Bulgars.

Once across the river, however, their route took them through dangerous territory all the way to Berza. *Chetniks* had been driven south from Leskovac and, living like bandits, infested the country. Near the hamlet of Druglica under Kimic they were fired upon, but rather timidly. The escort did not return fire, as it was partisan policy not to attack *chetniks* unless they could be sure of doing so without fighting civilians. The hamlet was known to have been a *chetnik* stronghold since the spring of 1942, and had existed by exploiting the ignorance of the peasants, distorting news, and representing themselves as protectors against the Communists, whom they maligned as worse than wild animals. Kenneth Syers was surprised to find the main plank of their propaganda was the presence of British Liaison Officers with Mihailović's generals.

The party had already stocked food for emergencies such as this and now carefully avoided villages and contact with peasants. Syers found a frontier had next to be negotiated by creeping across at night, for he had come on Kukavica to the new Hitlerite Bulgarian Frontier that now ran between Royal 'Bulgarian Macedonia' and

Jordanka with her hand grenades leading an attack to liberate a frontier village

The baker martyrs of Litakovo: Maria and Haiden Haidenov and their bakehouse with basket as put out for the partisans

Serbia. Once he reached Berza he was in pro-partisan territory. All the villages in that region of Leskovac Polje had organised *odbors* (Communist committees) and partisan companies.

On the night of 25th April he came to within a few kilometres of Leskovac and saw the enemy searchlights probing around the barracks and aerodrome. Then, with Radan Mountain ahead and Kukavica behind, on the way to the new base through Petrovac to Vujanovo the whole party was able to relax. The strict and orderly column dispersed to march at ease in an atmosphere of real security. Only on the fringes of this 'liberated territory' did hostile raids occur, sheer terrorist raids led by a Captain Mihailo Zotović, O.C. Serski Straje at Leskovac, and from farther east by Major Stikić. The burned-out houses were evidence enough, apart from the first-hand atrocity stories which every village had to tell.

This new territory of Syers's mission was self-supporting and comparatively rich, needing only such necessities as riding saddles, sugar and 'imports' which could be bought with dinars or levas on the 'black market' in the garrison towns. The peasants were still accustomed to move freely in and out of Leskovac, where, in the town itself, controls were said to be very slack.

Syers set up his station with his two colleagues, Henneker and Farrish, and began collecting every possible kind of information which his operators coded and got away by radio to headquarters. Even in this new partisan area he found the same homogeneous pattern, the military discipline and organisation with its inspiring technique of marching songs and political slogans as he had observed when attached to the 'Typical' mission at Tito's headquarters. Endurance and sincerity had made their mark on the peasants—characteristics most obvious to Kenneth Syers and his mission when on their last march crossing the snowfields of impassable mountains, they had seen the partisan escort unload the five ponies and toil several hours with the wireless telegraph gear on their own backs, plunging on and on through the snowdrifts.

On Radan Mountain both peasant and partisans were suspicious of all townsmen, not just of those in Leskovac. The peasants especially regarded townsmen as traitors and recommended their towns be destroyed, so they praised any news of Allied bombing. There was a great interest in this part of Southern Serbia about America and Americans, but when Syers tried to find out how the Royal Yugoslav government was regarded, he met with a conspicuous reserve and lack of enthusiasm.

At the end of April his work of collecting information began in earnest. On the 27th a German deserter was brought in for an interrogation which revealed that he had been at Leningrad with

H

his battalion which moved through Norway and then to France. He had now been sent to the battle school at Nish, where a staff of 200 Germans with very young officers were training Bulgarians under severe discipline. The prisoner himself claimed to have been a member of the Communist Party before Hitler's accession to power. Pay-books of such prisoners, regimental numbers and details of uniforms, statistics of enemy distribution, economic facts, mining information—all were details to be collated in Kenneth Syers's reports. The Germans were hurrying troops into these central Balkans, even using air force personnel and paratroopers armed with rifles and mortars, as if they expected some sudden happening.

Though from time to time his wireless operators listened, they could pick up no signals from Frank Thompson's mission. He began to find evidence of the Russian White Guard officers conducting vicious terrorist operations against Serbians in the Šumadija, and, on the other hand, of *chetniks* under Jagoljub Jovanović helping the partisans. At the same time documents from deserters and prisoners clearly showed the amount of collaboration with the Germans via the Nedić Army.

News began to arrive about the famine and destitution of the families at Tserna Trava. The partisans devoted their attention to bringing out the 300 families and spreading them across the farms on Radan Mountain.

Every day, as Kenneth Syers arranged with the partisans to set up a watch recording railway traffic, it became more evident that German troops were pouring into the district. For example, on 30th April he knew that 400 *Luftwaffe* arrived at the agriculture school barracks at Leskovac. Transport and fighter planes came to the aerodrome. Fifty transport planes towing gliders arrived at Kruševac from Kraljevo and heavy reinforcements came to Prokuplje. He formed a special detachment for a courier and liaison work with railway workers. Next he managed to contact and operate a spy in Leskovac itself, a man who enjoyed the confidence of the Germans and had actually worked as interpreter for them. This agent reported the sudden arrival of 4,000 Germans and motor transport with their Divisional staff, and sent word that they said they had come from Hungary but he was certain they had been brought up from Greece. A further 30,000 were expected and were to be billeted in the villages. A tank division had come in from Prokuplje also and there was heavy military traffic along most roads.

The next weeks brought many reports of German military infiltration in strength. Syers's wireless telegraphy station was kept busy coding and transmitting the information of tanks, ex-Africa Corps lorries, artillery, and heavy guns, noting olive-branch emblems, or jaegers with edelweiss on cap and sleeve, the shield-shaped pennants with black cross on blue ground. Besides Germans there were Austrians, Russians, Italians and Romanians, all well-equipped, ten to fifteen per cent of them having automatic weapons.

Something was pending, but neither Syers nor his spy knew enough to be certain how the Germans anticipated that D-Day and the Second Front of the Western Allies would be directed to these crossroads of the Balkans via Greece and the Adriatic and that the activity of the British missions had helped to convince them.

Billeting of enemy soldiers went on during the next weeks in the villages round Lebane and Leskovac. In out-of-the-way townships all the larger buildings were requisitioned. The district seemed to soak up the thousands and their lorries, in batches of 500 at a time accompanied by ten petrol pumps for fuel supply. By 6th May Syers and his spy, to whom he gave the code name 'Kwang Tcheng Tze' (later, after protests from the de-coding girls at H.Q., changed to 'Abdullah'!) estimated a total 10,000 troops had arrived. The 'parachute assault troops' designation of particular detachments indicated to Syers some intended resolute action.

As the build-up of the enemy went on, divisions coming in that had fought on the Dnieper and at Stalingrad, the traffic on the railway also increased. Syers prepared to go 'on the run' and made radio arrangements accordingly. On the 8th he recorded 300 tracked motor cycles as passing. On the 10th his spy in Leskovac reported the arrival and billeting of another 1,000 German-controlled troops, but declared the incursion appeared to be easing. The Germans had begun using churches as magazines and ammunition dumps. Rumours of a Bulgarian collapse had begun to circulate. As the new army seemed not to be working for an offensive, speculation suggested it was merely an insurance against a Bulgarian mutiny. 'Abdullah' reported that relations between the Royal Bulgarian Army and the Germans in Leskovac could not be worse.

Next day, 9th May, a small offensive began very close to the mission headquarters. Four tanks came up to Beli Kamen and 24 M.E. 109's dive-bombed the partisans there, fruitlessly, and after half an hour flew away. 'Abdullah' had been able to give warning of this raid two hours before it took place!

The day following was the important day for Syer's headquarters. After the successful Tserna Trava operations, Tempo arrived with his chief of staff, deputy, and one member of the Macedonian Initiative *odbor*. He intended to stay one week and then go on to Tito's headquarters to report on Tserna Trava and Macedonia and to inform Tito of the two-pronged march into the Bulgarian interior by the First and Second Sofia Brigades.

Great expectations were aroused by these, even if the only result were to take the enemy pressure away from Macedonia. In these afterdays, it is clear that none of the participants had any idea that their operations were pin-pointing to Hitler a fictitious zone for the long expected D-Day, thereby drawing into the vacuum of the Central Balkans huge armies to await an invasion that never came.

On 12th May word arrived from 'Abdullah' in Leskovac that two more enemy divisions totalling 30,000 men were expected into the area, and that these completed a transfer of the Hungarian army of occupation, together with a concentration of German troops arriving from Greece. Tempo and Syers speculated on these manœuvres but could only assume their presence indicated some action in Bulgaria.

Major Dugmore, Sergeant Rogers and their British mission had arrived with Tempo, and in conference all agreed the recent Bulgarian offensive did not fit in with the new manœuvres and the enemy forces concentrating from Greece. Major Dugmore's mission were of the opinion that the offensive against the partisans had not been pressed to the utmost. Clearly they thought—and Tempo agreed with them—something was expected to happen in Bulgaria.

Not until 14th May did news come in from Syers's spy 'Abdullah' of the resignation and escape of three Ministers in Bulgaria and of wholesale arrests there. The spy also warned that Tempo's new partisan headquarters were being suspected and sought after. Tempo also had news of serious attempts by German agents to penetrate the area; two had already been captured and shot, others were under suspicion and being watched. As it was, a certain amount of high-level bombing had begun over open ground nearby, very similar to the bombing Major Dugmore had seen at Tserna Trava. During the next few days it became increasingly more accurate, indicating that some agents were getting information through to the Germans.

Syers himself was now becoming bolder and arranging to plant a radio station for daily train reporting in a village close to Leskovac.

Major Dugmore's mission, with Syers's co-operation, now began to busy itself with the prospect of aiding Tempo to make contact with Tito, hoping to fly him to Bari. Tito's consent was necessary first. This caused communication difficulties which emphasised the isolation of those missions. More than that, it highlighted the isolation of Tempo's colleague, General Apostolski, who had the political as well as the military responsibility for all South Macedonia, and who had no British mission at all allocated to him.

Accordingly, on Tempo's urging, both Dugmore and Syers agreed to press for a mission to Mihailo Apostolski.

The joint missions now began to prepare a landing ground on the 17th, hoping to make it suitable for Lysander planes to land. A large grass meadow sloping slightly south-west was chosen, just one kilometre north of Bojnik. A road with its ditch on the east and drainage ditches on the north and west borders ensured a sound surface that could take two landing strips of 650 and 630 metres respectively. To an R.A.F. man like Kenneth Syers the making of this airfield gave pleasure and satisfaction, while everyone in both missions welcomed its construction as a step in removing their sense of isolation. A path across the field was filled in by one hour's labour at night and a request sent to H.Q. for a replacement of the field indicator which had been lost when 'on the run' during March. The plane bringing in the next sortie was asked to photograph the ground and comment.

In the night of 17th May Tempo had his special couriers and escort waiting outside Lebane. Soon after the appointed moment, two companies of the Royal Bulgarian garrison, fully armed and equipped for a campaign, stole out from their barracks on horseback, led by their officers. The partisan couriers saluted them, exchanged the agreed password and led them to the mountain village where billets had been arranged.

Next day a parade was held in a clearing of the deep forest. The full strength of the Bulgarian companies numbered 225. They were led by the lieutenant—acting captain—then commanding the Lebane garrison and ten officers. All were well groomed and smartly turned out in neat military uniforms. Tempo arranged the parade to obtain the maximum dramatic effect. He himself made an impressive figure in his Serbian forage cap with the red star upon it. As he addressed them with forceful gestures, his powerful voice rang out across to the forest which seemed to throw it back and magnify with the suspicion of an echo. He invoked the cause, the heroism of Comrade Tito, the brotherhood of all Balkan peoples, in rapid phrases intersected by momentous pauses. The British missions looked on as the rhetoric made the speaker larger than life, though not all understood exactly what he said.

Since 1935 this Montenegrin, born near the home of the great hero Njegoš, from being the Belgrade lawyer Svetozar Vukmanović, had been known by his party name Tempo. Three times he had been imprisoned for so-called political offences and three times he had been released after hunger strikes of a week or so. During the war in East Bosnia at the time of Užice he had been with Tito, and now, after campaigning in Bosnia Herzgovina, spoke as Tito's personal representative. He had a typical Montenegrin sense of humour, slightly satirical, not to say mischievous, which could be blown away by a generous and hearty gale of laughter. When Tito had refused to receive British missions, his chief anxiety had been, as he confided to Dugmore and Syers, in case he should be involved with one of the numerous British missions to E.L.A.S. in Greece.

Today, however, he exploited his involvement with the British to the utmost, displaying the teams of Major Dugmore and Kenneth Syers in their British uniforms, pointing them out individually to the Bulgarians and invoking their presence as a pledge that the Western allies backed the partisan cause. His speech swept the Bulgarian soldiers into his own torrent of enthusiasm. They responded with applause and rousing cheers.

After the parade the officers attended for interrogation by Syers. He found them suspicious of questioning, for though they had come over to fight they had the professional soldiers' reluctance to do 'spy work', and their own military sense of probity jibbed at anything savouring of betrayal. Apart from this, they were pleasant and talkative men of up to forty years of age, one of them a qualified medical officer. None liked publicity. All hated the fact that Bulgaria was made to serve foreign interests and disliked the German grip on their army and nation. At the same time the Allied terror bombing of their capital was resented. They knew of the O.F. (Fatherland Front) organisation, though they could only say it was run by secret groups. Among them all there was a restless anxiety to do something for their own country rather than act as policemen for the Germans.

All that May there hovered a sultry tenseness over those Central Balkans between Nish and Skopje, as if a terrible thunderstorm were due any day. The Second Front had been so long coming that everyone wondered. The Red Armies were on the move, but the Western allies were poised. Anti-parachute troops and *Luftwaffe* personnel poured into the district, cavalry and mountain regiments took up strategic positions and the railways from Greece assumed an active and vital importance.

Syers and Dugmore could learn nothing about the separate marches of the First and Second Sofia Brigades into Bulgaria, but the spy 'Abdullah' continued to send news of the Royal Bulgarian Army's troubles. Suddenly he had surprising news to send. There had been a mutiny among the Leskovac *chetniks*. Mihailović's commander for central and south-east Serbia, Major Radoslav Djurić, accused of being 'Bolshevik', was under arrest. Vera Pesić, who had been his secretary, had been taken out and shot.

As forceful and dynamic as she was attractive, rumour had made her the most colourful character in South Serbia, associating her with espionage for the Germans, for the *chetniks*, for the partisans, for or against the man she momentarily favoured. Whether she was the Mata Hari of her day may never be known, her end was so swift. The scraps of information picked up by 'Abdullah' were transmuted into a larger story when Djurić presented himself at Tito's headquarters on 30th May, some weeks after his brigade commander Jagos Vuksanović had arrived there.

Radoslav Djurić was interviewed by Tempo and his commander Stamsulić almost immediately, actually only half an hour after his arrival. Kenneth Syers was also present and noticed he was in battle dress, jovial and very much at ease, self-assured, lively and anxious to make a good impression. His symbolic *chetnik* beard had been shaved away. He gave the impression of an alert and shrewd soldier with every confidence in his future.

It became clear that on 13th May Djurić received a personal letter from Mihailović dated 8th May, pointing out the help his *chetnik* commanders had received from the Germans and stating, with regard to the difficulties of fighting on two fronts, "At present our most dangerous enemies are the Communists. Therefore I order that every kind of action against the occupier's forces cease, but the occupier will be attacked in propaganda."[1] Djurić replied that he could not promise to do more than defend himself if attacked by the partisans. He then went off on an inspection of troops, during which his officer in charge, Captain Jovan Stefanović, received a personal telegram from Mihailović ordering him to arrest Djurić and convey him to Mihailović's headquarters. On 18th May Djurić was apologetically arrested and put under 'protective' guard, though he insisted on retaining his weapons—which even then, with Tempo interviewing, he had still with him. His two subordinates now found themselves responsible, Major Ranko Stošić in charge and Captain Manić as operational commander. A Major Stikić, a Nedić officer working for the German Gestapo came on the scene and began to arrange for the delivery of arms and ammunition.

At this confused moment, 21st May, the partisans attacked and dispersed Manić's troops. Manić came to Djurić in despair and begged his advice, which when given was of course the only possible —to re-group forces. Djurić ordered his guard away and was able to forget being under arrest. Another clash with partisans on the 24th demoralised Manić's forces completely. Djurić's advice was once again sought. He advised withdrawal, which was happening fast

---

[1] *The Chetniks*, A.F.H.Q. Handbook, 1944, page 26.

enough in any case. Meanwhile he unobtrusively disappeared, hid
for a time and two or three days later found shelter in an Arnaut
(Albanian) house. During the two days he lay concealed here, he
contacted the partisan First Serbian Division. He was uncondi-
tionally guaranteed life and safety "without prejudice to further
enquiries".

Tempo was favourably impressed, but declared it was a matter
entirely for Tito who would acquire all the known facts about him.
In the meantime Djurić openly identified himself with the partisans
and issued a proclamation calling upon all his *chetniks*.

Both Bulgarian and *chetnik* defections were symptoms of the
pressure intensifying. Some great event, some enormous flare-up of
hostilities was expected, whose uncertainty increased with its very
delay. Syers had planted observers to check the increasing numbers
of troops and supply trains on the railway from Greece. A Bulgarian general with half a dozen German officers came to investigate
the desertions at Lebane. About seventy lorry loads of troops were
rushed in to fill the gap. German planes made several bombing
sorties on adjacent villages, and a punitive column was sent out in
an unsuccessful search. Indicative of the new spirit was the information that ten Bulgarians in this column had been disarmed by their
colonel for refusing to commit vicious brutalities against the peasants
while burning their village.

The spy 'Abdullah' had now a wireless set and a capable operator
in Leskovac itself. He began sending more details and rumours that
the Bulgarians would be withdrawn to Bulgaria, that Nedić was
ordering a new mobilisation to replace them. He reported an attempt
of the Germans to disarm the Bulgarian army in Nish, which resulted in the deaths of thirty Germans and some Bulgarians. Two Bulgarian generals there had escaped. The new Bulgarian regiment in
Lebane had put itself on the alert against any attempt by the Germans to disarm it and was awaiting the chance to join the partisans.
The Germans had closed the frontier to Gerdelica, cutting rail and
telephone communication. There were new reports of unrest in Bulgaria, and anxiety and nervousness among the Germans as if some
crisis were near.

Both Syers's mission and that of Major Dugmore were not left
isolated, constant and regular sorties came through, providing not
only arms drops for the partisans, but everything for the maintenance of radio communication, charging sets, batteries and personal necessities. And yet, for all the information gathered by his
carefully-planted spies, Kenneth Syers saw no results. That month
the railway from Greece–Skopje–Belgrade, and Belgrade–Sofia had
ever-increasing use, enemy troops of every kind and nation poured

into the district or went through on their way to Greece, but no Allied planes came to bomb them. Often even his telegrams reporting such events went unacknowledged. It seemed, he lamented, as if all of Serbia were bombed except that one crucial district.

None of the British missions could be aware that the great distraction of enemy troops down towards the Balkans and Greece was only part of the vital strategy previous to the Allied descent on the shores of France!

18: Thompson's Private Army: the Long March Begins

The column of the Second Sofia Brigade had moved from the battle of Tumbi Mountain on 13th May, congratulating itself on escaping encirclement and glad now to be away from that danger spot at 'Wooden Well'. The smoke of burning Kalna was left behind, though they knew the Fascist army was gathered round it. They were marching in the direction of Krusa Vrana towards their own mountain of Kom, marching, not in the dead of night as Tempo's partisans were wont, but in the broad light of day. They sang as they marched, not only the universal Botev song but songs of joy and peace as well—"The Beautiful Danube", in fact every Bulgarian song they knew.

The fiery spirit of Jordanka Nikolova ran ahead of them as she threw back her head and led the singing, or called party names across to their leaders for whom she, as secretary of the Politbureau, acted as a registrar of each man's prowess. She knew and every one of them knew, that the Abwehr had demanded of the Royal Bulgarian government that the entire partisan movement must be exterminated before the leaves could grow and clothe the forests to hide guerrillas. Well, the woods were green; spring had burst upon shrubland and woodland and spread its blessed cloak of concealment; the partisans had survived to enjoy the leafy shelter of summer shade!

Except on the heights, plum and cherry blossom was already over. Apple blossom was out and even falling. The Second Sofia Brigade felt itself an army of revolution now and was not disposed to lurk in the shelter of those welcome woods.

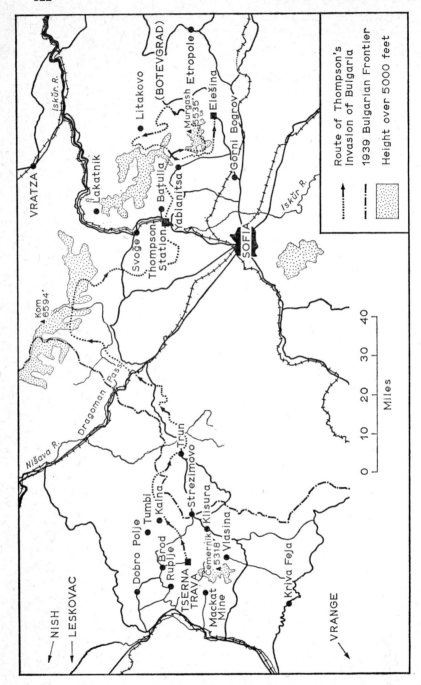

When they crossed the old frontier into Bulgaria, they held a meeting and made inflammatory speeches. On their own soil, once more they took the partisan oath with redoubled fervour. The Hristo Botev Battalion congratulated themselves on coming to their native land in the cause of the poet-hero Hristo Botev. The Levski Battalion similarly celebrated their association with Vasil Levski, in whose name they would free Bulgaria. They ate a good and hearty meal, provided by the people at Krusa Vrana, who shared in the festivities and gazed open-mouthed at Jordanka Nikolova as she made the most fiery speech yet, waving her pistol and hand-grenades; and when the time came for leaving they lined up to cheer, making a village guard of honour and crying, "Come Again! Do not forget us!" And then, in more Balkan fashion, "God keep you alive, and kill the dogs!"

The birds sang and the partisans cheered, and then along the ridge towards the Dragoman Pass they went as if to a holiday festival. As Sergeant Scott remarked, "It was like a Sunday School treat!"

Several, as they noticed the long line of 200 men and three women gradually extending across country, wished Misha had been with them. Sergeant Walker, Misha and Nikolić Stoikov had been great friends. Jock Walker had given them lessons in football as played in Newcastle. Misha, a former Soviet naval officer, had appointed himself instructor in guerrilla warfare—Soviet pattern—and had whiled away the winter evenings giving military lectures on tabulated subjects: war in rough country, war in forests, revolutionary war, war in the streets, war along river banks, preparation for attack, look-out posts, guards and spies—in fact he had covered every aspect of theory on the war they knew, especially the Russian system of instructing on care and protection of weapons in ice and snow, the care of hands, feet and faces in frost and how to lie on the ground in the snow. In every lecture one particular piece of advice was always straightly given: never should a partisan be taken alive! He himself had once jumped out of a train going towards the Mačkat mine and escaped despite the guards' rifle fire.

Both he and Nikolić Stoikov had gone south with the First Sofia Brigade, and it was rumoured poor Misha had been killed after the Tumbi break-out. This dividing of the brigade into First and Second had led to many partings. Nikolić Stoikov, quiet, earnest and attentive, had been with the mission since the beginning and had been attached to Nick, the original interpreter, who was actually a Croat born in Canada. Stoikov enjoyed the thrill of taking duty at the dropping grounds after the wood had been piled up for the fires. Frank Thompson remembered it was he who had helped him out of his parachute when he first landed, and regretted he also had gone south with Trunski.

Heartened by the enthusiasm of those frontier villages, Thompson shared in the general high spirits. He was leading his own private army—and not as an old-time general proud with the distance of command, nor directing from the rear, but in a fine company where all were equal. Not for him the mistakes of Lawrence. Had not Caudwell shown that freedom was secreted, not in the instincts of domination, but in the relation of man to man?[1] S.O.E. were still working on those old-fashioned methods of T. E. Lawrence, the pouring-out of arms, money and ammunition to resistance groups located in specific areas, which only resulted in demands for more. Not only that, but Yugoslavia was proving that supplying the population at random really meant promoting devastating internecine war, such as Nedić, Ustashe with *chetniks*, against Tito's men. Was it justified in any case, when the reprisals it brought down upon the civil population were so appalling? The political Bulgarisation by the Royal Bulgarians was one thing, the Gestapo-directed reprisals were another; *chetniks* burnt out villages where Communists had stayed, Communists destroyed villages suspected of *chetniks*. Everything was ruin to ruin.

The stinking ashes of Kalna still reeked in everyone's nostrils. S.O.E. should leave their desks in Cairo and come out to see. Why had they refused to apply the design of Wingate's new methods of guerrilla warfare? There had been enough talk of it in Cairo after the Ethiopian venture. This revolutionary march into Bulgaria would instance the worth of Wingate's 'penetration' ideas. Action would lead to action in partisan mobility. For the militant Communist like Caudwell, action must always precede thought!

Alas, if only he knew, Frank Thompson was far in fantastic idealism from either thought or action. Anyone as different from either Lawrence or Orde Wingate would be hard to find, for he lacked the utter ruthlessness of the one and the adroit adaptability of the other.

The first serious hitch became apparent to the British mission when the Second Sofia came to the valley of the Nishava River west of the Dragoman Pass. The marching column had become so drawn out that, though at first the valley seemed empty, before all the brigade had waded the river and crossed the Belgrade–Sofia railway lines, a train came puffing slowly up the pass and went by with at least quarter of the partisans still waiting there. Heads stared from windows, passengers—military and police—all looked out, fascinated with interest as the partisans stared hopelessly. But the train had its

[1] Caudwell, essay on liberty in *Studies in a Dying Culture*.

schedule to keep and puffed and puffed and went on! Not one shot was fired, neither did the partisans cut telephone wires, though as they thought about the implications, it was decided that the brigade should divide into two groups. This would keep their movements more compact and perhaps confuse the enemy garrisons at Odorovits and Smilovtsi.

Along the ridge of the Vilich *planina* the brigade came together again. The Levski battalion went first, led by Delcho, and the Hristo Botev followed. Jordanka, Vlado Tričkov and the staff section kept closely together. They had fourteen horses and mules. Thompson and the British mission had a pony specially allocated for the British radio station, but neither he nor his sergeants knew that loaded upon one of the staff mules was another set.[2]

This mysterious set, with the two Bulgarian radio-telegraphists, was being secretly conveyed to the Plovdiv Party headquarters to link up communication with Georgi Dimitrov in Moscow. They hoped to set it up with the forest partisans Boiko and Vurlo near the historical village of Batak. Both the telegraphist Ivan Pejchev and Pavel Tservulanov kept their purpose hidden from the British team. Vlado Tričkov himself, though he spoke English and had many long talks with Thompson at Kalna as well as on the march, kept his counsel about this secret. Nor did Nacho Ivanov and his wife Vera Nacheva appear to have any knowledge of this; and they should have known. Since they had come from the Sredna Gora general staff at Plovdiv with the special duties of arranging for the supply of arms and equipment, they had been both assigned to look after the British mission. To help them communicate they had Gočo Gopin, whose knowledge of English was now catching up with Thompson's expertise in Bulgarian.

Vera Nacheva and her husband had made a survey of the many groups of ten to 100 partisans scattered over the mountains of central Bulgaria. Both resented desperately the police suppression of their people and were convinced that in one revolutionary effort these young partisans could free the land. All their conversations with Frank Thompson reverted to this one subject. They had shared the same houses in the Kalna villages—always just a two-roomed dwelling in which Thompson had one room while Scott and the sergeants in the other worked the radio station. There was usually a stove in one room where Vera Nacheva did the cooking. She had already been sentenced to death in Bulgaria, had escaped and hidden on Mount Vitosha near Sofia. Her husband had spent two years in the concentration camps of Gondo Voda and Sveti Kirich near Assengrad.

[2] Trunski Neotdavna, Bulgarski Pisatel, 1965, page 586.

As they marched it seemed to Vera Nacheva they were going empty handed. They had delayed so long expecting arms in the Kalna district. Thompson had been always urging them to press on even without arms, for the lack of which he had given varied reasons ranging from bad weather to the need of planes for the Second Front which everyone knew was bound to come that summer. Even when the weather was good, only one or two planes had ever arrived, and this caused some doubt. Thompson, making use of Wingate's theory, answered by insisting they must penetrate the country and then as they travelled they would gather, first information, next supplies and then military support. Nacho and Vera Ivanov had argued that this, the partisan effort, was the Second Front, and had done their best to delay, explaining their procrastination as due to concern for the safety of the mission rather than expectation of more equipment.

None of the partisans was unarmed, Thompson was able to point out. The transporting mules and ponies were all loaded, and once they had their headquarters established and a dropping ground arranged, arms would come. His tall, lean figure grew more and more thoughtful as the heavy march continued, and he pulled on his pipe with a wry smile, no doubt reflecting how easy it would have been if that projected air-lift to the Sredna Gora could have been arranged.

19: The Anti-Communist Policemen: a Tangle of Agents

Nacho Ivanov and his wife Vera had reason for their anxiety in that sense of urgency which the long sequence of resistance disasters in Bulgaria had given to all its activists. They could not, however, at that time have known the extent of the double dealing which the Fascist repression in Bulgaria controlled, the sinister intrigue that had undermined many of their colleagues who had been picked off one by one.

British anti-Communist involvement in Bulgaria is said to date from the visit of John Swire when he came out as Reuter's correspondent to write his book[1] on the Macedonian murders.

He is alleged to have buttonholed acquaintances such as Lazar

[1] *Bulgarian Conspiracy* (Robert Hale, 1939).

Popovsky and, using them, began a prompting campaign to suggest that the only way to fight Communism was to draw in and suborn leading Communists, manipulating them to disorganise the growth of the movement itself. The seeds of this infiltration policy were sown in the house on Denkoglou Street where lived the Sultana Racho Petrova in the centre of Sofia, not so far from the Czar's residence. Her husband, a famous Bulgarian general, was anti-Russian. She herself was known as one of the wittiest and most talented women of Sofia and was reputed to have been the mistress of Czar Ferdinand. Delighting in music and the arts, a hostess whose refinement and grace of manner appeared to have been inherited from the best days of the previous century, she kept her salon as a society rendezvous.

When war broke out, international industrialists and Bulgarians with British sympathies found a congenial atmosphere at her home, for, although by now an elderly woman, she was actively engaged in collecting details of trade with Hitler's Germany.

Bulgarian loyalties and sympathies had become tripartite. The Royal family and court circles were secretly pro-British, commercial and middle-class Bulgarians were quietly pro-German, the lower classes and masses generally were by tradition pro-Russian, making a constant Communist threat to security, a fact which precluded any declaration of war by Bulgaria against the Soviets.

As the war proceeded the possibility of a Soviet victory directed the Czarist court and the Sultana Racho Petrova to more devious matters than mere trade. The future of Communism in Bulgaria became a more urgent problem to be viewed on the lines of John Swire's suggestions in addition to straightforward police repression.

The co-called chief of police, Peter Dragolev, had a more powerful colleague, Nikola Geshev, who took charge of this and by means of his direct access to the royal court, with his responsibility for all political supervision, enjoyed far greater power than his nominal superior.

As chief of Section A, Geshev had been entrusted with the critical task, not merely of outwitting political enemies of the Czar, but of combating Communism in particular. He had been in the service some seventeen years and had climbed to the top from the ranks, scout, chief of group, inspector, chief of service to chief of section. Authority trusted him. Ministers, new governments, chiefs of police, all might come and go but Geshev remained. He was authority and could over-rule, for everyone knew that by reason of his direct access to the royal court his activities were privileged and not to be gainsaid.

He quietly associated with the Sultana Racho Petrova and her circle, and, as the war progressed, subordinates in Section A noticed a lack of energy on his part in fulfilling Gestapo demands. He made only a pretence of discovering activists who had assassinated individual German officers and personnel in the streets of Sofia. The power cable connecting the important German radio observation station at Boyana Village was constantly being sabotaged, yet Geshev was always reluctant to search for the perpetrators and paid no attention to Gestapo anger. To those closest to him in his secret service he expressed pro-British sentiments and openly confided that he was certain the British would win the war. More than that, he took one or two into his confidence about the policy of Communist recruitment.

In 1943 the Sultana Racho Petrova had drawn Ivan Tutev aside and suggested he got in touch with 'progressive' circles. She advised him to cultivate connections who would arrange his admission to the Communist Party so that he could work himself into a leading position within it. Tutev, experienced intelligence agent as he was, could not refrain from expressing horror at such heresy! The Sultana, however, insisted that this plan represented the policy in which the British government was interested. After the war, when Soviet influence might establish itself throughout the Balkans, only by such infiltration could there be any control or indeed any knowledge of the intentions of the Soviets and the Communist Party.[1]

Suppers at the Restaurant Zdravé, masonic connections through General Zhechev, aide-de-camp of the Czar, dinners beside the red plush of the Grand Hotel Bulgaria, made a web of collaboration which balanced those extractions by torture in the cellars of the central prison, where Nikola Geshev's methods were more brutal and direct. By 1941 the Communist Nikola Pavlov had been arrested for the third time. On 3rd July he was sent to the Gonda Voda Concentration Camp to mix with the central group of captured Communists. He let it be known he was in danger of a death sentence. He had the nickname 'Komara' (Mosquito) for he was always pestering acquaintances, being ever in motion and over-eager to start gossip and idle chatter. By October he escaped with four others, including Anton Yugov, but was soon conveniently recaptured in the Rhodope forests and transferred to the Eni Klui Camp, from where, about 22nd March 1942, he was taken to police headquarters in Sofia.

---

[1] Tutev indeed carried out his instructions and played his part so well that in 1947 he had become Director of Foreign Trade; but the year following, in consequence of the betrayals by Kim Philby that led to the Traicho Kostov trial, he had under 'confessions' extracted by Moscow-directed Communists, every cause to repent bitterly of the whole policy.

Eleshina town hall

The Bulgarian frontier forests

Frank Thompson's grave above Litakovo

Thompson Railway Station, Bulgaria

He well knew there had been a great collapse of the central committee of the Bulgarian Communist Party, but, perhaps as a blind, his own wife had been detained. At his post-war trial, he described the only interview he admitted, with Geshev in his police office: "I found him sitting at his desk and rummaging about in the papers there and he did not even raise his head to see who was entering the office. After a little while he raised his head, tearing his eyes from the papers, and, after having looked me up and down from head to foot he said, 'Mosquito, the printing press . . .' "

Threats appear to have been enough, for Pavlov made no afterplay of having been tortured to justify his breakdown, and easily enough after his complete examination he signed the declaration to renounce political activities with the customary affirmation: "I will take up my stand on the front line in the service of the State." Geshev sent him back to prison to associate with Communist captives.

After this, action against the Communist resistance accelerated. On 29th April 1942, no doubt from information obtained by such methods, the police seized the secretary of the Communist central committee, Traicho Kostov, in his underground lodging at 11 Pateritsa Street. The collapse of the central committee seemed complete and events shaped towards the 'Trial of the 62' in which the bravest of the Bulgarian Communists were done to death, including the poet hero Vaptsarov.

Traicho Kostov, veteran Communist of many previous arrests—as the result of which he already had a crippled back—found himself undergoing a course of three police beatings. Four colleagues one after the other were brought separately before him. Each denounced him as the most active member of the central committee. After ten days he was called for questioning to Geshev's office. At first he persisted in denying Geshev's assertions, but this did not anger such an experienced interrogator.

"If you consider well," Geshev suggested with a plausible smile, "your refusals to answer cannot lead to anything good. First of all, because the beatings will go on and finally you will have to confess, but even if you should be able to bear the torture, which is almost out of the question, we have at our disposal enough evidence against you, as you know, circumstantial evidence as well as depositions, all all of which has the force of proof and will be sufficient to have you condemned to death."

One quarter of an hour was allowed the victim to make up his mind. Kostov, reflecting that the German Blitzkrieg against Russia had failed; that after the war Geshev and the Germans would go together, when nothing would hold him to his promise; agreed,

I

signed the required declaration and affirmation, and proceeded to a long written deposition in which he betrayed all the members of the committee and also the military organisation led by Colonel Radoinov. He gave his undertaking to collaborate under the direction of the political police.

Taking up the final deposition, Geshev declared that collaboration need not begin at once, but at the end of the war after release from prison. "For whatever the result of the war may be," Geshev insisted, "the Communist Party will obviously continue to exist and we will need a collaborator of your rank at the very source so that we not merely learn intentions, but influence policy."

Geshev now worked out a scheme by which new, innocent depositions were made for submission to the court and by direct intervention of the Czar, via the Minister of War, the judges exempted Kostov from the death penalty, finding attenuating circumstances, hard family conditions, "bad health and ideological circumstances". Except for one similarly treated, the others on trial were all shot, Radoinov and his parachutists having been executed before.

After this, prison life for Kostov improved. Nikola Chausev, one of the few who by 1949 at Kostov's post-war trial was not in 'residence' at Sofia Central Prison, told how in June 1942 he, Chausev, was examined by one of Geshev's assistants and most cruelly tortured, beaten unconscious, bastinadoed and burned in the nose with cigarettes. He was put into Kostov's cell, but something made him suspicious, although he answered all Kostov's questions about his personal life. Kostov knew the Morse Code and so made contact with neighbouring cells. Nikola Pavlov often came to the peep hole of the cell. Kostov had no sign of torture upon his body but was calm and often sang happily. His food was good and nourishing, quite distinct from that of the other prisoners and through the toilet he received newspapers which he whispered were put there for him by a 'progressive' policeman.

Kostov remained in Sofia Central Prison until March 1943, when he and the group of political prisoners were transferred to Pleven jail to a milder regime. Here he gathered round himself a number of others who had also broken under Geshev's methods, each pledged to uphold the other's secret. Emissaries from Geshev came and went and it must have seemed to the chief of Section A and also to the Sultana Racho Petrova that they held the whole future of the Communist Party in the palms of their hands.

Now, as the Bulgarian partisans were invading from the frontiers and making what seemed to the authorities in Sofia 'big talk' of nation-wide rebellion, Geshev sent Kostov orders to write letters to the central committee in the Sredna Gora to neutralise any partisan activity towards aggression. At the beginning of 1944, when he had a closely-knit group of political prisoners around him at Pleven, Kostov sent out a letter by underground routes to the Chavdar partisans questioning the central committee's decision to pass over to an 'all-out offensive'.

'You are bidding too high!' he wrote, underlining in Draža Mihailović fashion the need for preserving the organisation till after the war, declaring himself opposed to the increase of partisan activities against the police, instancing the victims of partisan encounters and the draconian repressive measures they caused.

Though this fatal letter is supposed to have been rejected, it coincided with an energetic campaign by the Royal Bulgarian police and the military which drove the Chavdar partisans eastward and effectually prevented them moving to link with the Second Sofia Brigade and Major Thompson.

But none of this subversion was known to the young Britishers or to the happy revolutionaries who led that invasion march, rejoicing on the new spring turf of their native soil, and they had no key to read the coming indications of it.

20: On the Bulgarian Mountains

When the long columns of the Second Sofia Brigade reached the slopes of Kom Mountain, the weather reverted in typical late spring Balkan fashion. Snow fell, as Vera Nacheva remarked, "in cupfulls".

The attitude of the peasants changed at the same time. Like the bitter winter wind, their faces seemed to harden; they became furtive and then openly hostile. Everyone was shocked to notice this, something so vitally different from those days at Kalna in Yugoslavia—not merely terror of incrimination by the police, but a real fear as of the vicious bandits which partisans had been represented as resembling. Frank Thompson now began to realise how desperate this resistance movement was, Bulgaria being the only nation on Hitler's side where there was a partisan effort.

As they were approaching Kom, the general staff of the brigade, finding food could be bought in Dolgi Del, had come right into the main street, bringing the column with them up to the houses. Urged on by the enthusiasm of Jordanka, they called an improvised

meeting of villagers in broad daylight. Speeches about the O.F.
(Fatherland Front) did not receive the applause so customary in
Kalna. People wanted to get back into their houses and close the
doors and even the money by which the British mission paid for its
food had been taken furtively. The brigade ate a good lunch but
hurried away. The chill of that forced welcome was so significant
they knew there was no time to lose.

The first impact of police opposition came near those hamlets of
Govejda and Dolgi Del. The rear of the long column had no idea
of what was going on until suddenly those weary marchers became
aware of a struggle at the head of the line. Dencho was ahead
leading the Levski battalion when he saw a figure silhouetted against
the ridge.

"Who's there?" he challenged.

"And who are you?" came the retort, simultaneously with a rifle
blow that struck across his arms and was repeated three times from
a carefully concealed trench. Dencho fell into the trench, instinc-
tively firing from his own automatic and shouting to alarm his comrades. The police, underestimating the partisan strength, ran forward
using bayonets and knives in close hand-to-hand fighting, probably
under orders to capture prisoners alive for interrogation.

Before the main column could halt, it was all over. One partisan
had been killed and one policeman shot dead. When the general staff
came up, Dencho was found to have three knife wounds. Another
policeman had been disarmed, seized and made prisoner.

A torrent of words burst from the despairing captive as he was
brought down to Vlado Tričkov for questioning. He spoke so fast in
his pleading that Thompson could not understand what he said till
afterwards. He was not a Fascist, he declared, in a frantic effort to
gain sympathy. He was not a soldier, certainly not a policeman.
He was a conscript, which any one of them might have been. He
would have escaped, just as they had, if he could. A man must live.
What could he do? A married man, he was; and had three children,
and a wife—four lives depending on him. What could he do? And
now he had surrendered! Of his own free will, he was a prisoner!
Still pleading, he was searched and his papers dragged out of his
clothes. As they were read out to the little group standing there,
he fell silent and began to tremble, for there it was in black and
white! He was a single man, and a regular member of the police.

At the same time a runner came down from the Levski battalion.
The band of police had re-grouped and were making another ambush
directly across the column's intended route. The partisan column
turned away from them to go up the heights of Kom. The prisoner,
no longer a source of useful information, but only an embarrass-

ment, was passed to the end of the column where men of the Botev battalion smashed in his head with rifle butts. As the British mission passed him lying beside the trampled pony track, it seemed an unhappy, tragic omen.

Scanning the slopes with binoculars, the partisans gradually became aware of the police tactics. Trenches had been dug and everywhere on heights where trackways met or some visual advantage prevailed, small outposts were manned with groups of half a dozen policemen. The men occupying them were unused to combat conditions for they could often be seen leaving carefully masked shelters to stretch their legs and smoke a cigarette or two. The defeated ambush posse had deserted their useless position and were trailing after the column. Now and again a shot far out of range indicated some police observer had spotted the brigade. Every time some scattered police post caught sight of the partisans they would signal by such a gunshot, which served also to warn the Second Sofia, and keep the stragglers to the column.

The strain began to tell. Under the heights of Kom the general staff held a meeting to discuss tactics. Their objectives were clear. The Levski battalion, with Georgi Chankov (Jordanka's husband) as secretary of the regional committee, was to establish itself on Murgash Mountain with a view to operating in the Sofia zone with the Chavdars of Botevgrad, the Hristo Botev Battalion to continue to the Sredna Gora headquarters base at Plovdiv with the general staff, eventually linking up with the Rhodope resistance bands. The little group of Chavdar guides with them were expecting at any time someone from the Chavdar partisans around Botevgrad to make contact, for they knew nothing of Geshev's police subterfuges and Kostov's letter.

The column had now exhausted its food and was tired and hungry. Moreover, following that snowfall, rain had set in and the men were soaked and cold. Should they not wait and regain their strength? Only one night's rest, claimed the more experienced soldiers of the Levski battalion.

"How rest with no food?" argued others. "It is food the men want as well as sleep! Let us get to a village and take supplies by force if they are not offered, if they are withheld!"

The fiery enthusiasm of Jordanka broke down all opposition against continuing the march. She was wearing an English golfing jacket the mission had given her, a partisan beret on her head and on her feet only tourist shoes which did not keep out the water. As she spoke she conveyed the impression of an overwhelming reserve of energy, accumulating, almost threatening. They had now outdistanced the enemy, who were even then digging trenches behind their route. The police were confused, she argued. They could keep on the upper ridges. In one day they could link with Chavdar who would bring them food—another day and they would be on the Stara *planina*. What a welcome they would get in Koprivshtitsa! First Rebellion Town; Only tomorrow they could all be marching past Botev's home! She stood with her quiet girl friend beside her. The fierce enthusiasm changed to an incisive threat as she pictured the fate awaiting them if they stopped. The dreaded word 'encirclement' was enough. Reluctantly all agreed to press forward.

It was decided that news of the existence of the British mission, the English officer and his three sergeant radio telegraphists, must be kept secret; even their own village adherents should not be aware they had Englishmen in the column. No one was to speak of it for propaganda purposes. Higher and higher, across open country, the march continued, always avoiding any track or known route which might conceal an ambush.

The mission still had a small supply of their special packets of provisions, conserves, salami, rum and coffee, but by sharing with the partisans around them it was dwindling to almost nothing. Their one pony was beginning to look thin. The brooks on the mountainside had become torrents which the animal objected to crossing even when a plank was put down to give him footing. After one near-disaster when with the enemy close at hand and in the face of gunfire, Kenneth Scott saved the radio set, baggage and also the pony from destruction, Frank Thompson organised a support squad to get the precious equipment over brooks. The pony was bolstered and surrounded by partisans. Once again, in the dark of night this time, there was a mishap. The animal went down with two legs deep in a wash of bog. Had not Nacho Ivanov and Kenneth Scott plunged underwater into the pool and pulled up the load while the men heaved the pony across, the set would have been lost.

After ten days marching towards Petroshan, dawn overtook them as they realised they were on the north-east side of Kom above Berkovitsa. By continual passing over trackless country on the mountain slopes the normal distance of their march had been magnified many times. The food situation had become desperate, so they waited restlessly for the couriers to return after contacting the villagers. As by now had begun to be suspected, they reported no co-operation could be obtained. Everywhere the partisans had met reticence, alarm and closed doors.

They learned that the Germans were in the village. Under their orders all the milk for miles around was commandeered and the villagers had been mobilised to work in the newly enlarged factory for processing milk into *kashkaval*, the famous yellow cheese, renowned for its high quality. This was now all being regularly despatched to Germany. Though the villagers had themselves declared they were entirely without food, the factory warehouse was stacked with cheeses ready for transportation. Such intelligence was enough to spur the brigade to action. Telephone wires were cut. Outposts were set up to ambush any transport and blockade the village. Recklessly without plan or hesitation, the factory was attacked, the doors battered down and the stores plundered. Before leaving, the entired place was demolished, vats, machinery and transport, everything reduced to ruins as contributing to the enemy war effort. The whole operation took scarcely half an hour, after which the brigade re-assembled without any casualties. As they moved on they lamented the lack of bread and onions and many tried to loosen the taste of cheese with edible green shoots and forest leaves.

The rain had begun to ease off. The general staff decided to send ahead into villages asking peasants to set aside bread after the baking in chosen places so that it could be given without risk and collected without danger. They marched as much as possible in the night now, taking only an hour or two to halt and rest the mules and ponies. Dawn came up suddenly as they were recrossing by the stud farm near Petroshan. They had passed the Ginska River and came upon the new road which the 'labour boys' had built in about the year 1935 by forced conscript labour, a useless effort in road-making, going idly and forgotten through Petroshan towards the ridge of the Stara *planina*. Now its deserted condition was welcome enough and took the column on until the brigade turned away to make for Murgash. Occasional appearances of distant police puzzled them, as did certain strange inauspicious happenings.

On the road from Bakovo village their scouts had apprehended an unusual wanderer who was dressed in a civilian jacket but still ominously wearing police uniform trousers beneath it. He admitted he was a policeman, but insisted he had nothing to do with any operations against them for he was on leave. He was only looking for his lost cattle. Yes, he admitted he was alone. No, there was no one else searching for the cattle.

Some time later they came to a solitary house standing beside the woods. Once again their binoculars showed it was a carefully arranged police post in which they noticed one woman. As they rushed forward, the police fled, firing their way out in a compact group. But the woman had disappeared. They knew she must be hiding in that house, yet though they searched everywhere, she could not be found. Walls were broken open and ceilings pulled down, but to no effect. If they had been Fascists, they would have burned the house down. As it was, they gave up the search at last and pushed on. The police had fled directly along their line of march so, to avoid another ambush and confuse the enemy, they deflected to the right.

Later, in the depth of the forest, all the brigade heard the sound of horses and cattle bells. Incredible as it appeared, an enormous herd of cattle was being driven across them and into their line of march so as to interfere with and hamper their progress. To those hungry men the temptation to halt and refresh themselves with a feast was almost irresistible. The leadership suspected the trap and gave orders to drive the cattle out of their route and hasten speed. They dared not load themselves with carcases of beef. Already, so as to lighten the horses, they had buried and concealed both their typewriter and duplicating machine, but that mysterious radio set which gave them independence from the British mission and could make their link with Moscow any time, that was retained.

In the late afternoon as they were crossing a glade in the forest, they surprised a charcoal burner leading two bridled horses. He was not travelling on any recognised track but across open country. He could give no reason for being there, nor could he account for the horses, nor why they were bridled. Without further enquiry he was seized and made prisoner, for at the same time the Botev battalion had another mysterious wandering civilian brought to them.

These coincidences brought a change of attitude to the whole brigade. The old atmosphere of Tserna Trava and Kalna was lost. Instead of welcoming peasants, of village deputations of congratulation, their own countrymen were being pushed across their path as spies. Every Bulgarian in forest or field had to be regarded as an enemy and made prisoner.

The scouts sent out to seek food now came back with yet more gloomy reports. The police were emptying the entire district, taking civilians and their livestock down into the valleys and leaving nothing in any hamlet the brigade was expected to enter.

The next two prisoners the partisans took were men more secretive and discontented than themselves. They were 'contrabandiers', who, not knowing what was afoot, had come up to these hill villages to buy food to sell on the Sofia 'black market'. Hungry and tired, they were anxious to get out of this 'scorched earth' district and pursue their lucrative calling elsewhere. Their intentions were so shamelessly expressed, as if the two adventurers regarded the partisans as on a level or even as worse criminals than themselves, that their story had to be accepted, though it did not gain them liberty.

One morning the partisan appointed to keep watch at the brigade's halting place reported to Dencho that near their camp he saw soldiers leading a saddled horse. No peasant or partisan would have such a good saddle, and the circumstances worried the staff. They had no choice but to continue. They had made speed coming round through the Petroshan Pass and went by Zanog village and Zimevitz on their way to Lakatnik. Sometimes there would be food that could be bought for which Thompson would pay with his store of English golden sovereigns or Bulgarian paper money, though he never had direct dealings for the staff kept the mission out of sight, wedged in between the vanguard of the Levski battalion and the Botev detachment who now brought up in the rear. The partisans showed extreme concern for the safety of the British mission, despite their own danger, though all the Bulgarians remarked that neither Thompson nor his sergeants would ever accept the proffer of riding on the horses, which were kept for the over-fatigued or the women. It has been suggested that Frank Thompson and his sergeants were hemmed in so as to be kept in ignorance of the partisan radio, but there can be no doubt there was also genuine care for their safety. They were regarded still as having the power to conjure supplies out of the heavens, although the nearer they came to the Red Armies the less need there would be for such magic.

From the time they began to come south of Kom, dodging road-ways and keeping to goat tracks, skirmishes would develop, more often now in the rear. This was regarded as a good sign that they were outdistancing their pursuers, who had no idea of the brigade's intended route.

As they came round Koznitsa Maxale, the advance party caught another mysterious, solitary wanderer who was identified as a resident of Lakatnik, a known Fascist. He was forced to accompany them with his hands bound. Next day police were seen approaching. As the brigade moved away a skirmish began in which this captive was killed, but whether by partisans or police was never known. A rearguard action now developed with the pursuers until dusk. The police seemed to be accompanied by military using mortars and obviously attempting to get ahead of the partisans and cut them off. These manœuvres still proved unsuccessful, for though the partisans could not entirely disengage themselves from the enemy, every indication of the hostile presence in pursuit quickened the march of the brigade.

Coming down in the direction of the Great Isker River valley, Vlado Tričkov and his friends on the staff anxiously consulted the representatives of the Chavdar partisans. Why had not the comrades come to meet them? The men of Chavdar were as worried as anyone. This was strange country to them. They did not know any of it. Secretly they feared their own partisans were waiting on the wrong mountain. They could only murmur "Murgash" and "Etropole" (names of Chavdar haunts) and shrug their shoulders.

Frank Thompson began to be anxious. He realised he was only a consultant to that closely-knit committee of Communists. As a foreigner, far from being its leader, the equal voice he was supposed to have had difficulty in making itself heard. The tight Communist organisation, with commissars and commanders who looked after politics and tactics, made his power and purposes very different from anything Lawrence had ever engineered. And though he might reflect on Wingate's 'penetration' methods of partisan warfare, he was fettered from any attempt at taking the lead. They were all leaders here—it was nobody's private army. So how could the dash and nerve that was behind Wingate's 'penetration' succeed in such a situation?

The young Englishman made speeches. He threw himself, to Kenneth Scott's great concern, into political identification with the Communist committee. His ideas were applauded by them, but, when each meeting was over, nothing was more than a pipe-dream, for the committee went their own way.

The brigade was now so tired that although it was the end of May, always it seemed to be growing dark when the order came to pick up rifles and march on. The days seemed to have disappeared, for after dawn the order would come to halt, and through the bright daylight the brigade would get a fitful sleep under rocks or brushwood. Quite suddenly during that last week of May, in the dead of night—and darker than night in that forest—the advance guard halted abruptly. The column looked to their rifles and listened. Someone on horseback was coming through the woods towards them. The heavy plunge of hoofs on the hillside seemed ominous. The rider was coming up so as to cut right across their path. So fatigued were they that, as soon as the men realised it was only one solitary rider, they sat down just where they were and fell fast asleep. Even when prodded forward again by their more alert comrades they were dozing on their feet, neither caring nor comprehending.

The peasant on horseback had deliberately sought them out and rode alongside as they trudged on. He declared himself a revolutionary from the days of the 1923 rebellion and an activist of the Chavdar partisans. A glad murmur of "Chavdar!" went through the ranks as those near the general staff caught up the word. But the news he had to tell was of despair rather than of hope, for he reported that the Chavdar partisans had been defeated a whole month ago when they were assembled at Eleshnishkia Monastery. A month ago! That was when the two brigades were massing to move away from Kalna! Apparently as soon as the police had news of the march of the Bulgarian resistance, instead of attacking the Second Sofia Brigade, they had set about conducting a campaign against the Chavdar all around Botevgrad, and even now they were being driven further east. Chavdar were all hunted, fighting for their lives, and could not break through the police and military cordon that bore down on them. That was why no partisans had been able to reach the brigade. In his own case, the horseman declared, he had risked everything to tell them—his wife and family, his homestead, all he had. If he stayed with them, he would risk being compromised still further and be no use to anybody. He galloped off, leaving behind him men so tired and reconciled to fatigue as to be impervious to the calamity of such news which, during the last two days, they had already come to anticipate.

That was one of the worst nights of the march and, dark as it was, the mist arising after midnight made it darker and heavier. When it was darkest, one of the horses on which Ilyo, commissar of the Botev battalion, was half asleep, suddenly slipped, throwing Ilyo into the mud and going at a plunge down that slope into the depths of the valley. The Botev battalion spent four hours searching for it, an accident which resulted in them being cut off from the Levski battalion. Only when it dawned did they find the horse, a mere hundred metres away from where it had slipped. Far from galloping away towards some village as they had feared, or even just straying, it had fallen fast asleep at the bottom of the slope, never making the least effort to get back on its feet.

The general staff began to get worried about their direction and bearings, wondering if they had come too far south, for sometimes through the night at the end of the Isker valley they caught a breathtaking glimpse of the bright electric lights of Sofia spreading and sparkling as the capital slept oblivious of war. Unknown to them, from his headquarters Nikola Geshev was receiving details of their movements, although his reports grossly exaggerated their numbers into thousands.

Tired as they were, however, the column was still ahead of the enemy, who never dreamed the partisans would venture so near to Sofia. No doubt this is how they crossed the Isker so easily and in broad daylight, once again traversing a railway. Down by the riverside there were labourers who were supposed to be guarding both ends of the cable bridge, but when the Levski battalion rushed forward towards them, they threw everything away and fled. Even without any enemy opposition it was no easy task to get the horses and mules across, but by surrounding each animal with strong helpers every one was pulled to the far bank. When they were all safely over, the partisans, breathless and tired, were too exhausted to give their usual cheer and they crept on uphill to the cover of the bushy ridges.

21: Ambush at Batulia

As they faced the bare hills opposite, the staff paused a moment to take stock of the situation. The police now pursuing had come from Vratsa, but in their avoiding efforts the brigade had come south and Sofia was now nearer than Vratsa. If the police came out after them from the Sofia barracks they would be trapped. They needed to hurry on to the Murgash Mountain, but without rest this was impossible. The urgency to unite with Chavdar had gone. A police cordon separated them from their allies. They had lost days and days wandering round the Kom and Koznitza mountains. The brigade general staff were mostly townsmen Communists: the sun, the stars and the mysteries of mountain weather were insoluble to them. They ruefully contemplated the zigzag course that after ten days of hardship had brought them to this climb within sight of Sofia itself. They had come much too far south!

Thompson and his sergeants showed on their maps with a compass exactly where they were, roughly equidistant from Sofia and the top of Murgash, whose summit 1,687 metres high, was due east. The general staff nodded their heads at the map and the compass in that very positive oriental negative so characteristic of Bulgarian determination.

"Distance on the mountains," asserted Vlado Tričkov, "is different from distance on paper. We have learned that. None of us know the villages on Murgash, nor indeed where the forests are. We must have local guides and take them with us; then we can be sure of finding the way east and round Batulia."

They set watch-posts and laid an ambush on the Sofia road while the brigade rested out of sight in a fold of the hills, but they had not long to wait before two men on ponies were brought up to the staff, loudly protesting that they were not police but civilians, travelling on the main road. They had nothing to do with the war, with partisans, or with Germans. They were traders, they affirmed, dealers in fuel —coal and charcoal. They had done nothing wrong and had no weapons and no food. Dencho Znepolski, Vlado Tričkov, and

Blagoi Ivanov lay on the grass and listened to their protestations of innocence. "You live in the district and you know the mountains," Vlado Tričkov decided in persuasive, mollifying tones. "You can come with us to act as guides. Be our friends and live the good life for a little. Just for a few days, helping to free the nation from the Fascists!"

Pleasant as was the invitation, its rejection was immediate and clamorous. They could not stay. They must be in Svoge, the village six kilometres along the road, on the 23rd without fail. They were brothers but not friends. They lived apart from each other. They were in dispute over a property, in a lawsuit, actually: one against the other. The whole matter was to be decided in Svoge. They must be on their way.

Armed partisans stood round them. The path back to the road was barred.

"You will come with us," said Dencho Znepolski.

"We need a place to lay up and rest out of sight. Somewhere secret that no one can find, where partisans can sleep safely," urged Vlado Tričkov. "You know the district. Show us, and we will be grateful. Refuse—and we know you prove yourself Fascists!"

Quelled by the tone in his voice, fear silenced the brothers, and cunning united them. "You must go to the long wood," advised the older of the two. "Follow the river towards Yablanitza, and you must find it after four or five kilometres."

"You shall take us," coaxed Tričkov, smiling, "and then we shall be able to thank you."

The brothers looked at each other and then, with an effort, spasmodically agreed. They led the way, chatting and joking with their captors, giving out random shreds of information about the air-raids on Sofia and enquiring about the battles in Yugoslavia, their energy and vivacity contrasting with their tired guards who listened with drooping shoulders replying in monosyllables. Those partisans who looked southward shivered as they saw through the early evening the lights of Sofia again spreading across the plain, no longer radiant, but cold, hostile and dangerous.

Frank Thompson lit his pipe as they moved on. He of them all realised the tragic contrast only too keenly. They had set out to raise the land, to call for recruits, to hold meetings in the style Tempo held them in Macedonia. They had the fine embroidered banner, the good hearts and the orators. The cold eyes of the crowd in Dolgi Del had been a significant warning, but who could have foreseen it would have come to this, to be compelled to make prisoners of any peasants or civilians they might meet and hold them as pledge against betrayal?

The march to the wood went uphill and away from any tracks. When they arrived, all agreed the site filled every requirement for a secret camp. Without the two brothers they would never have found so ideal a place. The location was covered with sparse hills and close-set scrub and taller bushes, along which, sweeping to the north beside precipitous cliffs, stretched a long dense wood, thick with new green leaves that shone against the rocky crags and red-brown earth of the hills. Facing the north it appeared denser still by the accumulation of deep shadows.

The two coal dealers looked at Dencho Znepolski and Vlado Tričkov expectantly.

"This is a good place," Tričkov summed up approvingly, as he realised there was not a sign anyone had been in the wood since the grass grew and the leaves came after the winter. "We shall spend the day here."

"What do you call this wood?" asked Znepolski.

"Marina Murtvina,"[1] came the reply. "And that great red rock over the cliff, they call that Kamen Kurvav.[2] No one comes here except the gipsies."

"It will suit us very well," said Vlado Tričkov. "And you shall stay until we leave."

Once again the two brothers began to protest. The lawsuit! The court at Svoge! They had lawyers to pay. The action took months, and had just come to be a hearing! Lament as they might, it was of no avail. The guards took them away, while the brigade filtered into the wood, beating out secure little nooks among the bushes.

'Claridges' also settled down, Sergeants Walker, Monroe and Scott with Major Thompson, all, tired as they were, lamenting the lack of food and concerned that in such an isolated place there would be no prospect of acquiring any victuals when they woke up.

Fatigue overcomes even hunger. Casualties of the whole brigade at least had been very light. From this secure refuge different operations could be planned next day. They watched their pony led away with the other horses. It was a comfort to know he would get some good grazing at last.

The command staff came along and settled down close by. The Levski and Botev battalions pressed further in, but the thicket was so dense that, beat the bushes down as much as they could, they all seemed to vanish as if the woodland swallowed them up. Vlado Tričkov and Dencho Znepolski gave orders for the posting of sentries, sentries who were as tired as the general staff, and who stood with their backs to the trees but slid down into the same slumber as the rest of the brigade. Silence returned to the long wood, a silence as

[1] Dead Sea.   [2] The Stone of Blood.

deep as that which overhung it when they arrived. The birds that had been frightened away seemed not to return.

Everyone was asleep except for the two least tired of all, those two brothers. They had not been tied up, perhaps out of gratitude because they had brought the brigade to such a good place. After a while, one of them slipped away, excusing himself from the guards by the natural excuse and saying he would be back in a short time. At least an hour went by when the other, realising how sound asleep were his guards, crept silently across the dark to rouse his brother. He was shocked to discover he had not returned, for his place was empty, though the men beside him still slept on. His first impulse was to rouse them, to shout alarm, to have his brother brought back and prevented from stealing such an advantage from him.

As he stood irresolute, he reckoned his brother might have been gone a couple of hours, might indeed be well on the way to Svoge by now. Quick as the thought, he made up his mind and crept stealthily out of the wood. His brother might get to Svoge and win or not win their lawsuit, but if he went in the other direction to the nearer police garrison at Bukovits, he could be sure of being well paid for his information. If he stayed the partisans might shoot him because his brother had gone.

So, while the birds sang next morning in the long wood and the loudest singer of them all could not wake one partisan, the first brother arrived at Svoge and declared that concentration of the Second Sofia Brigade to the police station; but the second brother had arrived first at the Bukovits garrison where he made his separate report. The telephone wires were at once ringing to summon armed police and military detachments from Vratsa, Mezdra and Sofia.

The tactics of the brigade in marching by long columns of single file had given rise to such exaggerated accounts of their numbers that the authorities were not inclined to believe their new informants estimate of only 200. Every available man was mustered and the wood quietly surrounded by machine guns and mortars. The inveterate enemy of partisans, Captain Gočo Stojanov, was summoned to take charge of the offensive.

Not till midday did a partisan sentry notice a figure in uniform on the slope very high up but in immediate proximity to the camp. Vlado Tričkov when called could see nothing and calculated that even if one or two policemen were there, they would never dare to attack in the light of day. That slope, however, with its red cliffs went right up and overhung the whole wood. Some time around five minutes to two, as it is remembered, the police began to hurl a shower of round pebbles from this ridge just above where the Hristo Botev battalion had established themselves. The one large pebble that struck the arm of a sleeping partisan—a veterinary surgeon's assistant—caused him to shout with surprise and alarm. He leapt raging to his feet and awakened the whole camp.

The immediate stir and bustle below indicated the success of this stratagem. Chaos broke out as the police opened fire. Their machine guns raked the trees and sent the young leaves flying. Until the partisans came to their senses, they began firing everywhere, answering the enemy at random. Some ran down the valley towards the ravine, which was the very worst direction as the enemy had foreseen this route. The Levski battalion kept in a compact formation and, moving under the brow of the slope, made straight for the road, fighting their way through. Preserving military ranks, they emerged almost without loss while the enemy fired into the leaves behind them.

Dicho Petrov, commander of the Botev battalion, was slain in that first fifteen minutes when the battalion came under the first onslaught. The general staff and the Botev battalion drew together as the enemy began to lose fire concentration and fire recklessly. Frank Thompson and his sergeants came in towards the general staff. During a pause in the firing, Vera Nacheva left them and ran towards her husband, who was lying full length by a bush.

"Are you alive?" she cried.

"Yes!" he replied. "But don't you come near me! That's an order!" He looked round and grinned, " Another order for you! Keep alive!"

"Why?" his wife asked, joking.

"I want to have someone to write the words on my tombstone," he said with a wry smile. "So you keep alive!"

She went back to the mission, where Frank Thompson was actually writing in one of his books.

"Whatever are you writing?" she asked, in Bulgarian. "There is no time for that!"

"There is plenty of time for what I write," he said. "All my life— a lifetime."

"But what are you writing?"

"I am writing my obituary," he declared sardonically.

The mortar shells began to come near at that moment. Seeing the futility of defending such a hollow, Tričkov gave the order to move. As he passed the word along, the partisans automatically came into their column formation. He lead them up the ravine along a woodland track, hoping to find a gully that led out beyond the thicket. But there was no way out. The track was blocked by the bare and dusty cliff under which tracks were diverted to right and left where cattle had once turned along the bushes.

A fusillade of shots from the ridge announced the enemy had once again located them. Frank Thompson felt a sudden thud in the back which sent him flying forward. He was surprised as he recovered to find himself unhurt. The bullet had actually lodged in a dictionary in his pack. Kenneth Scott felt a smart in his hand and saw it was bleeding. A bullet had passed directly between his fingers, doing no more harm than ripping the flesh.

The column scattered as hand grenades lobbed towards them. Sergeants Walker and Monroe sped down the ravine and found the stream. As they came into the open, a machine gun picket mowed them down. Vera Nacheva also ran down river, but before the edge of the wood she saw a dense blackberry tangle and crawled under the brambles upon a ledge and lay there. She saw the Fascist helmets passing below and heard the policemen cough and whisper as they paused to reload and fire. She found she had now one bullet only left in her revolver and treasured it, reflecting it was the one thing that could stop her being tortured before execution if she were discovered. She lay there until dusk when she crept out and went towards Murgash. By hiding all the time and watching, she linked up with Blagoi Ivanov, Delcho Simov and other fugitives, making a little group which eventually found the Chavdar partisans in the Sredna Gora near Plovdiv.

Vlado Tričkov had turned uphill. Jordanka called to everyone to follow and went back at grave personal risk to rally the brigade. Only a little group of that 200-strong expedition got the signal. The din of machine-gun and mortar fire, the yells and curses of the police, who from their safety on the heights constantly bellowed for the brigade to surrender, drowned her cries. She found that not more than a score were left together, including Major Thompson and Sergeant Scott.

"We must gain the heights!" shouted Tričkov. "Let us get beyond the ridge or we are lost!"

The three women had come together, for Nikolina and Mary had joined Jordanka. Nikolina had left her shoes behind in the scramble and going barefoot over those stones had to be supported by her friends. Suddenly they came to a cleft out of which water flowed. The track stopped here and the only way forward was to climb up the rough bed of the stream, a slow and dangerous task with risk of slipping any moment.

Vlado Tričkov, with easy-going bravado, stopped in this place to light a cigarette and reckon whether the enemy were following. As he debated this with his comrades, the track below suddenly filled with men wearing police helmets who opened fire, causing the partisans to rush for the bushes on the right, but not, however, before Vlado Tričkov had been shot in the leg. He lay there concealed a moment while other partisans hurried up—including Jordanka who raged at them for stopping. The machine gunner Valentin Andreyev also managed to climb up here despite his wounded arm. He seemed to represent their last world in ill fortune, for his machine gun, on which they had counted so much, had been put out of action by the first burst of fire when an enemy bullet had by chance directly jammed the barrel. Jordanka tore her dress and bandaged Vlado Tričkov's leg.

Aiming to extricate themselves without casualties, they continued to creep up the slope below the enemy who kept up a never-ending fire. At the same time the police pursuit party could be heard beating the woods. They kept crashing on, aimlessly throwing grenades and shouting, "Give yourselves up! You are the last survivors!"

With relief the partisans realised they were out of view and completely hidden. This was the critical test of a really cold-blooded partisan, for the woods were very thick and all that was needed was confidence in concealment. Though the police were still arriving and pouring into the wood from the side nearest the village, their very shouting and random firing proved they could not see the partisans. They had no dogs. They talked aloud and held open conversations as they came down the narrow paths, never breaking into the thorns and bramble thickets, making such a disturbance it was as if they determined to frighten the partisans away from themselves.

Those police above now began to leave the ridge and come down, firing as they descended. Seizing the opportunity, Vlado Tričkov's party jumped into the open by a now deserted ridge which ran along to the cliff-top above the river. Once up there, they lost no time in departing, creeping down any hollow or going up in the shelter of one of those dusty red ridges. There were no more than twelve of the general staff, Jordanka and her two women, Nikolina and Mary, with Thompson and Scott. The crackle of machine-gun fire, the bombs and the shouting seemed to be actually increasing in the long wood below them.

Suddenly a party of police appeared on the foot-path opposite on the far bend of the river. They were leading the mules loaded with supplies. To their dismay Thompson and Scott recognised their pony with the precious wireless set, the one link with S.O.E., being led away. There was no time to run for cover. The fugitives squatted on the loose gravel and stones, keeping their heads down and relying on the hollow to conceal them. One more partisan caused alarm by joining them as they lay there, although the noise of the firing had died down by then.

To Frank Thompson's anxious enquiries about Sergeants Walker and Monroe, this new arrival replied that he had last seen them crossing the river at the lower end, but there was savage fighting just there. The main party and the Levski battalion he thought had got away. (Actually one party with Dencho Znepolski had escaped and was campaigning towards Trunski to link up with the First Sofia. Another group with Trifon Balkanski and the one or two Chavdar emissaries was retreating to Yugoslavia.)

At about 1800 hours the little group lying in their hollow noticed a policeman who was coming up the path on the far side of the river. As he was staring across towards them, one of the partisans, in pressing closer out of sight, slipped and dislodged some pebbles, making a spurting avalanche of gravel. The policeman stopped and at once pointed his rifle. Immediately from unseen locations there was a crackle of machine-gun firing. Bullets began to ricochet about the rocks. The partisans with one accord made a dash to climb the hill. Ivan was shot in the ankle as he crossed that exposed country west of the river, but his wound was bound up and they all pressed on intending to go straight towards Murgash.

A party of police, however, was seen crossing this road so they moved towards Eleshina. The road from Ogoya was closed by an ambush and they had the impression they were being pursued. Their track had taken them between high cliffs in which they could well have been trapped, but first Gorazd and then two or three others climbed to the top. They turned again and bound their rifles together, making pulleys and slings to drag everyone up to the bushy summit of an impregnable hill where they lay in the thicket all night, not close together this time, but in little groups so that any disturbance of one would alert and bring assistance from the others.

22: The Trap

Next day they shared out weapons and towards night, realising it was no use making for Eleshnishkia Monastery, where the Chavdar disaster had occurred last month, they moved northwards towards a small village, hoping to scout for food there. Since both Tričkov and Ivanov were wounded, Slavcho Lazov was now chosen as commander, Gorazd commissar and Mladen deputy. Gočo Gopin stayed with the mission, still acting as interpreter to Frank Thompson. There began an argument whether to turn back to Kom. This would have meant again crossing the Isker River, the railway and also the open road from Sofia to Vratsa. Nobody viewed that lightly. Ivanov had a friend upon whom he was sure he could rely in the village of Arab Konashki, fifteen miles farther east in that high pass between the Murgash and Etropole mountains. Everyone knew of the forests, the precipitous cliffs and mountains there, and the Russian monument of 1878 at the top of the pass. It was the heart of Chavdar, they would be safe, they would live well there till the Soviet armies came. After the talking, towards which Jordanka contributed an exhortation not merely to live well but on their task as liberators of a new Bulgaria, their spirits plucked up and they moved away in the direction of Etropole.

Vlado Tričkov's wound was bad. Carrying him was difficult. After each kilometre they found it necessary to stop and rest. It was level country but bare of trees and without much cover. Slavcho Lazov and Mladen went out in the dusk to reconnoitre and found three lost partisans from the Botev battalion. This raised hopes of finding others, even of assembling the brigade. Thompson and Scott had no such illusions. It seemed to them the only way to penetrate to the Sredna Gora and reach the partisans at Plovdiv was to infiltrate across the mountains in very small groups. Some might be caught, but some would succeed. They rightly suspected that this was what was happening with the majority of the brigade in any case. The leadership was deteriorating; torrents of words were no substitute for military action. Without a radio set the British mission was useless to the partisans and in fact was an encumbrance. They resolved to disengage at the first opportunity. Thompson had a compass and map, but the partisans always seemed determined to rely on a hearsay knowledge of the lie of the land—from which, when deflected by some police action, they became lost.

That evening was spent in a winter sheepfold and then, moving on through the dark, the forlorn little band arrived at Bakovo, which it was said had a month previously supported seventeen partisans. They reached the highway here and rushed into a very poor cottage to seek a guide. They now fully comprehended how vital was time and this chancy wandering towards the east through unknown places had been the cause of all their misfortunes.

Their sudden appearance threw the family in that ramshackle dwelling into a state of terror. The eight children cowered on the bed-shelves and the woman shrank back behind her husband. When she understood the partisans intended to take away her man to guide them, she came forward like a tigress. She begged and she wept. Her voice cut the air with declamation and hysteria. The police would kill him: they would burn their cottage: the children would starve. The terrified youngsters began to wail, but the partisans seized her husband and dragged him away. She became demented and began hysterically fighting like a wild cat. Scott and Thompson stood by outside, appalled at the shrieks and commotion. The door was roughly shut upon her as her husband struggled with his cap and coat.

"There is no other way," grumbled the two partisans who prodded their unwilling ally on either side. "When the glorious Soviet Red Armies arrive, you will be rewarded."

The pressed recruit led them across to the sheep-walks of the Mremikovski Monastery. He crept through by the sheepfold and passed within the walls. But it was empty. There was no one there and nothing to eat! The survivors of the Botev battalion had already been through it and cleaned out every scrap of food. There was only a bin of old chaff from last year's harvest. Full of rat droppings as it was, it contained grains of real wheat and so was shared out. Thompson and Scott actually filled match boxes with reserve supplies.

Whilst the younger and more active were searching in lofts and attics, four more survivors of the Botev Battalion appeared. Glad as the company was to see them, there was also the bitter reality that they represented four more mouths to feed.

The company—they can hardly now be referred to as the Second Sofia Brigade—began to move off at ten o'clock when they were accosted by the macabre apparition of a tattered and dishevelled partisan who gibbered and gesticulated. He was one of the Botev survivors whose mind had become unhinged. He did not associate with them but ran wildly round like a demon and climbed upon the monastery walls.

There was no doubt he had attracted attention, for the partisan on sentry watch outside reported soldiers were moving along the ridge. Once again the company had to abandon their chosen route and go down by the river. So the days passed and the nights went by, seven of them; time enough they had spent for a healthy man to walk easily across Bulgaria.

Sometimes they could buy bread, sometimes it was given them, but for long periods they starved. Walls and stones were searched for snails. Thompson and Scott looked for the larger garden variety, which they shared when they found a cluster; filthy and sticky, raw as they were, they kept stomachs moving but left a gluey, thick flavour in the mouth. Frank Thompson lamented he had not paid more attention to the culinary aspects of botany, for such grasses and herbs as they found hardly took away this devastating taste which remained in the head long after it left the mouth.

In one village near Litakovo a brother and sister provided what bread they could. A wicker basket as if for waste was hung outside the bakehouse in the night and as much bread as could be baked concealed within it. This was one of the few occasions in the whole fortnight when the partisans found real support. Otherwise it was threats or gold that induced assistance. Once a 100 leva note of Kenneth Scott was refused because it had a torn corner and only its replacement by a golden British sovereign mollified the shop-keeper. The bread from near Litakovo carried them on for a time, but only into another barren land where other survivors seemed to have been before them.

As it does towards the end of May the summer rain began to set in, lasting unceasing for days. Without the help of the sun, the general staff once again lost their way. They were always either pur-sued or facing ambushes which deflected them from their course. They were Bulgarians in their own country and insisted on their leadership. Thompson with his map and compass was not entitled or allowed to assume command of their route, though his own mis-givings increased daily. The dangers seemed to magnify in imagina-tion as well as in reality.

Mladen and Lazov, out at dusk on one of their reconnoitring ex-peditions, found an abandoned hut with a store of old withered potatoes and dry beans. As it was night no fires could be lit for cooking, but it was essential to share them out. The men devoured them in the raw. They were now in a state of starvation and stomachs were empty. Only a few hours passed before the whole company was doubled up with excruciating agony. Their digestive pains lasted for days and made the general gloom unbearable.

Seven partisans had been killed in a sequence of petty ambushes as the partisans wandered to get east of Murgash Mountain, and now even Jordanka's propaganda and excited exhortations about the endurance of the Soviet peoples could hardly prevent many from wishing themselves dead, so extreme was the effect of that old and mouldy rubbish they had eaten. There were three avowed an-archists among their number who had been the first to grumble and curse about the shortage of food. They also had gone for the beans and potatoes more voraciously than any, and now at the first twinges of indigestion they burst out into flagrant revolt, cursing the expedition and everything connected with it. Vlado Tričkov, whose wound was festering, quelled their demonstration with harsh words and harsher threats, which had immediate effect. His authority,

however, was resented by Jordanka as inappropriate to the principles of true equality and Communism. She challenged him before
them all.

"Why do you act so?" she reproached him. "Don't you understand that in our present position we must show tolerance and have
nothing to do with severity. All we need to do is to explain that
tomorrow things will change and may not be so bad!"

She took the three on one side and chatted and sympathised with
them for a long time. Whatever she said was effective, for the three
grumbling anarchists ceased their outrageous complainings whenever she was about and, in the words of Slavcho Lazov, 'endured'.

There were now two men besides Vlado Tričkov whose wounds
were becoming so serious as to incapacitate them entirely. They
knew they were a burden and a hindrance to any progress. At last,
partly on their own volunteering, partly by suggestion, it was agreed
that these two, Valentin Andreyev and Bonka, should separate from
the compatriots and try to reach the village of Željava, where they
might lie up and get well. Valentin had faithfully served the whole
time without having a rifle, so Jordanka made him a present of her
own. The general staff let them go sadly, for no one knew what the
two wounded men could expect in these police-ridden villages.

The culmination of privations and crises came on 29th May
when three partisans attempted to leave. The sentry saw them silhouetted on the skyline against the moon and gave the alarm. The
pursuers dared not fire to bring them down, so that only one was
headed off and captured. The other two made the most of their
lead and ran on down to the village.

The effect of this desertion was electric and sent a shudder
through the camp. A meeting of the little company was held.
Really it could have been termed merely a gathering, but the general
staff rigorously formalised it into a routine Communist Party meeting. The commander took charge under his party name, 'Thomas',
and issued orders for future procedure. He lectured on the code of
Communist Party conduct and discipline on lines drawn up by Vlado
Tričkov and Nacho Ivanov. Jordanka's tolerance was over-ridden
entirely. Deserters and recalcitrants were to be shot. Anyone who
stole food from his comrades or who plundered the communal store
would be tried and executed. All expressed agreement and concern,
especially the captured deserter who stood by in a state of terror,
desperately anxious to retrieve his status and save his life.

Scott and Thompson stood by silently. The meeting seemed to
seal the blundering desperation of a Communist committee hide-
bound by Communist rules on which the partisan leadership relied,
and as they listened they comprehended the dilemma facing them.

It was clear the only hope for that venture was its free dispersal into units of twos and threes, yet the whole company now relied on the British sovereigns the mission held which were all that would buy them bread. How could they now honourably detach themselves? And Thompson's own stance as a comrade precluded him from taking command.

The company moved on through the night and came to that great slope below which, in the valley beside road and railway, lay Eleshina village. They stopped by the stream to wait before taking action. As the point duty for the watch was changed, it was noticed that one of the two sentries posted along the approaches had disappeared. Whether he had deserted to the village or been captured was never known, but most thought he had surrendered.

After all this suffering, all these days of wandering, they were back almost to where they had fled after the battle, yet no one gave that point any reflection. The villagers of Eleshina were alive. They lived on bread! There would be bread in Eleshina. In the dark the partisans all moved downhill. They dragged themselves on to the highroad where they straggled boldly along without hindrance till they came to an orchard at about 2300 hours.

Seven partisans, led by Slavcho Lazov and Gorazd, were chosen from volunteers to steal into Eleshina and obtain bread, provisions, food of any kind. Thompson once again supplied them with gold. The rest of the company climbed into the orchard and began picking the green plums and cherries, cherries which were so unripe they had no stones. Warnings about empty stomachs went unheeded. Whatever could be reached in that eerie moonlight was devoured. All taste had departed from those hungry mouths that had sometimes been thirty-six hours without drinking water; ripe or unripe, sweet or sour, had no significance. Day after day Thompson and Scott had whiled away hours going through the inside linings of their pockets, clothes and kit, hoping to chance on crumbs left over from better times.

The foragers returned much more quickly than expected, and empty-handed. The first tavern at the roadside was lit at every window. Watching from the shadows they had seen an armed sentry on guard outside. As they caught glimpses through the open door, they realised it was full of police and also contained an army unit. Something was expected. Sentries were going down to Eleshina. The village was invested.

"It is no matter," said Vlado Tričkov. "We shall proceed through the night and find food in another village."

There were murmurs of horror at the thought. The partisans resolved themselves into another formal meeting. Everyone had his say in turn. Vlado Tričkov's untreated wound was angry. He was weakened by the pain and exhausted. The stamina of every person there was failing. Each was growing deaf and losing reason from sheer starvation. Only Jordanka's eyes shone more feverishly than ever, but she could not bring herself to urge those pitiable survivors back over that mountain.

It was decided to send the five strongest men over the pass towards Rashkovo. They could get bread from the friends in the Litakovo village, ten kilometres away at most, taking the abandoned cart-road all the way. They could do it, and be sure. The five stalwarts took their bags and trudged away along the cart track beside the stream. The partisans went back to picking cherries and then, leaving a sentry to watch the road, went up into the wooded slope north of the orchard.

Next morning dawned. The partisans were in the same place. A night's march had been lost, but through the early summer mist the five volunteers returned and they brought bread, a share for everybody—yet it was bread which was to cost the lives of the young woman and her brother who supplied it. The five partisans had entered three houses and found everyone friendly. As she ate, Jordanka began to make a speech. Nikolina applauded her as she told of the love of the Soviet people for the partisans, but the others were silent. Every scrap of bread was eaten. Thompson and Scott held their hats under their slices so as to catch any crumbs, and they went to sleep and slept through that morning of 31st May.

As the sun shone and the Balkan warmth of summer increased up the valley towards noon, the partisans awoke to remember with misgiving the sentry who had disappeared. Throughout the villages there had been proclamations and announcements making much play, not just of rewards for betraying partisans, but a free amnesty. Even supposing that sentry had been captured, would he not break under torture?

Suddenly, upon a hill only three hundred yards away from their camp, a police post was discerned. Orders were given for no-one to leave the shelter or stir from those leafy bushes. At 1400 hours a police squad of twenty men marched out from Eleshina. For a moment it looked as if they were advancing towards the hidden camp, but they continued marching north and did not approach the fugitives nor even cross the river. Slavcho Lazov and one comrade were deputed to track this column and report whether it intended action against the camp.

At 1600 hours shots were fired into the wood. The enemy began machine-gun and mortar fire from the ridge above and the road below. Slavcho Lazov and his comrade hurried back from observing the northward column and found the wood impenetrable and encircled by Facist police and military. They could only conceal themselves and wait.

Within the wood the partisans, already in their customary column formation, moved quickly downhill, rifles at the ready and on the watch for targets at which to fire. Frank Thompson decided this was the moment to separate. He and Scott climbed higher towards the ridge and when halfway up the face of the hill moved round the eastern slope. The trees clustered more thickly here. They chose a spot where, between four trees growing close together, the old leaves had piled against the thicket of saplings and derelict branches. Their overcoats and capes were camouflaged and as they crept within to hide it seemed a perfect sanctuary.

Down below the partisans came into action. A devastating uproar of small-arm and rifle fire broke out, answered by mortars and machine guns. Over it all rose the wild cries of Jordanka as she screamed defiance and ran openly to throw grenades against the enemy. As they lay there, a crashing above them told that the column that had been seen marching north had turned back and, reinforcing the encirclement, were making a sweep through the wood. As the battle began to sway back uphill, another squad suddenly entered their copse from the east to take up position close beside them, some of these Bulgarian troops being only ten feet away.

Suddenly one soldier saw the two Englishmen and jumped to his feet, firing as he did so directly at Scott and taking such a point blank aim that Scott saw the flash from the very muzzle and sensed the puff of explosive gases from the barrel. Yet, wounded as he thought he was, he felt nothing. He had not been hit. As he and his companion were dragged out, he realised his adversary was cross-eyed! Four soldiers had hurled themselves upon each man. As they were being kicked and struck in a panic of fists, revolvers and rifle butts, a senior N.C.O. arrived and barked out orders. The struggle ceased and they were taken to the military post on the hilltop.

There one partisan had already been tied up. Thompson's hands were secured with a belt and Scott's with ropes that went tight to the bones and cut off all circulation at the wrists. This inflicted severest torture upon his wounded hand. The earlier injury from the bullet wound in the first ambush had become poisoned and discoloured, causing the whole arm to swell and inflame.

Other captives were brought up and secured. Jordanka and her friend, when their grenades had been used up, had crept into an elderberry thicket and hidden, but the horde of troops had flushed the woods like hounds after a fox, and they too were dragged out and taken alive to the same place as the British. Lazov and his comrade lay above the wood long after the operation had finished and everywhere become still. Then in the dark, realising they were the only survivors, they climbed up to the ridge and marched east through the night.

23: 'Prisoners of War'

Meanwhile the prisoners had been taken down to Eleshina, where they were stood up in the courtyard of the town hall and exposed to the whole village. The houses emptied and everyone came out to mock them, singling out the British prisoners from the others, gradually, as they understood the guards approved, growing bolder, swearing and spitting and endeavouring to get near enough to punch them with their fists or strike them with anything that came to hand.

Frank Thompson was terribly shaken by this. Catching some of the meaning of the Bulgarian phrases used to revile them, he whispered to Kenneth Scott they were being blamed for the loss of life in the Allied bombing of Sofia. Starvation and the privations of that long march had taken heavy toll on his constitution. The green *planinas* that stretched away above the houses began to sway before his eyes, and then grow dim. He lost balance, collapsed and fell in the courtyard.

There was a momentary hush upon the crowd. Someone brought water and the two Englishmen were taken into a small building. A resident of Sofia who knew a few words of English and French but who pretended to know a great deal more was brought in to help with the questioning. They were not searched, but asked to place all their possessions on the table. Scott and Thompson declared themselves as 'prisoners of war according to the Geneva Convention'. They laid down the golden sovereigns that had survived from Scott's original ten and Thompson's fifty. A stream of questions came at them about the British mission, of its purpose, the Second Front.

Scott and Thompson replied to the orthodox questions, giving name, number, nationality and rank, but refused to answer more, calling attention to the necessity for them to be treated as prisoners of war. The questions were rough and ready. The interrogators supplied the answers when Scott and Thompson did not reply. They seemed to have no prior knowledge of the British mission.

Scott and Thompson were not soldiers, it was asserted. They were partisans, rebels and bandits, plundering villages, murdering peasants, the uniformed officer declared with an emphatic gusto more impressive to his audience than to the captives.

Frank Thompson and Kenneth Scott were now taken through the crowd to the cellar below this square, two-storeyed building that was the town hall. Horizontal barred windows only two feet above ground level allowed some light to enter the dismal room where a large bench was the only furniture.

Suddenly the door was thrust open and a clean-shaven civilian, smartly dressed in city-style suit, entered, followed by policemen, soldiers, and as many villagers as could crush themselves inside and around the doorway. He carried a truncheon some thirty inches long of the type used in Bulgaria for official beatings, rubber-covered with a hard core. Not a word was said. He ran forward and began to strike the two Englishmen where they sat on the bench, moving up and down to get harder blows in the confined space. All the soldiers and police stared in idle curiosity. Suddenly, as abruptly as he had begun, he ceased and went outside. The spectators left. door was shut, leaving Scott and Thompson nursing their bruises and their bewilderment.

Actually, as the captives learned later, this civilian was an evacuee from Sofia whose wife and family had been killed in the city by the Allied bombings the month before.

After some time a guard entered to take the prisoners for interrogation. Major Thompson was brought out first. Outside the cellar were steps and on that side the path ran between the buildings to the road with the bright evening green of the *planinas* extending above. There were two guards upon the steps. Thompson bent down. He ran his hand along the woollen sock where it was folded against his military breeches. At once the soldier behind shouted alarm and with the muzzle of his rifle forced him against the stairs. The others held him down and began a search. The neat little hand-grenade contraption of S.O.E. was wrenched out of his sock and brought upstairs to be placed with the other exhibits which were displayed upon the table. Here all articles taken from both Scott and Thompson had been arranged. As Frank Thompson came drearily up the steps, the door banged a destruction on that forlorn hope of desperate escape. All Scott's signals, plans and ciphers were there, together with the crystals which he had retained in order to make contact with Trunski's column, the First Sofia Brigade that had marched southward and was also in possession of an S.O.E. set.

This building beside the town hall of Eleshina was apparently the headquarters of the military unit located for that district north of

Sofia. The officer in command conducted the interrogation by means of a lance-corporal who had once been a pupil of the American School in Sofia. Frank Thompson's knowledge of Bulgarian blended with Russian also helped to communicate. The interrogation proceeded on much the same lines as the previous hasty questioning, though conducted in more military fashion and, as could be expected from the higher ranks in charge, in a more intelligent manner. Major Thompson repeated his assertion that they were both soldiers in military uniform taken as prisoners of war and therefore must be treated as such according to the Geneva Convention and that neither must be compelled to reveal anything except name, rank and number.

The military commander gave his assurance that this would be the case. He showed himself as interested as his subordinates in the venture of these Englishmen and exerted himself to convince them he knew everything about the British mission. He knew all the facts in detail about the engagement at Batulia on 18th May, his information obviously having been extracted from captured partisans. He showed some exasperation when he found that neither Scott nor Thompson would add anything to his stock of military intelligence, shrugging his shoulders and indicating how useless reticence was as he already knew everything. He ordered both to be taken back to the cellar, where they stayed for two hours.

All the time sightseers came and went, crowding into the room as thick as they could stand, coming from all the villages around. Most of them had never seen any live partisans, whom the Czarist propaganda machine had represented as bandits and murderers of the worst type history has known, reviling their activities as those of "sub-human criminals and bestial butchers".

Among those coming to that courtyard was Nada Bojilova. She and her school friend were evacuees from Sofia. The drum had been beaten and all the village people commanded to march past the bodies of the slain partisans where they lay exposed in the open courtyard. Newspapers covered the necks of each corpse because the heads had been severed and taken for separate display, but all their waists had been bared so that the peasants could see the sunken stomachs resulting from starvation, a warning to those who might feel tempted to go on the mountains, as the policeman on duty said, to show how they feasted up there!

Nada had a brother in prison and another had been a partisan from 1942 since when she had had no news of him. She felt sick with horror, but as she turned to slip away unobtrusively with her friend, two women were dragged from the cellar under the town hall where a crowd was loitering. She was shocked to recognise Jordanka as one of these prisoners—Jordanka, whom she had known in Sofia and with whom she had been in the concentration camp of Sveti Nikola. All the vivacious lustre had gone from her features. A wound gaped open across her face and a stream of blood flowed down her left leg. She had scarcely strength to walk. She turned to the policeman and asked for water to wash.

"So you tidy yourself up for this world?" sneered the policeman.

Even then she had not lost her innate spirit of defiance, and retaliated, "It is not in this world your own worries will begin!"

A soldier brought a basinful of water from the stream so that the two women could wash the blood from their faces before being brought upstairs for questioning.

Eventually at evening time a lorry drove into the courtyard. Heavily escorted, the partisans with the two Englishmen were driven away from that valley to the village of Gorni Bogrov only ten miles east of Sofia. Here Captain Stojanov had commandeered the school as his headquarters in that spring campaign, a two-storeyed building where the sentry's watch-tower overlooked the playground. (Today that tower still remains but holds only a bell to call children to lessons.)

A stream of clear water ran between the school and the road. On the playground boundary, a low wall fronting the clear roadside stream, had been stuck the severed heads of the partisans, a ghastly sight in that peaceful location. Yet neither Scott nor Thompson noticed as, exhausted with fatigue, they were pushed along the path to the high entrance steps and shut in the cellar room below the assembly hall.

Light could only filter through the small windows at ground level. Rough and clumsy masonry supported the joists holding the thick floorboards overhead. Rubbish and old barrels were the only furnishings below. In handcuffs and chains, miserable and squatting disconsolate on the floor, were the two partisans who had deserted on 29th May, together with the partisan sentry who had disappeared. The latter had been so savagely tortured and beaten that his face showed a mass of cuts and bruises. So severe was the damage inflicted upon him and in such contrast to the other two that both Scott and Thompson were sure he had never been a willing traitor but had been captured by force.

Other prisoners in that cellar were unfettered but dejected, keeping silence in a gloom of resignation. They were the peasants from the Litakovo district village who had supplied the bread which gave the company its last meal, a meal which served to doom the bakers.

As the two Englishmen became used to that cellar gloom, they perceived there were still one or two more partisan prisoners in the further shadows about the floor. Vanusha the Russian was there, even now wearing his mournful deprecating smile.

After a while the door opened abruptly and the new arrivals were pointed out to a German officer whose boots, uniform, decorations and arrogance denoted his high rank. He ran at Frank Thompson and Kenneth Scott and began spitting, kicking and beating them. Then he dragged out Vanusha, who seemed as frail and helpless as a bird anxious to escape. "There you see!" he shouted, in a raucous, polyglot mixture of words. "You see them, the British! What do you think of your ridiculous, stupid allies now?"

Some time before dusk a drum began to beat in Gorni Bogrov, summoning the people to pass by the schoolyard. The partisans were paraded for everyone to see before an assembly of all ranks of military and police as well as the motley crowd of local peasants and children. They came up into the playground behind those severed heads on the wall. Jeering remarks were made by the police on guard, who had been primed to instigate a tumult of insults against the prisoners. The woman in the corner house opposite the school raised her voice. Tall and lean, wearing golden coin earrings, she had those keen intelligent eyes which in some Bulgarian women are so remarkable.

"What do you want, my son?" she shouted to Frank Thompson, as if sneering.

He heard, and called back in Bulgarian, "Bread and onions!"

"Do you hear?" she sneered. "He asks for bread and onions!" And then again, "Bread and onions!"

The crowd looked confused, but in the anonymity of numbers began to understand and murmur, "Bread and onions!"

"Prisoners are guests. We do not starve guests! If we kill prisoners we do not starve them, under a roof or under the sky!" she raved, and then "Shall we give him bread and onions?"

The peasants began to mutter in a growling response, "Give him bread and onions?"

She spoke to her daughter who ran indoors and came out with loaves of bread. The police, still thinking it was all a mockery, looked on at first. Before they could comprehend, it was a reality. The bread was passed over, the onions arrived. The crowd must needs be humoured and the sentries could only look on and get the partisans back. The incident was effective, for by someone's orders food arrived, quite apart from the dishes of bread and onions which the woman with the golden earrings had sent over. Even into the cellar and till long after dark, the crowds of sightseers were encouraged to come and see the captured partisans. As if on some holiday excursion, they pushed and crowded to look past the guards.

There were two partisans who had never been brought out. Frank Thompson told Kenneth Scott he had learned that the two women, Jordanka and her friend Nikolina, had been lodged in the room along the corridor. Throughout the night they could be heard moaning and crying. When the last sightseers had gone, towards midnight there were piercing cries from that room accompanied by terrible crashing and thudding sounds, noises as if heavy furniture were being moved and flung from wall to wall. There were sharp, bitter screams, sometimes at first long drawn out, and then as the hours went by, deeper and unnatural, and they ceased just after the dawn broke. Those two women were never seen again.

In the depth of the night, about two hours past midnight, Major Frank Thompson was taken out of that cellar. Precisely what went on is not known, but he was brought back some three hours later. After the long interrogation, he was haggard and hardly able to keep on his feet. Sergeant Kenneth Scott was next marched out, and taken upstairs into a well-lit room in which beside the guards there were three civilians and the dominating figure in German uniform, the Gestapo representative.

The interrogation was precise and deliberate, not bullying nor ruffianly as he had expected, but clear cut and, for all the civilian clothes of his interrogators, conducted on military lines. The questioning, though persistent, had a pleasant and persuasive air about it which was obvious, even through the mechanical translations of the interpreter. On the tables beside the wireless telegraph set which he immediately recognised as his own was another set he had certainly never seen before. They asserted that this other set was captured at Batulia from the partisans on 18th May. They took up Scott's surprise at seeing the set and refused to accept his denials. They declared the apparatus was packed on the mules and captured just the same as the one Scott acknowledged. Again and again they insisted on this, returning to the subject with eventual exasperation. There was the second radio set, they argued. What was the point of denying it? It was there in front of them. Despite several whispered consultations, they could get no further than Scott's dogged refusal to admit any knowledge of this second set which he did not recognise. But the matter puzzled them, as it also puzzled Scott. Even during subsequent matters they would revert to some chance question involving the operation of the second apparatus.

They used scrappy bits of knowledge to try and convince their prisoner they knew everything there was to know about the S.O.E. signal school in the Middle East. They asserted that transmission must go to a nearer base than Cairo and demanded the whereabouts of this station. The whole energy of the interrogation suddenly concentrated upon this. Was the centre in Italy, or in Turkey? They knew it was outside Bulgaria, they persevered, resorting to devious assertions and cross-assertions, hoping to find its exact location.

It was when they came to their inquisition about other missions that Kenneth Scott was able to be more loquacious, explaining the absolute secrecy of the work and the steps taken to hedge that secrecy by making certain that each mission was self-contained, independent and isolated, in fact insulated, so that it was in complete ignorance of any other mission. The details of this lack of knowledge were so obviously true and in accord with standard intelligence routine that they were accepted. The matter which bewildered and discontented them, especially the Gestapo representative, was not so much the existence of the other set as the fact that Scott disowned it. As it was there, and so denied, they had two alternatives—to accept either that Scott really did not know of it, or that it was destined for some other mission, about which if he knew nothing, then Major Thompson might.

Kenneth Scott was able to disclaim any political association. No, he was not a Communist, nor anything else either. He was just a soldier. He evidenced his uniform and his paybook and demanded medical treatment as being a prisoner of war, calling attention to his swollen and discoloured arm, the inflammation of which was running up to his shoulder. He complained that he needed immediate attention for this. The Gestapo officer intervened here and expressed great concern and sympathy completely out of character with Kenneth Scott's expectations. It was agreed he should have treatment as soon as a doctor could be found.

It was almost morning when he was brought down to the cellar. He found Major Thompson had been asked questions very similar to his own, but had had a much more hostile interview. He had boldly declared himself a Communist, and had grimly delighted in the exasperation of the efforts by his interrogators to find out how he had come to learn Bulgarian and the many ways in which they altered their questions to get some explanation of how and why, whether he had been to Russia, what Russians or Bulgarians he knew and so on.

In the morning, to Scott's surprise, a military escort came for him. He was brought out of the cellar and marched to the doctor. The latter was a military practitioner and had obviously been primed, for he spoke English, and chatted in a friendly, affable manner in the course of which he asked quite casually how Major Thompson had learned Bulgarian and continued in an indirect way to pursue the subject—not unobtrusively enough, however, for Scott had been alerted by Major Thompson's account of how the interrogation committee had tried to probe for this, though why they should attach so much importance to it he could not understand.

The doctor's treatment was effective enough and his arm improved throughout the day, until he was actually able to sleep during some of the night. The number of partisans in that cellar dwindled. From time to time, singly, they were taken out and did not come back.

Next morning, 2nd June, the escort came, ostensibly to conduct him once again to the doctor. As he was being marched down the road, a large automobile arrived and drew alongside. An officer in German uniform curtly ordered the escort to put Kenneth Scott in the back seat of this car.

24: The Faked Trial:
Agent Murders Agent

All that 2nd June when Scott did not return, Frank Thompson waited, expecting to be sent for. At an appointed hour he was once again marched out with the remaining partisans as a public show. From the open curiosity and comments he knew he was that phenomenon, 'the Englishman partisan'. The peasant woman from the house on the corner came over with her bread and onions, together with a slice of *kačamak* or corn-cake, like the hominy he long ago had eaten in the United States. He saw her golden earrings and would have given her one of his British sovereigns if he had one left. That was something he resented the Fascists having. He wondered what had happened to Scott, and as the day passed forebodings about his comrade's fate intensified . . .

It was after Batulia that Geshev, the Bulgarian police chief, realised the full implications of that march of the Second Sofia Brigade. For at the very moment when he had locked up in his prisons enough infiltrators to give him control of post-war Bulgarian Communism, this Frank Thompson, a young English officer, an avowed Communist Party member—Russian, indeed, Bulgarian-speaking—with two radio stations giving contact with both the British and the Soviets, was about to join with the as yet uncorrupted Bulgarian Communists, Tsola Dragoicheva and Dobri Terpeshev, in the Sredna Gora. This was not in the plan that the Sultana Petrova

and the royal court had so carefully sponsored and nothing like it
had ever come from the British agents in Istanbul. To him the conception of a British officer being a genuine Communist was sympto-
matic either of double dealing or folly.

The reports Nikola Geshev now received on the interrogation of
Frank Thompson proved his existence both as a British Liaison
Officer to the partisans and as a sincere Communist with open and
orthodox Party connections, a most dangerous man who could
wreck everything the royal court had built up over so many years.

Manyo Nachev was a chief of section under Geshev at the time,
and was in his confidence and knew his anxiety that valuable
collaboration by his 'recruits' should not be destroyed. A plan was
now formed for Frank Thompson's removal, and Manyo Nachev,
it is alleged, was the official entrusted with the task of exciting the
townsmen of Litakovo against the Englishman so that he could be
killed in the provocation of a riot. He could thus be eliminated without complications; neither the Istanbul British connection nor the
Gestapo need be concerned . . .

Next day the peasants from Litakovo were taken out—the peasant
who had provided the flour and Maria and Haiden Haidenov who
had baked the bread. They were a sad pair, pale, with large eyes
and dark hair, and they seemed to accept the inevitability of their
fate with a smile and that affirmative Bulgarian shake of the head
without speaking.

The large cellar under the school began to seem empty, and the
tramp of police boots overhead more ominous. Frank Thompson
still had his pipe. One or two of the soldiers, as he got to know
them, were free of tobacco, and the food had begun to restore his
vitality. The parades around the playground seemed irksome now
and every morning the public washing beside the road more humili-
ating. Yet as the days passed Frank Thompson began to feel the
change upon the crowd coming to watch: curiosity was giving way
to a more open, if silent and unexpressed, sympathy.

To be walked across a school playground seemed strange, so far
from Winchester alleys and cloisters, the public washing here so
bizarre against memories of the College porter's washing tales. His
eye would catch sight of those ghastly heads drying on the wall
above where the women came to do their laundry in the stream. It
seemed he knew them, his friends from the Kalna days, and he kept
resolving never to look that way again. Daily, and sometimes in the
night, the remaining partisans were removed. One or two returned,
but most did not, and there was still no sign of his vanished sergeant.

On the third day he was taken out under armed escort to a
village square, where, thrown down on the flag-stones, was the

ragged emaciated body of a partisan, his face so battered and smashed as to be completely unrecognisable. Frank Thompson, though hardened by active service in many fields was shocked. He was halted beside the body. The villagers were on the far side of the square. Sentries played with their rifles in a suggestive and ominous manner until a military car arrived out of which stepped a Bulgarian officer in uniform who strode towards where Frank Thompson was guarded. He kicked the lifeless corpse and, turning the head with his stick, demanded of Thompson whether it was 'Bai Ivan' (Vlado Tričkov).

Thompson hesitated. No one could identify those ruined features.

"Yes," he replied, "Bai Ivan." He knew that, should it not indeed be 'Bai Ivan', by such identification the enemy might be led to discontinue their search for the chief of staff, Vlado Tričkov, if he were still at large.

"Good!" grunted the lieutenant. "Now you have helped us at last."

As Frank Thompson returned he perceived the attitude of the crowd, silent, almost reverent, so different from that evening at Eleshina, and, when he reflected in his prison cellar, he began to understand a deeper, classical significance in these Fascist presentation of the slain partisans, by which the enemy were weaving the self-destructive myth as dynamic as in the ancient days.

Every night there was the 'police hour' when at the signal all the blinds in Gorni Bogrov were drawn and no one was allowed to look out on penalty of death.

On the evening of 4th June there was more activity than usual around the school and it was whispered that Captain Stojanov had arrived. The woman in the house on the corner had arranged her blinds so that she could see through them. When her lamp was out, she had an open view of everything that went on around the school. That night, besides police and military vehicles, she saw the ominous lorry set out full of men and some guarded partisans carrying shovels.

The lights were burning in the school all night and next morning Frank Thompson and the remaining partisans were brought out very early and commanded to wash, after which their hands were tied. They were then brusquely loaded into military transport and driven away, accompanied by a heavily armed escort.

"Where are you taking us?" demanded Frank Thompson.

"Sofia," came the reply.

The convoy, however, was driving north and went up through the pass and through Botevgrad to Litakovo, where it stopped in the village square. As Frank Thompson and the partisans struggled out of their vehicles a grim sight met their eyes. The bodies of about a dozen partisans were stretched out in the square, their clothes still wet with the dews which had soaked on them through the night. Some had lain there three days. They had been brought down in the primitive manner on the two-wheeled ox timber frames whose runners trailed behind, constructed to drag their loads over the *planinas* like sledges. One corpse bound to the shafts by the wrists was just then being unfastened, the oxen standing by.

Thompson turned to the officer in charge of the party and said, slowly and sternly in Bulgarian, "You are not taking us to Sofia. You are taking us to be shot. I am a British officer in uniform and a prisoner of war. You will have to answer to my government if anything happens to me."

Before the entrance to Litakovo town hall he was held back while a uniformed officer of high rank, a general, it is said, from Sofia began to make a speech to the crowd belittling the partisan movement, denouncing Communism and ridiculing its leaders, indicating the corpses in the square as a fearful example of peasants playing at being soldiers. Captain Stojanov stepped forward to emphasise his superior's words. He caught hold of Frank Thompson and dragged him forward before the townsfolk, shouting, "Now see! This is the Englishman who has come to destroy our state. Death to all these bandits!"

Major Frank Thompson turned to the general and once again, in Bulgarian, so that all could hear, claimed protection under the Geneva Convention as a prisoner of war. This was something that beribboned general did not want to hear, for he strolled away as if deaf. The ruse to have Major Thompson killed in a public brawl while police were defending him from the crowd had hopelessly failed.

Thompson was hurried from the crowd and shut under guard in a side room by the porch in Litakovo town hall. The other partisans were lined up for the inspection of Captain Stojanov (nicknamed 'Babaitu'—bully) and his aide Mihail Dimitrov (known as 'Doctor' from his function as torturer). One by one, the partisans were brought up to identify the corpses, perhaps for military information but also as an object lesson in terror previous to the following proceedings. Those who showed any sign of hesitation in naming each dead partisan were brutally slashed by Stojanov's stick. They were then taken into the town hall for further inquisition.

The townsfolk of Litakovo were also allowed into the main hall, where some pretence of legal procedure was staged for their edification, half-judicial, half-military, as the presence of armed and uniformed soldiers everywhere showed. Lieutenant Colonel Manov presided. Associated with him were the sadistic police spy, Georgi Tonev Kukov, and Ivan Georgi Dinalov, with of course Stojanov and Mihail Dimitrov. They began taking the depositions they had already obtained by torture, and commenced calling in captive partisans to testify of their guilt. As they proceeded, the eyes of that Litakovo audience showed what they thought, even if their own mouths were silent.

Something seemed to have gone wrong at the beginning of the trial, for Captain Stojanov left the judge's table and came to the only telephone in the town hall, where the hall caretaker heard him engaged in a long and bitter dialogue with Sofia. Even now Geshev could have intervened, but the public avowal of Communism precluded any action on his part even as British agent. About half an hour later, according to the caretaker who was hovering close at hand and while the evidence was still being heard, a tall officer entered the porch. To the caretaker he seemed of the highest rank and behaved importantly enough to have been another general. As he came in, all the soldiers saluted him and he asked what was going on. He asked to see Major Thompson in the ante-room and began talking to him in English, so that not much is known of that conversation except that they talked about England. The officer spoke English easily and offered Major Thompson a cigarette. Thompson openly told him that he was a Communist, whereupon the visitor said, "How can a Communist claim to be a prisoner of war?" The officer was very friendly with Major Thompson and they talked for ten minutes. On his way out he paused in the porch for a short time talking. He told the peasants there he was on leave and just passing through, so he had stopped to see what was going on and make the chance to speak some of his English!

When Major Thompson was, at last, brought into the hall, there was a hush. Then a buzz of conversation broke out and the audience craned forward to hear him answer to his name, rank and military number. There was another murmur as they noticed he broke away from using the interpreter and spoke in Bulgarian with a good accent. He leaned against a column before the judge's table, listening sympathetically as the police tried to show him that some partisans had given evidence against him. Under the tortures used by those in authority there, it could not be a surprise if evidence were produced for or against anything in this world or the next.

Next, slowly and quietly, Frank Thompson answered to his political sympathies, declaring boldly that he was a Communist.

Then came the critical questions by which the court had already considered it must condemn him. "By what right do you, an

Englishman, march into our state and make war against us, not only as a soldier but politically?"

Thompson removed his unlit pipe and answered in Bulgarian, slowly and deliberately so that everyone heard. "I find myself here because this war is no longer a struggle between one nation and another. The most vital thing in the world today is the struggle of anti-Fascism against Fascism, of freedom against tyranny."

"Are you not aware that we shoot men with your beliefs?" came the challenge from the prosecutor.

And the answer came, precise and determined. "I am ready to die for freedom. I am proud that I die together with my comrades, partisans of Bulgaria!"

A powerful wave of emotion surged through the body of the hall and an old woman, moved to tears, stepped forward with that authority, that daring of the matriarch, which has always been wielded by the Bulgarian grandmother.

"I am an old woman," she anathematised, "and it does not matter what you do with me. However, you are in the wrong! Know you, we are not on your side, none of us! We are on the side of these brave folk!"

Her words were bitter and clear as a curse. For all that Stojanov knocked her to the ground and police dragged her out. There was a muttering right through the hall. Nobody's lips moved, but the voice of that nameless mob was obvious to those authorities. Moreover, feet began to move about and shuffle. Even Stojanov realised quite a number in the hall were far from well disposed and the proceedings came abruptly to an end. An abrupt conference at the table, the formal platitudes of so-called justice, and the death sentences were being read out.

Through the doors, Major Thompson and his comrades had to pass close by the gathered crowd. Partisans and Englishman together lifted clenched fists to salute and name the Fatherland Front, and to name, claiming as their own allies, Great Britain, the Soviet Union, America and all the free nations, shouting, "Long live Freedom!" and declaiming in unconcerted fervour phrases from the Botev song: "He does not die who goes in Freedom's cause!"

The original police plan to incite the people to attack the partisans, which had been started at Eleshina and which aimed to provoke a riot at Litakovo agitating the mob to kill the prisoners and so avoid the embarrassment between military and police of executing a prisoner of war, had fallen absolutely flat. The pseudo-trial also had been a failure and had only revived one of the most stirring inspirations in Bulgarian history.

A special firing squad and excutioner arrived from Sofia. Almost immediately, with the utmost haste, Frank Thompson, the quiet Russian soldier Vanusha and the Bulgarian comrades were conveyed above Litakovo, where, lined up against a sloping cliff with the valley below and the green of Murgash beyond, they raised their clenched fists in defiant proclamation of the defeat of Fascism. And as they fell before that firing squad, they renewed again the truth and the spirit not only of the Botev anthem, but of Frank Thompson's own words:

> Write on the stone no word of sadness,
>   Only the gladness due
> That we, who asked the most of living
>   Knew how to give it too.

The very next day, 6th June 1944 (D-Day), the Second Front developed, neither over the Aegean nor the Adriatic, but across the English Channel. The words and the deeds of those Englishmen fighting in the Balkans had not been in vain. Every German held down in the bitterness of the partisan struggles along the *planinas* had enhanced the Allied prospects of success.

But this deed had been done. Major Frank Thompson had been formally executed, not by the German Gestapo but by the Royal Bulgarians after a public 'trial' while he was still in uniform and claiming protection under the Geneva Convention as a prisoner of war.

With an eye to Allied victory and his British connections, Nikola Geshev began to feel insecure, and that June, soon after D-Day, his assistant Manyo Nachev was summarily dismissed, thereby providing his master with a useful scapegoat for the future.

25: Working 'Under Gestapo Orders'

The car into which Kenneth Scott had been snatched from his military escort drove south and, on reaching the main road, turned westward towards Sofia. The savage pain in his arm had improved, but it occurred to him that he might be going under police escort for special treatment, perhaps to some Sofia hospital. He was driven right through the centre of the city, where Allied bombing had devastated whole streets. He saw the bomb damage left just as it had happened. Main streets only had been cleared haphazard, leaving piles of rubble about and the blackened, broken windows plastered with paper.

His car continued to the west and drove out along the Radomir road for about four miles until it turned away along a lane towards a large, dingy white house standing in green meadows. The barbed wire and the armed military guards posted at the entrance and along the drive belied the peaceful appearance of the architecture. The alertness of sentries made it clear to him this was no hospital. He knew no Bulgarian and not enough German to communicate well. He was marched through the hall and taken to a back room.

As the door closed with a lock and a bolt, the first shock of complete desolation, of total inability to communicate, came upon him. The hours passed. Food was brought. There seemed always activity within the house: heavy military steps, sometimes voices— German or Bulgarian—but inside his room only the drop of water into an octagonal sunken bath dripping from the beaks of marble birds, slowly and spasmodically into a pool about three feet deep. As the bath was octagonal, so was the shape of that room. Scott passed the time by measuring and re-measuring the diagonals— twelve feet across, with just enough room between wall and water's edge for a bed. Light came mysteriously down into the interior and heightened the impression, once long ago of security and of privacy for the bathers, now of isolation for the prisoner.

No indication of former occupants remained, neither in the corridors nor in such parts of the house into which he could some- times get a sideways glance. He could speculate whether he were confined in the harem bath of some nineteenth-century Turkish civil servant or whether the former tenants were the entourage of some rich Austrian Jewish merchant from the early days of the Coburg Czars. There was a cold oriental style about the place which must have been not unsatisfactory in the summer days when water poured through the bird fountains. As it was, because of worn-out plumbing or possibly owing to bomb damage, the jets only dripped enough water for drinking, just enough to maintain the pool at level and prevent the use of all that centre of the room.

Outside the locked door it was very obvious there was a guard. Always a guard. And just a guard upon him. And a spy-hole through the door at which the guard's eye would now and again appear. Why should he be brought away from Major Thompson and isolated here? The pain in his arm was ceasing, deflecting dis- comfort towards keener awareness of the activities of his lice. The

warmth, the food, the inaction of his body began to make their depre-
dations unbearable. Through the night, the changing of the guard,
the military traffic somewhere outside, through all the long hours
the lice were like an army of sentries to keep him restless and alert.
The very passing of time was a menace hinged around with phantoms of beatings and torture, for it was obvious British uniforms,
army pay-book, the Geneva Convention, gave no more protection
here to any foreign soldier than to any Bulgarian rebel.

Next day the reason for his being singled out became clear. He
was conducted into a large room with windows overlooking the
countryside, green and peaceful meadows, trees and the rolling
planinas above them. There was furniture in the room, and indications of one-time human habitation, but of the six men who sat
at the table, three wore the blue Bulgarian uniforms and three the
insignia of the German Gestapo. Armed guards stood appropriately
at hand.

The interview began in a stereotyped military fashion, which soon
collapsed, for the three Gestapo knew neither English nor Bulgarian.
The Bulgarians gave no sign of knowing either German or English.
The interpreter was a Bulgarian who had to re-translate to an
over-earnest German N.C.O., who then re-translated forcefully into
Germano-English and vice-versa, in the course of which the bland
charm and persuasiveness of the three Gestapo soon became filtered
into a threatening intensity of purpose.

After sympathetic and friendly enquiries into whether his arm
was healing and if his hand and fingers were well, they made their
intentions curt and imperative, demanding that wireless communications be made with Cairo at once. Kenneth Scott was
ordered to operate his radio station under their directions. The
tone and method of the order left no doubt about the consequence
of non-compliance. Scott at once refused and made his formal
declaration of being a prisoner of war. This was brushed aside
curtly by the commanding officer, with laughter by his companions.
The prisoner was a technician, not a soldier, they asserted, a radio
telegraphist who had entered the country illegally. He had con-
sorted with bandits, and with such blood-thirsty desperadoes he
had gone through peasant villages, robbing and murdering the
peaceful inhabitants. No nation accepted robbers and murderers as
prisoners of war.

Kenneth Scott doggedly protested that he was a soldier under
military orders and claimed his rights under the Geneva Convention. He called attention to his uniform and produced his R.A.F.
pay-book. It would not be possible for him to do as they commanded and he must decline.

There was a hostile pause, followed by a renewed effort of bland persuasion. "You are not asked to give information," ran the argument. "You are only required to work as a technician. Other prisoners of war work on farms raising food, or repairing rail-roads. You must earn your keep by doing radio work. There is very little we do not know and still less you can tell us. As we know more than you, we do not ask you questions, but you must do radio work."

The chief Gestapo officer launched into a lecture, into which he shot significant pieces of secret information calculated to impress Kenneth Scott with his omniscience. His assistants chimed in with remarks on codes, from which it was clear that they knew at least one very secret code.

Reluctantly, and with studied hesitation, Kenneth Scott agreed. He and Major Thompson had had plenty of opportunity to discuss this possibility. Besides, S.O.E. and Force 133 in Cairo had also tried to establish some standard procedure for radio operators who should be captured and forced to work back their radio sets under duress. He had settled with Major Thompson that if ever they were prisoners and pressed to work the radio for the enemy they should feign reluctance before grudgingly complying. They planned to warn Cairo effectively by using the code so as to arrange for the last letter of each last word to take up the word 'CAPTURED' and in the same message to intrude the name of a girl.

Scott's acceptance was received not with joy or pleasure by the interviewers, but with curt military acknowledgement that he had saved his life but saved it only temporarily so long as he did his work correctly and obeyed instructions. The Gestapo commanding officer warned him with slow menacing sentences which only became more threatening in translation.

His captors were in earnest when they had demanded the set be worked at once. He was taken immediately to a large room entirely used for wireless telegraphy and set to work. A long and rambling account of the battle at Batulia was drawn up, representing the incident neither as a disaster nor a success, and indicating that the British mission would very soon give details so that a sortie could be received, arms and supplies being urgently needed.

Now came the divergence of theory from practice. German N.C.O.s came at regular times to give, receive or monitor messages which were carefully checked somewhere by superiors whom Scott never saw. He realised each message was always reworded! This thwarted part of his plan, but was encouraging in that it must make for a difference of style which might be noticed. He could also make a few mistakes such as an inexperienced, badly-trained operator might make. He left out deliberately his security check message. To his relief nobody came to point this out. Perhaps they did not know.

When that first message went out Kenneth Scott had the most trying time of all. If there had been no change in the staff at Cairo, they should suspect the situation at once. But if there were nonchalance in the decoding room, or haste or even sickness there, he might find himself responsible for calling out some Allied aeroplanes with their crews and equipment to be destroyed in the Sredna Gora Mountains. Or if the message were bluntly queried, he might be betrayed!

He need not have worried. At the British receiving station the absence of the security check message was noted with alarm and the errors seemed many more in decoding than even Scott had intended. The whole message stood out before the eyes of the S.O.E. chiefs as a warning signal. Kenneth Scott had the reputation of being one of the best operators in the whole Middle East field. Such mistakes would fail even a trainee operator and when coming from their most capable sergeant of signals could not be regarded as accidental.

At once they knew he was in German hands and sent out warnings to other missions to watch carefully for Major Thompson or any other survivors who might be in hiding. More definite than anything, however, Kenneth Scott by his bravery in making those mistakes had placed responsibility for the safety of his life squarely upon the shoulders of Force 133. If they showed any doubt or distrust, if they queried the authenticity of the message, or indeed if they failed to respond to any request the pseudo 'Claridges' might make, the Germans would suspect and Scott would be sacrificed to Gestapo torture and elimination.

The only solution was a careful game of bluff. No-one but Scott could work the set. Every sending operator's touch was distinct and recognisable. The Germans knew as well as S.O.E. that if they changed the operator the substitution for Scott would be detected. No one could play Scott in 'Claridges' but Sergeant Kenneth Scott, so while Cairo appeared to accept the messages, Scott's life was safe. Bickham Sweet-Escott was in charge at Cairo and vividly describes the anxiety there as they wrote out messages in reply to the masquerading station, stalling and stalling and finding reasons for not sending precious aeroplanes into Bulgaria. His department. however, did not have immediate control for sending out of signals, and sometimes the proposed messages would come back for attention or amendment by another department in words which would, if allowed, have destroyed the security of Kenneth Scott's bluff.

Sweet-Escott was not the man to allow himself to be over-ruled in matters of loyalty, and his department never permitted an unguarded reply to go out. The signals from pseudo 'Claridges' received even more attention than most from orthodox missions.

As the messages came and went Kenneth Scott settled down into a steady routine. He was regularly ordered to attend in the wireless room, where besides transmission a considerable amount of monitoring work occupied the staff. One particular day was occupied with a very long-distance message which was sent out by the Germans very slowly with the words repeated at regular intervals.

Transmission and reception from Cairo continued, time passed, and he could begin to guess from the nature of the excuses S.O.E. were making that they knew of his predicament. The Germans sometimes became querulous and restive, but he was able to allay this by proving that since the mission had come to Bulgaria it had not been possible to persuade Cairo to make one single drop, an assertion which the Gestapo could check to be correct. Their attitude remained threatening and implacable.

After a week the Royal Bulgarian Lieutenant Martinov in whose custody he now was, grimly announced that Major Thompson had been shot, not as a soldier but as a political agitator who had conspired with rebels to commit crimes against the Royal Bulgarian government. "Lucky for you that you have not mixed yourself up learning Bulgarian and getting into politics," was the object lesson of the announcement, coupled with the ominous implication that if officers were shot as simply, punishment of other ranks was no problem at all.

Kenneth Scott could not at first believe this cold-blooded news and begged his opposite number on the Bulgarian side, Feldwebel Konchev, who was now in fact his jailer, to find out. All he could learn in confirmation was that the Englishman "had died bravely", but Konchev had produced two photographs of Major Thompson and a Fatherland Front badge as if to prove the fact. Out of all Bulgaria why produce them via Konchev to exhibit to the prisoner? This question occurred and recurred in Kenneth Scott's mind, for there was ample time to consider the motives of the Bulgarian underlings of his Gestapo captors, especially after, some ten days later, he himself was taken outside and officially photographed.

It was now past the middle of June. The tiled partitions of the bathroom were prison walls from which it was a relief to be called at the regular intervals when he worked on assignments at the radio station. Time was escaping him, without friends, newspapers, books or even English conversation, except for a word or two with Feldwebel Konchev and the interpreter. He drew up a calendar date sheet on an old piece of official paper and ruled it off to mark away the days and months.

Thanks to S.O.E. super-efficiency, he had, unknown to his captors, a compass and a good map. The ruling out and marking of days emphasised and made more vivid the passing of time. Each tick, each mark on the calendar prompted the importance of escape, but when after much toil and ingenuity he prized up a marble slab from the floor, he found it was bedded upon thick concrete.

Gradually about this time his assignments began to alter. He realised the Germans were slowly taking over his set. S.O.E. at Cairo were wily and gave no sign that they recognised any change of touch in the operator. Whether this was an even wilier move on the part of the Gestapo to test whether S.O.E. were bluffing by whether they would challenge and question the alteration in the operating touch is too complicated a speculation. They did not, and nobody seemed wiser.

The imminent prospect of Allied air-raids suddenly caused immediate evacuation. All radio equipment was loaded into the six large vans in the yard. The important personnel, including Scott, were taken with them into the remote country, where they remained for weeks, working as usual, but in the more delightful surroundings of a Bulgarian rustic summer, living on regulation rations which were augmented by Feldwebel Konchev's purchase (as he said) of a sheep and a goat. Out in the remoter countryside the formalities between prisoner and jailers almost began to ease, so that he managed, wonder of wonders, to get the B.B.C. news! Breathlessly he listened to hear of the Allies over-running Europe, the Russians advancing through Romania, of Montgomery and Eisenhower, and of the R.A.F. over Germany. Konchev listened, frightened, anxious but hypnotised, begging Scott to keep the sound low, but anxious to hear and understand.

When the vans returned and Scott was once again locked within the octagon of bathroom walls, he soon perceived that the atmosphere had changed. He no longer seemed so necessary as a radio operator. Feldwebel Konchev was ingratiating, whereas the Gestapo were off-hand and insolent. In July a drunken Gestapo officer leered at him with the news that two Englishmen and six partisans had just been captured, and only a week after this Feldwebel Konchev prodded him with the information that his colleagues Sergeants Walker and Monroe had been executed, though Kenneth Scott was certain they had never escaped alive from Batulia.

The brief spell away in the world outside had made confinement within that marble room still more intolerable. He knew now the location of the sentries posted around the house and the gates in the barbed wire fences where the guard dogs patrolled all night. Outside his own door one sentry was still mechanically stationed, for the watch was maintained night and day. Feldwebel Konchev hinted that there was an argument between the Gestapo and the Bulgarians over his future and suggested the Gestapo were determined to execute him as being a useless liability, but that the Bulgarian officers objected and argued that as he was a known prisoner of war who had been taken under their charge, he could not now be so conveniently exterminated.

One July night there was a celebration with merrymaking, drinking and all kinds of riotous fun that echoed throughout the whole building. Feldwebel Konchev came during the evening. "The Germans are visiting us," he declared in a whisper. "The guards have gone down to drink. You can escape tonight."

He handed his prisoner a revolver and urged him to get away that very evening. Something deterred Kenneth Scott. The sentry had gone from his post outside the door. The music and singing from the party grew even louder. Nothing seemed more simple, but some intuition prevented him from acting. He was not feeling well, the lice were troubling him, nothing about Feldwebel Konchev inspired him with optimism. He decided to put off the attempt until next night and hid the revolver. Tomorrow he would be able to store food, make his plans and prepare himself. It would be no use running out there and then, merely to fire off his revolver.

Next morning Feldwebel Konchev arrived in a state of agitation. Why had Scott not gone? He had lost the chance and now must give back the revolver. Scott was reluctant and protested, but Konchev demanded in a panic and began searching, grumbling and cursing as he dragged out the bed and tore off the bed-clothes to find Scott had ingeniously knotted the blankets to make a fold where the weapon reposed unobtrusively. He snatched up the revolver and made off muttering.

Scott does not say so, but it seems obvious that he had narrowly escaped a standard escapist assassination plot which would have conveniently removed him both as evidence of Major Thompson's treatment as a prisoner of war and the matter of the operation of the pseudo 'Claridges'. He expected at least an enquiry or some punishment. Instead, nothing at all was said and the *Feldwebel* went dumb about the whole affair.

The German attitude towards him continued to harden into a chilling coldness, while the Bulgarians became more and more friendly, a contrast which carried the menacing implication that something was intended with regard to his disposal. As he ticked the passing of the days on his makeshift calendar, the map and

and compass so cunningly contrived by the 'Firm', and still secreted undiscovered by his captors, began to have a hypnotic impulsion to drive him out of that confined space, away from the marble prison and the dripping water. The sentries standing in the corridor outside always seemed as dull and bored as he was himself. There could be no communication between guards and prisoner other than scrappy Bulgarian phrases, bits of German and French, gestures and sometimes just grins.

At last a newcomer to the guard happened to be a young Bulgarian soldier who knew some English, asked questions about England and America and passed the time by improving his own knowledge of the language in improvised conversation lessons. Gradually and cautiously a friendship developed. The sentry confessed he was discontented. He knew the war was lost. He and Scott discussed the progress of the Red Armies and speculated how long before they crossed the Danube. The sentry asserted that he intended to join the partisans. Kenneth Scott boasted he could take him to them and introduce him if he helped to arrange an escape. They worked out a plan and agreed to put it into action on the occasion of the sentry's next round of duty.

At thirty minutes after midnight it was arranged they should steal out with just enough time to reach the railway line, where at a regular early morning hour a goods train gradually lost speed up a steep incline on its way towards the frontier of Yugoslavia. Kenneth Scott, in the style now of an old campaigner, filled his pockets and every possible receptacle he could with bread, and turned in to sleep fully dressed in his boots, equipped to step out of bed and walk to freedom. Also in the style of a veteran, he dropped soundly off to slumber. Nobody woke him. When he jumped out of bed, it was broad daylight. The sentry had deserted to operate the plan without the encumbrance of an English prisoner. The door for the first time was unguarded, but by now, not only were the guards in the yard alert, but that railway train must have reached Kustendil at least.

Events now began to move more quickly. Food improved; the behaviour of the sentries underwent a transition from the respectful to the deferential. The vans no longer filled the yard and the wireless signal-room seemed to be going out of gear. As the Germans became fewer, the Bulgarian soldiers relaxed—not into inefficiency or indiscipline, but they became less mechanical and more friendly with one another.

On 5th September Kenneth Scott was taken to that huge prison building which, as the Stoletov, still dominates the little slum houses and courtyards of the Western suburbs of Sofia. At that time it was used chiefly for the incarceration of political and military detainees. Here a great fuss was made about de-lousing. Usually prisoners were made to strip in batches, but Scott found himself the only unit in his section.

In full view of all the surrounding windows in the open prison yard, he was compelled to wash down stark naked at the tap. Nevertheless he soon realised he had become a more important guest than the average prisoner. The lay-out of the prison was explained to him. He was shown a flat, pockmarked wall where they openly machine-gunned undesirable prisoners in batches. Adjacent to this was a long low shed with machine guns installed at one end for more secret executions. "We keep the population down here," the official commented grimly. "It is very bad and unhealthy when overcrowded in summer."

His cell, though it over-looked the prison yard, provided a welcome contrast to the cold marble of that oriental bathroom where he had existed for fourteen weeks. Prison ablutions freed him from the lice, so he expected, as he settled in, to be in some greater ease and comfort. Disillusionment was swift, however, for that cell had a population of jumping Bulgarian fleas described by Scott as "large as lady-birds", even larger than the omnivorous bugs that seemed to appear from nowhere and vanish into the half-shadows without a movement.

Next morning there was an ominous spatter of machine-gun fire from the long low shed, and some comings and goings of which he could just catch glimpses from his window. But the warder only shrugged his shoulders and nodded his head, declaring it was only practice. But who was practising and why?—unanswered questions which left Kenneth Scott most uncomfortable.

26: Liberation Day

Far over Kenneth Scott's head and out of his comprehension, as either member of the British mission or prisoner of war, events had been sweeping away authority and personalities in Bulgaria like an overwhelming tide. As long ago as 1st June, after the heavy Allied air-raids, the Bulgarian leaders had realised the Nazi weakness and, sensing defeat, they had decided to break away and make peace with the Western allies. On this day a non-party government was formed led by the former minister, Bagrianov.

M

He attempted to play the double game of placating Germany and pleasing the Allies, arranging for German troops to withdraw safely from the Black Sea ports, yet delaying shipments of Bulgarian food to Germany, while offering the Soviet Union consulates in some of Bulgaria's larger cities. The Fatherland Front distrusted him and refused to co-operate. As soon as he had come to power on that 1st June, he had been faced with the incursion of the First and Second Sofia Partisan Brigades. The presence of a pro-Russian peasant army sponsored by the English Major Thompson with his avowed Communist and revolutionary political sentiments had introduced into Bulgaria a feature that could have negatived the intentions of Bagrianov and all the ministers of the Czarist government. Such a revolt would give Bulgaria to the Red Armies.

The minister's representative was therefore urgent in ensuring that the leader of the British mission, Frank Thompson, be eliminated from the scene, and it may indeed be this representative in person who appears in contemporary accounts as well as in popular tradition as an un-named 'general' or 'colonel on leave' hovering in the background at Litakovo. Had not the Gestapo fastened upon Scott, the wireless operator, hoping to develop the methods of 'turning round' which they had so successfully used in France, there is no doubt Kenneth Scott would have been executed simultaneously, with his major.

Bagrianov, having reduced the partisan threat, began to release insignificant political prisoners, and sent the former Speaker of Parliament, Stoicho Moshanov, to Turkey to start armistice negotiations, on 17th August, officially announcing in Parliament his intention to withdraw Bulgaria from the war. On 26th August, alarmed at the progress of the Soviet troops in Romania and the Romanian armistice, he announced that Bulgaria had "officially withdrawn from the war and regained neutrality". The difficulty of negotiating this with the Western allies in Cairo and the Soviet government's rejection of his declaration of neutrality destroyed his confidence and he resigned.

Now developed one of those curious two-faced sequences, the interpretation of which confuses history and breeds hostility. On 2nd September the new cabinet of Muraviev-Mushanov-Guichev, instead of immediately deferring to the nearest Allied armies (the Soviet Union's), temporised. Moreover, this cabinet contained four members who had deliberately refused in 1942–3 to participate in the Fatherland Front. Since the Fatherland Front observed that the members of the new cabinet were noted to prefer the Western allies to the Soviet Union, it now flatly refused to co-operate.

Though Muraviev ordered Moshanov to conclude an immediate

armistice, the Allies now broke off contact with him on the pretext that Moshanov's credentials were not now in order. On 5th September this new government decided to break off diplomatic relations and to issue a declaration of war against Germany! The Minister of War, Ivan Marinov, now dug his heels in and refused to agree, demanding a seventy-two hours delay to enable Bulgarian troops to escape capture by the Nazis and to get safely out of Macedonia and South Serbia. This very delay also allowed all German troops with arms and equipment to withdraw comfortably from Bulgaria!

The victorious Red Army was not likely to check in its triumphant progress from the steppes and Stalingrad to meddle in the devious Balkan intrigues of a Coburg Czarist government, and on 5th September the Bulgarian minister in Moscow was presented with the Soviet declaration of war against Bulgaria.

This sequence of delay followed by swift action enabled some to point to the Soviet Union as a bullying opportunist, others to accuse the Western democracies of participating in delaying intrigues to maintain the Bulgarian royal house and 'wealthy' classes, and still others later to blame the Churchill-Roosevelt-Stalin pacts which gave away the Danube countries in 'spheres of influence'.

Events in Sofia now accumulated. The transport workers went on strike on 6th September. They assembled in a huge protest meeting among the tangle of tramlines in the Central Square before the great blackened fabric of bombed and windowless hotels. They moved quickly about, not wanting to press too closely, for this Central Square had a nasty reputation for police bullets. The Minister of the Interior, V. Dimov, publicly declared that the wartime laws could be severely enforced against Fatherland Front elements. Next day, 7th September, police forces began to put down socialist demonstrations throughout the country, attacking partisans in Pernik as well as Sofia. A worker was killed in Sofia and partisans were slain in Pazardjik, Assenovgrad and other places. It was on this day that Kenneth Scott had heard the 'practice' machine guns shooting in the long shed at the prison.

On the same 7th September Marshal Tolbukin issued his proclamation "To the Bulgarian People! To the Bulgarian Army!", and on the next day, 8th September, the Red Army crossed the Danube at Roussé and the Soviet Fleet came into Varna. All over Bulgaria the prisons began to open and partisans to stir from their far *planinas* toward the valley towns.

The excitement penetrated into Scott's prison. Unknown people, some uniformed, some just ordinary workers, came to his cell to rejoice and bestow all kinds of gifts upon him—melons, peaches, fruit, vegetables, flowers, everything came in a rush that was quite confusing. There was an amnesty. Some said that half the prison population had been freed. People were walking in and out as if it were an hotel.

Towards evening it was rumoured that the Soviet tanks were advancing and would come to the city along the main road from Plovdiv. The anti-aircraft battery at Govedartsi and units of the Second Engineer Regiment joined an armoured Bulgarian regiment moving towards the general post office. The training company of the military college, with the Searchlight Group 'Slatinski Redoubt', proceeded to surround the Ministry of War and all the principal seats of government in the central city, while the Engineers shock battalion came in from the opposite side of Sofia. Partisans and a huge crowd of sympathisers occupied the most hated of all buildings, the central police headquarters. Shots were heard from time to time across the city, but to the ordinary civilians there appeared to be no resistance, only a fermenting fever of expectation for the arrival of the Red Army.

Next morning, 9th September, Kenneth Scott had a visitor far different from any who had previously entered his cell, which was now unlocked and unguarded. Of rather short stature, his hair brushed well back, this newcomer was neatly and expensively dressed. He spoke very good English and seemed well known to everybody. "Even the Jews and foreigners there knew him." He went through the prison just as he liked and was treated with great respect.

As he talked, as the smooth and easy flow of standard English came from him, Kenneth Scott was baffled to assess the visitor's intentions or purpose. He had been an isolated prisoner for fourteen weeks, during which he had heard no real live English like this. The visitor had the politest address and an engaging, charming manner. He declared himself as a British agent; yes, he was on the side of the English all the time. He could trust the English. He seemed to want to stay. Gradually Scott overcame his bewilderment to veer the conversation round directly to ask why he had come and what he wanted. Oh, he wanted to talk English, to have the pleasure of meeting an Englishman, to know how an Englishman thought about the war in Bulgaria. Nothing more than that, to be pleasant and to talk English! Conversations pursued to no purpose become boring. When some purpose unknown to one participant is exercised at length, the situation becomes frustrating. The stranger's charm extended to an extreme reluctance to leave, as if he had a matter of importance to convey and did not know Kenneth Scott sufficiently well to say it. Once or twice he might have been on the brink of asking something. But he did not, even though he checked himself at the door and left promising to come again.

Who was he? Could he have been the arch-enemy, chief of political police, Nikola Geshev, scouting for a refuge, some asylum, or way to Britain? Scott, having no inkling of Bulgarian machinations, was in no position to determine.

Soon after this a uniformed official came and Kenneth Scott, still a prisoner, was taken off to the centre of Sofia by tram to be left, abandoned, in a side street. His guard just spoke a few words in Bulgarian to him and went away. Kenneth Scott waited and waited. Several hours passed. His indignation mounted. He was a prisoner! So used to being watched, so acclimatised to incarceration that this deprivation of guards, this dumping into freedom, struck vividly into his conditioned reflexes as a grave injustice. He protested and went on protesting until he found someone who spoke English and took him to a telephone.

He still had his S.O.E. map and his concealed compass, but with everyone so friendly, saluting his uniform, shouting greetings in Russian to him, this was hardly the time to make for those bare frontier mountains! More than that, he was depressingly hungry and had left all that cornucopia of food in his cell!

Very soon in response to the telephoned 'protest' a Bulgarian army N.C.O. arrived. He was taken at once to a Bulgarian restaurant nearby to be treated to a good meal and then conveyed to the main guard-room in the central city. Three Italians and one Russian soldier were there already, in a relaxed atmosphere as little like that of a guard-room as may be imagined.

Rumours were flying. The troops had mutinied! The Germans had gone! The Russian tanks were only twenty miles away! The government had fled! The Bulgarian troops were shooting their officers!

Throughout the early afternoon people poured onto the streets. Hastily improvised banners and placards began to appear. Scaffolding went up around the equestrian statue of the Russian Czar Liberator before whom a huge picture and text of Lenin appeared! Motorcycles went mysteriously to and fro and people began to take up their stands on the pavements. Towards mid-afternoon a procession began to form in the street leading to the central square. Partisans assembled behind their ominous automatic rifles. Citizens joined in with weapons and military equipment. Some weapons might have been dragged out of antique oriental depositories, and some by their condition seemed to have been that very day demanded or cajoled from possession of the regular troops.

As the parade moved off, photographers appeared. This was the signal for everyone to press into the procession as it moved along, swallowing the onlookers like a huge sea creature with ever-enlarging tail. Voices were raised in slogan and in song. Clenched fists were uplifted in salutes, hands and handkerchiefs waved, and kisses blown.

Only now had the Chavdar Brigade of partisans come to Sofia, a weary, emaciated little band that had been persecuted right up until yesterday. They stood in the main square, the women with clean laundered linen holding the banner, their men still in heavy Bulgarian caps with broken peaks. Todor Zhivkov, thin as a rake with living rough, bare-headed, his shirt open-necked, came out to greet them all and individually, while the citizens looked on, anxious to be seen applauding and cheering, staring with some wonder at these inhabitants of their mountains whom the Czarist press and the police posters had up to last week denounced as bandits more brutal than the wild beasts.

Not till evening and after another meal did Kenneth Scott and the three Italians trail down to the railway station, led by a very anxious Bulgarian officer. From his shaky irresolution it was clear he counted on the prisoners to protect him. The Russian prisoner had disappeared and no one knew or cared where. The official trams were not running. Home-made, rough and ready placards showed the hammer and sickle. As groups of young men and women linked arms across the street to make up their own separate little processions, they moved along shouting in unison the new catchwords of freedom—"Long live the Fatherland Front!" "Glory to the People's Partisans!" Uniformed soldiers whom some declared to be Russians cut heavily through the people, roaring past on their motorcycles.

The Bulgarian officer who, to use Kenneth Scott's own phrase, 'had a shake on' was stopped and hectored, sometimes by burly groups of workers, sometimes by private soldiers to whom, the formalities of saluting abandoned, he made faltering explanations of the importance of his 'guests' and so, despite his officer's rank and uniform, managed to reach the railway station alive. The crowds were thinner here and across the open spaces shots could be heard from the central city. From the Germans? From the Russians? Executions, probably, explained their guide with a shudder.

Grouped on that platform there were about a score of South African and United States air force men, all anxious to find a train, but equally anxious that it should be travelling in the right direction. Most of them had formed the crews of two bomber planes which had crashed recently. After some days in hospital they had been brought out suddenly and dumped here. To Scott's amazement all were loud in their praise of Bulgaria and the Bulgarians; as a British ex-partisan prisoner, he listened to glowing accounts of their V.I.P. treatment with some cynicism.

The one train that seemed prepared to leave eventually pulled out of Sofia and took the ex-prisoners slowly and reluctantly towards the greener land of the Maritza valley. The United States airmen marvelled at its sluggish progress and debated whether it would reach Turkey before the Russian armies commandeered its services. They speculated and took bets on their chances of being drafted into the Red Armies. Young, full of life, as they were, almost innocent of war which they had only seen from the heights above, these American airmen could only imagine such an event as another episode in their own individual serials of adventure, but to Scott and his Italian fellow prisoners the prospect was a different matter.

Near Plovdiv another train joined them, carrying some 200 airmen from the prisoner of war camp, and on they chugged towards the Turkish border, no longer furtive prisoners skulking out of the country by the back way. News of this trainload of soldiers had preceded them. All along the railway line the population turned out to cheer and wave. Bulgarian troops hurried out of barracks and formed up in salute beside the line. Rifles, old guns and pistols were banged away, oriental style, in greeting. Clenched fists were raised everywhere and even the occasional solitary peasant let off his gun, for everyone thought these were the Russians and this was their first glimpse of the glorious Red Army!

This impression was not maintained at the Turkish frontier, where the United States embassy was represented in full force and at highest power. Every man came out of that train and was shepherded across with the minimum of formality. While officials were arranging for their accommodation and transit, they learned how they were only just in time. The frontier was about to be closed! Bulgarian Czarist politicians and officials, police, German agents and other undesirable refugees were beginning to flock across to an extent that could not be allowed to complicate Turkey's neutrality and relations with the Soviet government.

As Kenneth Scott sampled the good food served with the charm and politeness of old Turkey, he seemed to breathe in another world, a world into which the steam of everlasting prison *borsh* (bean, cabbage, or beetroot soup) had never penetrated. There were two more days ahead, however, before, after travelling across Turkey, all the ex-prisoners arrived at Aleppo in Syria to be flown in grand American style to the U.S. airfield at Cairo.

Once in Cairo, Kenneth Scott could be said to know his way about. He reported next morning to S.O.E. headquarters like a spirit who had re-crossed the Styx. The news he brought of his companions was sad indeed—though for three months now it had been guessed—but did not prevent S.O.E. from giving him the welcome he so richly merited. His old flat was restored to him with its bathroom, clean laundered sheets and the real luxuries of the 'Firm', whose two surviving pieces of equipment—the map and the compass—he could now joke about!

After the usual reporting he came back to routine duties, preparatory to being granted leave and returning home in December 1944. Bickham Sweet-Escott, his chief at S.O.E., had recommended him for the D.C.M., which he eventually received at Buckingham Palace in December 1946. In the meantime he had gone out again to Cairo as representative on the Allied commission for dealing with Bulgarian war crimes. No criminals or putative offenders came within reach of his office here, for there was no long-drawn-out trial like that at Nuremberg to deal with the perpetrators of the vicious police and military crimes in the heart of the Balkans, where retribution was more immediate.

27: Retribution

On that 9th September, when Kenneth Scott was on his way to Sofia railway station, the Royal Bulgarian occupying authority in the Tserna Trava district and all across Macedonia and South Serbia was collapsing. Soldiers in the ranks took charge, officers and officials fled. Some, like the hated advocate Georgi Hotinov, the agent for Bulgarising Macedonia, disappeared into anonymity for ever. The treacherous mayor of Brod, Stavro Milenkov, detested for extorting information from helpless women, was seized and publicly executed at Dejićev in front of his victims. The police officer Pelivan was arrested at Bitvern and his colleague Ivan traced to Pernik jail; both were condemned to death.

Whilst Kenneth Scott was sitting with his Italians and the Allied airmen waiting for their train to pull out of Sofia for Istanbul, on the western side of the frontier in Yugoslavia Bulgarian soldiers and officials had crowded into another train at Pirot and were anxiously waiting for the engine to pull out in the direction of Sofia, hoping to race from Serbian retribution across into Bulgaria.

But a pack of partisans had already come upon the platform and were passing down the train in a search for escaping Fascists.

Tričkov Gergur was casually glancing into the windows when he saw a civilian cowering down in the carriage corner behind a group of Bulgarian soldiers. At once he recognised Dimitar Dražev Savov, the Fascist Bulgarian mayor of Tserna Trava. He shouted to his Tserna Trava friends who were parading with their rifles and grenades at the far end of the train. In an incredulous stampede, they charged down, invaded the carriage and dragged out the terrified head-man under the eyes of the Bulgarian soldiery. Protesting innocence, disclaiming his identity, he was carried off to be handed over to the partisan authorities. Formal depositions were taken and he was condemned by the court set up by the people's *odbor*, sentenced to death, and returned to Tserna Trava for execution.

Early one October morning the square in Tserna Trava from the early dawn began to fill with peasants.

Here, by the monument before the town hall in April of that very same year, the square had been almost deserted except for Royal Bulgarian soldiers and police. Before the old monument which still stands in the centre, that Fascist mayor had had one wounded Italian brought out.[1] There had been an execution parade, the mayor had read the condemnation, after which the prisoner had been forced to kneel and was there and then decapitated with a woodman's axe. In medieval viciousness the head had been struck on the wall and the body left exposed, but on Friday 26th April, a little band of peasants had crept up in the dead of night and carried it away for burial.

It had been springtime then. Now it was autumn. The square was packed with widows, orphaned children, and women in mourning black. Just before eight o'clock, door and windows of the town hall suddenly opened and Dimitar Dražev Savov, one time Royal Bulgarian mayor and magistrate of Tserna Trava, whose authority struck terror into the homes of shepherd and peasant across the *planinas*, was pushed onto the balcony by the rifles of militia men. Once again his appearance on that balcony struck a chill that seemed to freeze the crowd back with a sullen hiss.

Somebody shouted, "Death to Dražev the Criminal!"

[1] After the capitulation many Italian soldiers were conveyed to the Mačkat mine for slave labour. Often they escaped to fight for the partisans, many of the bravest losing their lives in the March offensive; but this one had been caught during a search of Kozarnica when the peasants were giving him shelter and tending his wound.

The crowd took up the cry with a savage roar and stormed towards the town hall, demanding to strangle him with their own hands; but the militia men formed out and held them back with rifle butts while the group around the mayor shot him down in front of all. Just as the partisans had been left in the square when slain, so the mayor was abandoned on the balcony, nothing to see but a corpse in clothes on which the children spat.

The Red Army, the Fatherland Front and the partisans of Yugo-slavia united to form committees to track down, arrest and despatch the war criminals, who, if they had been active in the occupation of Macedonia, found no refuge in Bulgaria. Boris Gorćilov Tasev, the Royal Bulgarian army captain at Brod and Dejićev, was caught, identified by Tserna Trava partisans and sentenced.

In Bulgaria itself, the Fatherland Front sent Vera Nacheva and her colleagues up to Litakovo, where a people's court was set up to hold another trial in the town hall. The mayor of Litakovo and those of his associates guilty of assisting in the betrayal of Major Thompson and the Second Sofia Brigade were brought before it. The few survivors, relatives, witnesses from Chavdar, made their grim depositions, which allowed for no mercy. In the words of Mrs Thompson, Frank's mother, to me years later, "They butchered the lot."

In its new virility of power and freedom, the Bulgarian Fatherland Front was not disposed to have truck with any reasons of diplomatic policy that might perpetuate the old regime. Everyone in the highest places concerned with "involving Bulgaria in the World War against the United Nations and the misdeeds connected therewith" was arraigned before the First Chamber of the People's Court consisting of thirteen members, prominent amongst whom was the name of Vera Nacheva Ivanova.

On 1st February 1945 the long list of death sentences was announced, name after name, from Prince Cyril of Preslav Saxe-Coburg, generals, regents, prime ministers, cabinet ministers, deputies and members of parliament. Death, confiscation of pro-perty, deprivation of rights—the stroke of retribution was savage. In the last words of the proclamation: "The sentence is final and not to be appealed against."

But it was as if the soil of Bulgaria cried out, over-thirsty for blood as in Byzantine times. Captain Stojanov had anticipated his fate and by suicide in Sofia on 9th September had cheated investi-gations, courts and gallows. His superior, Nikola Geshev, subtlest war criminal of all, had vanished, perhaps to Turkey, perhaps on the same train as Kenneth Scott, to live happily ever after, as some say, in Ankara. He took with him his knowledge, no doubt, but he left behind the most tangled web of intrigue and suspicion—threads of which came to light in trials such as that of Traicho Kostov— which confused both the new rulers of Bulgaria and the Western allies. The traditional British agents from whom Geshev had expectations had been replaced by Kim Philby, who now had access to all Geshev's files in the British archives. The work done in the torture chambers below the Sofia police headquarters and the central prison, which had turned Communists and politicians into double agents, passed into the hands of a still more sinister double agent, for Philby used his information ruthlessly on Moscow's behalf and played the old Bulgarian Communists against each other, sending them to their deaths from the safety of his desk in Turkey.

28: Left-wing Double Agent against Right-wing Double Agent: Kim Philby versus Geshev

On 7th September 1944, Nikola Geshev was furiously burning documents from his secret archives, anticipating his own flight to Istanbul. On that same 7th September Pleven Prison was broken open by the crowds. The prisoners were all set at liberty; but as a little group of them, Kostov and his 'recruits', began making their way to Sofia, a terrible fear clung round their hearts that some discovery of police dossiers containing evidence of their collaboration might convict and destroy them.

Directly they reached the capital, Kostov's fellow prisoners Pavlov and Bogdanov, busied themselves with the task of searching these out in the archives. Concerning Kostov they found only a 'doctored' document which revealed Traicho Kostov as a true Communist. This they handed to Kostov who read it with satisfaction and returned it. Pavlov and his comrades, however, had not received such consideration, for their incriminating documents and declarations reposed forgotten in the files. Pavlov, aptly nicknamed 'Mosquito', destroyed everything referring to himself, but handed the details convicting his colleagues to Kostov, who now felt both secure in his own freedom and powerful by the secret knowledge through which he could dominate his party.

In 1944 in the British Service there was a newly created Section (Section IX) "for the collection and interpretation of information concerning Soviet and Communists espionage and subversion in all parts of the world outside British territory".[1] Kim Philby, prompted by his Soviet masters, obtained the position of head of this department in which all documents and files concerning the European agents would be accessible to him. He confesses that in 1944 he had arranged his staff to obtain the volume of wireless traffic concerning the national liberation movements in Eastern Europe.[2] He admits that he manipulated the organisation so as to keep the whole field of anti-Soviet and anti-Communist work under his own direct supervision.[3]

In 1946 he became First Secretary with the British Embassy in Turkey, a cover style for his position as head of the secret intelligence station from which he dealt with Balkan affairs.[4] Istanbul was then the main southern base for intelligence work directed with regard to the Soviet Union and the socialist countries of the Balkans and Southern Europe. Philby had access to what he chooses to term "a trickle of low grade information from Bulgaria" from refugees and this, on page 120 of his book, is the only mention he makes of any relations or dealing with that country, a tactful quiescence which is significant since he admits his contacts with the Soviet secret intelligence in Istanbul.[5] (He did not leave for Washington until 1949, when the Kostov trials were over, Burgess having come out to see him in 1948.)

There can be no doubt that he fed back to the Soviet Union all reports in British possession concerning Communists and others who had been in Geshev's hands, and that Moscow used them, however unreliable, to overthrow those undesirable to the Soviet Union. The fates of Kostov and of other 'home Communists' therefore lie at his door, and the assortment of intelligence obtained from the unworthy sources he mentions was used to make Bulgaria subservient to Soviet policy. But worse than that, under the guise of British requirements and influence he tempted and blackmailed the old Communists, who had twisted under Fascist torture, at the moment when they had become free to pursue their ideals once again.

The author of that letter to the Chavdar partisans, Traicho Kostov, for example, had by no means escaped the net of Nikola

---

[1] *My Silent War*, Kim Philby, Macgibbon & Kee, 1968, page 75.
[2] *ibid.*, page 79.   [3] *ibid.*, page 87.
[4] *ibid.*, page 97.   [5] *ibid.*, page 111.

Geshev, ex-chief of Section A. Now at the head of the Bulgarian
Communist Party, in November 1944, Kostov found himself, by
some mistake or perhaps a trick alteration of date, alone at a
lunch on Masaryk Street, Sofia, in the house of General Oxley,
British representative of the Allied Control Commission. After that
lunch he alleged that another British representative drew him aside,
speaking in Russian, and suggested he knew in detail all about
Kostov's transactions with Geshev from the time of the Bulgarian
Communist Party's collapse as far back as 1942. To Kostov's
indignant rebuttal, this man countered with confident self-assurance,
revealing that the British still kept up a connection with Geshev,
who, he insisted, had been carrying out their instructions for a
long time, and that it was precisely on these instructions from the
British that Geshev recruited his victims. Moreover, Geshev had
supplied the British not only with evidence in writing but with
Kostov's own extorted declaration of collaboration. This individual,
noticing the distrust on the face of his listener, went on to instance
and prove by detail that the documents received from Geshev were
being kept by the British in a safe place. He began to claim that
Kostov render to the British that service promised to Geshev under
duress. The threat implicit in the possession of those documents
was unpleasant and dangerous. "Thus," complained Kostov, "I
found myself hard pressed!"

"It became clear," continued Kostov's deposition, made under
the stress of his trial, "that the dossiers were at the disposal of
British Intelligence, of which it is known that, let it only once take
hold of a man's little finger and it can always pull out the man's
arm and after it the whole man himself. Because of this, I did
not even think of resisting and gave him my consent."

It seems extraordinary that any Englishman should have been
assigned to such a dubious and unpleasant task, extraordinary until
it is realised that at the head of the organisation hovered Kim
Philby, working under Moscow's orders.

After 9th September, the Fatherland Front had taken power in
Bulgaria, a government not predominantly Communist but in which
the control of the police and the courts was in the hands of the
Communist Anton Yugov. As Minister of the Interior, he established the 'People's Militia', which seized 'enemies of the people'
and brought them before his people's courts. The Communist Tsola
Dragoisheva reorganised local government to a Communist pattern
answerable to the Communist Party. The tide of blood began to
flow: 2,138 death sentences, 1,948 long-term prison sentences were
announced—a red terror as remorseless as that white terror of
1925!

As soon as those Communists in exile—Georgi Dimitrov, Vasil Kolarov and Vulko Chervenkov—came back from Moscow, they began removing obstacles from the path of Party supremacy, while Philby was actively dabbling in British Eastern European Intelligence. The day after the United States ratification of the Paris Peace Treaty on 4th June 1947, Nikola Petkov was arrested and a disgraceful sequence of persecution led to this leader of the opposition being executed by hanging (on 23rd September 1947), an appalling official murder as bad as those of the royalist regime, but setting the new tradition in Russian fashion—elimination by trial, confession and execution as against the old Balkan style of assassination.

For now Moscow had all the treachery Philby could give them. Even to have been in one of the concentration camps or in Sofia's central prison, as a member of the resistance meant the possibility of having been 'turned round' by Geshev. When Georgi Dimitrov came from Moscow with his Macedonian sympathies, with the weapon of 'Marxist-Leninism' cultured in the Soviet academies, it was easy for anyone only a 'home Communist' to be proved an 'enemy of the people'.

In complete power, Georgi Dimitrov (Prime Minister 23rd November 1946 to 2nd July 1949) supervised the adoption of the new 'Dimitrov Constitution'. A Bulgarian patriot who had outfaced the Nazis in the Reichstag Trial of 1938, he had renounced his Soviet citizenship two days before the elections in October 1946. His mother was a Macedonian, his first wife had been a Yugoslav, his second a Sudeten German. He stood for the international understanding of Communism and desired a Bulgarian-Yugoslav rapprochement, especially over Macedonia.[6] His own determined idealism led him to an outspoken statement in Bucharest about the creation of an East European Federation.

This, together with the agreement between Yugoslavia and Bulgaria at Bled, alarmed Moscow. The idea of a South Slav United States (with Bulgaria as the Seventh Federated Republic) reaching from the Adriatic to the Black Sea and which would command both the food production of the Danube and the mineral resources of the Balkans, was welcome only so long as Yugoslavia seemed to be a docile satellite. Once Tito showed independence, Stalin reacted with harsh disapproval and determined to liquidate any in Bulgaria who might lead aspirations of independence or attempt to solve the 'Macedonian Question' by union with Tito's Yugoslavia.[7]

[6] Milovan Djilas, *Conversations with Stalin*, Hart Davies, 1962, page 37.
[7] *ibid.*, pages 157–9.

Dimitrov became ill and went to Moscow at the beginning of 1949, where in suspicious circumstances he died in a Moscow sanatorium on 2nd July 1949. No one who embarrassed Stalin ever lived happily or long in that Russian climate. In the meantime Traicho Kostov, his Deputy Prime Minister, found himself accused of 'Titoism'. Chervenkov, as ever dutiful to Moscow, pressed forward the persecution of the old Communist veteran, who was prosecuted and went the way of Petkov, being executed in December 1949.

Kostov bravely contradicted his confession at the public moment of the trial, so that his judges resorted to discontinuing his examination and had his written deposition (which no doubt had been made under inquisitional pressures) read aloud, but not before he had been cross-examined in that court, voluntarily admitting the matters involving his relationship to Geshev, the police agents, the partisans and the Western allies.

Communists though they were, all Bulgarians who could be considered to harbour comradely associations with Yugoslavia became suspected and were persecuted. Military pressure on the Yugoslav Macedonian-Bulgarian frontier intensified into a 'total cold war'. Bulgarian partisans who had fought in Macedonia fell into marked disfavour. The 'Moscow-trained' variety of Communist led by Chervenkov and his ally Chankov (who had once actually been married to Jordanka) controlled the government, and it became a crime to be accused of 'Titoism', as Kostov's execution had demonstrated.

To Moscow's satisfaction the 'Macedonian Question' and the ideal of a Balkan federation fell into abeyance. The wiser partisans in Bulgaria became quiet and accepted disgrace, if disgrace were impugned, for the tongue in peacetime becomes a dangerous and uncouth weapon to the soldier. Bulgaranov was discharged from the army in 1949. Even the renowned Slavcho Trunski, who from leader of the famous First Sofia Brigade had become commander of the Third Army Corps, was imprisoned in 1951.

Only when the 'little finger' of Stalin ceased to wag in 1953 did the pendulum of events swing back and the influence of Chervenkov and Chankov decline. Bulgaranov was 'rehabilitated' in 1953 and elected to the central committee in 1954. Trunski was freed to become commander of the military academy, Sofia, in 1954. The partial (and posthumous) 'rehabilitation' of Kostov came two years later, in 1956.

No one has interfered with Nikola Geshev. He has lived happily on in exile, his dossiers having served both sides so maliciously. Now even Philby tries to 'rehabilitate' himself in print, garnishing his so-called 'leftish' aims by using names of whatever people were unlucky enough to have made his acquaintance.

Frank Thompson's role as a folk hero has never been revived. Peasants seldom come up the hillside to where the gypsy horses have broken through the palings of the grass-grown grave enclosure. The paint blisters and peels from the board which has fallen from its monument. Only rumours that British agents and anglophile royalists were responsible for his execution and the seizure of his mythical gold are circulated from time to time by those who think love of the Soviet Union equates with dislike of the Western powers. And in the West no one in authority desired his image to survive—whether because of a guilt complex, or whether perhaps swayed by such sentiments as those expressed by General Ironside with regard to T. E. Lawrence, who can say?

It had not been the destiny of Frank Thompson to ride into Sofia leading a national army, as T. E. Lawrence had done into Damascus. His long march, though a tactical failure, had been a strategic success by directing Hitler's armies towards a pseudo Second Front and by scaring the Royal Bulgarian Army from advancing to crush Tempo's partisans. The important strategic effect had no relation to what Frank Thompson himself set out to do, so, whether or not he actually possessed the ruthlessness of a Lawrence or the brilliant adroitness of a Wingate, though in fact he achieved nothing, he had succeeded in spite of himself. He had read and digested that estimate of Lawrence by Caudwell: "He slew and plundered and was ruthless and contracted his aspirations to the narrow hopes of an Arab leader. Lawrence . . . never fully realised how completely he had betrayed them all. He had brought into Arabia the very evil he had fled."

To the last Frank Thompson held to his vision of the 'new spirit in Europe' for his 'brave company'.

He and his mission had obtained a successful strategic result they did not know about, for to this end the controllers of S.O.E. were moving them in the field like chessmen. Justification for the sacrifice of young officers in this way may be difficult to find by such an anomalous body as Special Operations Executive. If Frank Thompson had pushed their intentions too far into a private war to advance his own ideology, his moral right to do this may be questioned, but his death in an unyielding and defiant gesture ennobles his campaign into more than a mere adventure. After a war the victors may become splendid, but those who die unyielding in freedom's cause grow gigantic, larger than life, as in the Bulgarian hero-poet's famous song.

"They do not die, They perish not, Who fall for Freedom's sake."